IMAGES of America

ROCKINGHAM COUNTY

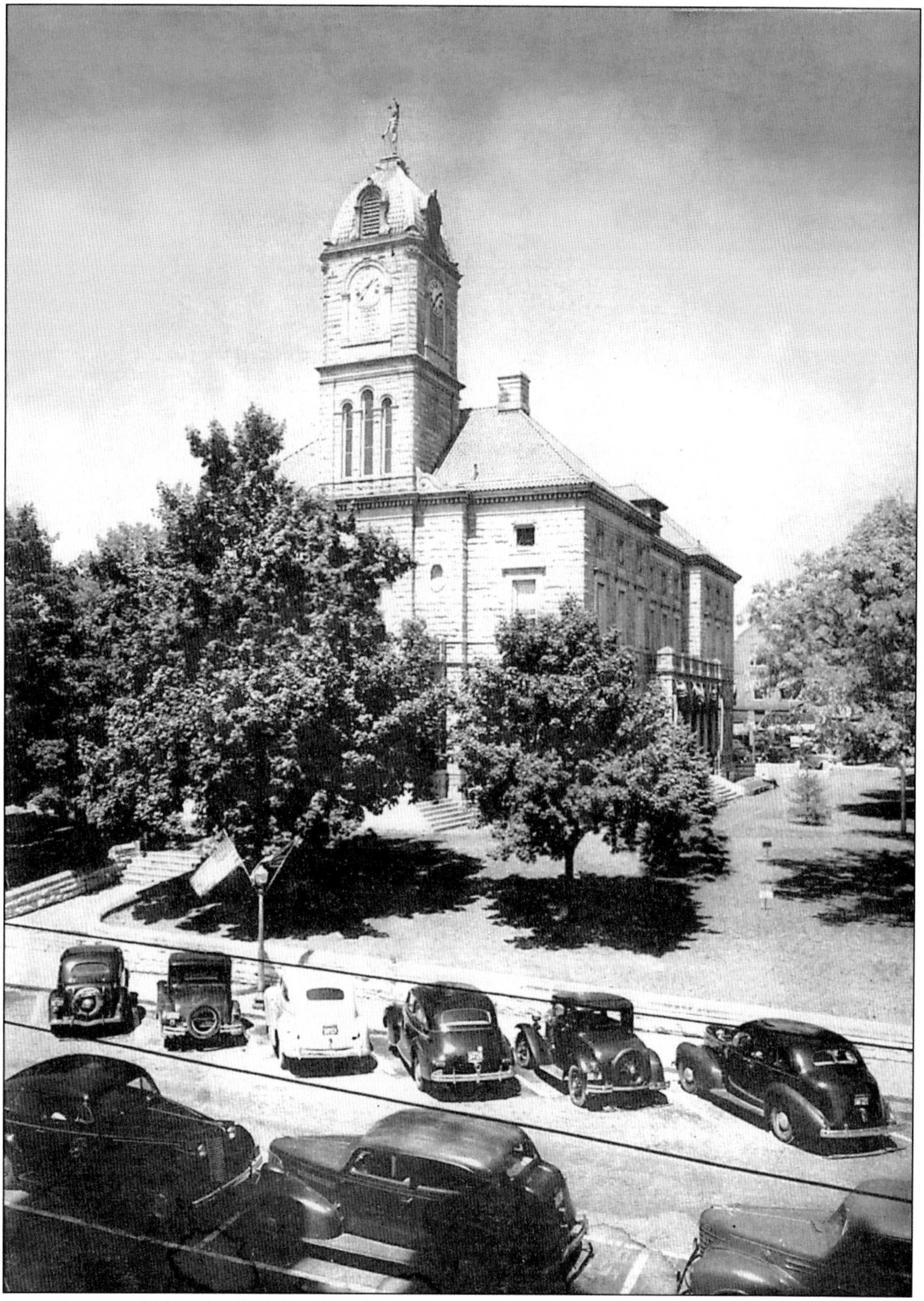

Completed in 1897, the fifth Rockingham County courthouse still graces the downtown square of the county seat, Harrisonburg. (Private collection.)

IMAGES
of America

ROCKINGHAM COUNTY

Scott Hamilton Suter and Cheryl Lyon

ARCADIA
PUBLISHING

ISBN 978-0-7385-1724-7

Published by Arcadia Publishing
Charleston, South Carolina

Printed in the United States of America

Library of Congress Catalog Card Number: 2004111539

For all general information contact Arcadia Publishing at:
Telephone 843-853-2070
Fax 843-853-0044
E-mail sales@arcadiapublishing.com
For customer service and orders:
Toll-Free 1-888-313-2665

Visit us on the Internet at www.arcadiapublishing.com

Dedicated to the memory of Agnes Virginia Kline (1898–1983)

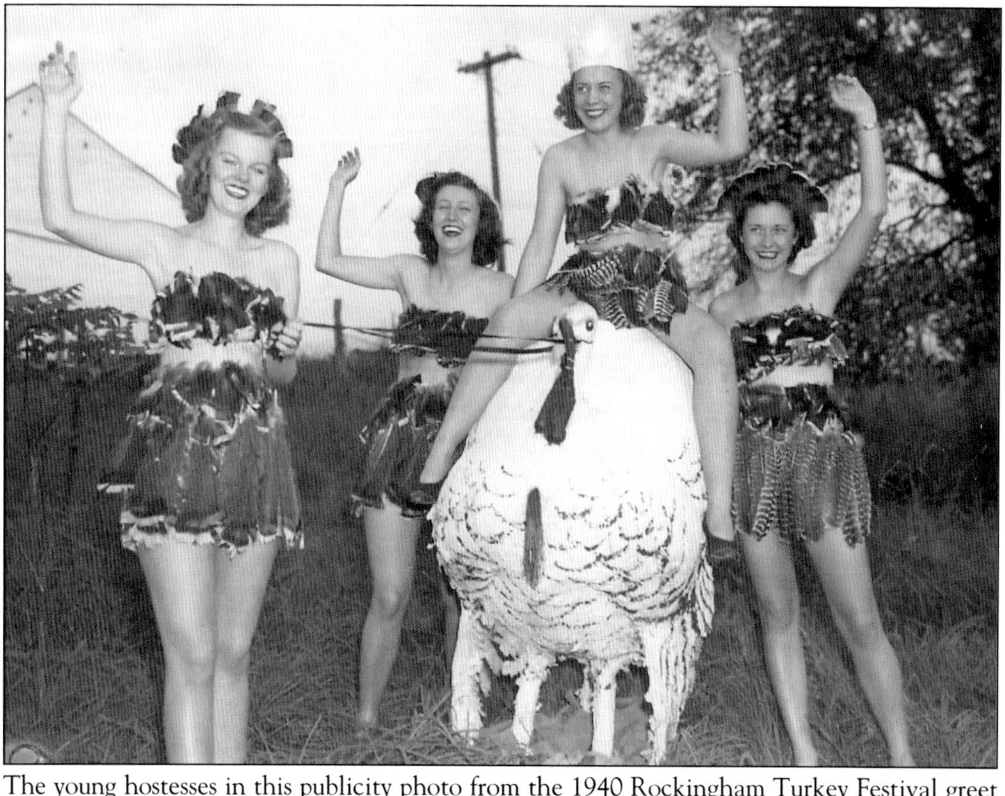

The young hostesses in this publicity photo from the 1940 Rockingham Turkey Festival greet visitors at the beginning of this photographic survey of Rockingham County. (Harrisonburg-Rockingham Historical Society Collection.)

CONTENTS

Acknowledgments

We would like to thank the following individuals for granting us permission to reprint photographs from their collections: Hubert Wine, Kermit Early, Harold Wood, Kent Botkin, Jim Suter, DeRay and Mary Miller, Greg Evans, Jeffrey S. Evans, and several other private collectors. We also thank the following institutions for permitting the use of their archival material: Bridgewater College, Eastern Mennonite University, the Harrisonburg-Rockingham Historical Society, James Madison University, and Massanutten Regional Library. Numerous individuals helped in a variety of ways; we extend our gratitude to Terry Barkley, Lois Bowman, Weldon Click, Janet and Earl Downs, Betty Heatwole, Harold Huber, Richard D.F. Martin, Kerry and Brent Showalter, Roger Simmons, and Norma and Stanley Suter.

Selected Sources Consulted

Downs, Janet Baugher, Earl J. Downs, Pat Turner Ritchie. *Mills of Rockingham County*. 4 volumes. Dayton, VA: Harrisonburg-Rockingham Historical Society, 1997, 1998, 2000, 2003.

Giedion, Siegfried. *Mechanization Takes Command: A Contribution to Anonymous History*. New York: Oxford University Press, 1948.

Hess, Nancy. *The Heartland: Rockingham County*. Harrisonburg, VA: Park View Press, 1976.

Koons, Kenneth E. and Warren R. Hofstra, eds. *After The Backcountry: Rural Life in the Great Valley of Virginia, 1800–1900*. Knoxville: University of Tennessee Press, 2000.

May, C.E. *Life Under Four Flags in North River Basin of Virginia*. Verona, VA: McClure Press, 1976.

Rockingham County, Its Past and Present Illustrated. Harrisonburg, VA: *Harrisonburg Daily News*, 1909; Harrisonburg-Rockingham Historical Society, 1998.

Suter, Scott Hamilton. *Shenandoah Valley Folklife*. Jackson, MS: University Press of Mississippi, 1999.

Wayland, John W. *A History of Rockingham County, Virginia*. Dayton, VA: Ruebush-Elkins Company, 1912.

INTRODUCTION

This is not simply a *history* of Rockingham County; it is a book of *impressions* of the county. The photographs included in this volume offer the views of many people, mostly natives of the county. Certainly the opinions of the authors are here, although quotations from others are included. Most vibrant, however, are the visions of the people who appear in these images along with the buildings and landscapes they have created and experienced. The story spun in this collection is one that often escapes history books.

Many of the images here were taken by anonymous photographers who, with Kodak Brownies or other simple cameras in hand, recorded life in the county through the years. Although they may not have expressed their thoughts in words, the photos they shot reveal what they felt was important, sometimes on a personal level and other times on a civic or historical plane. As we searched for photographs to include in this collection, we were delighted to find two small albums of images taken in and around Mount Crawford about 1900. The lack of a professional skill level and aesthetic quality in many of the shots is not important; what is important is the reflection of that photographer's vision of life in that town at that time. Because of his or her foresight we have a unique record of a brief moment in the history of Mount Crawford.

We dedicate this collection to Agnes Virginia Kline, a name that will have meaning for some readers but may not resonate with all. Agnes Kline was born in 1898 in Rockingham County, attended county schools, graduated from Bridgewater College and George Peabody College, and then served as librarian at Bridgewater College for 40 years. We choose to remember her because she was not a trained historian, but a historian of the life and values of the community around her. Throughout her life, she wrote about her memories of Rockingham County and interviewed older community members, making copious notes of their stories. She kept scrapbooks of newspaper items that may have pertained to county life at the time. She took photographs and wrote two monographs about Rockingham County's past. Most significantly, she kept all of her work and found a home for it at the Historical Library at Eastern Mennonite University. Agnes Kline died in 1983, but we still have her window to look through to the past.

This is not only to praise Agnes Kline, but to make the point that recording contemporary life through photos, notes, diaries, or interviews can play a significant role in the future. The anonymous Mount Crawford photographer may have been only having fun, but because of that amusement we have a clearer picture of the lives of that town's residents. Understanding our past can be instructional as we look to the future. In 2004, the agricultural systems that have been an integral part of Rockingham County's economy and culture for more than a century are facing change. As national businesses withdraw from the poultry industry, farmers are turning to the past as a source of inspiration. In order to protect their investments and maintain employee jobs, growers are exploring the formation of a poultry cooperative much like those created in Rockingham County in the 1940s. Similarly, just as market forces encouraged farmers to switch from raising wheat to poultry and livestock at the beginning of the 20th century, the same forces are compelling crop growers to consider new avenues such as a wholesale produce auction. Such a move would radically affect the types of crops planted. Once again, old ideas are re-fashioned to fit the changing times of the present.

We hope that presenting these images of Rockingham County's past will help us recognize the value of preserving the county's agricultural and rural heritage. We also hope that the book will encourage a realization of the importance of recording the county's culture and maintaining its past, whether mundane or extraordinary.

One

Agriculture

While agriculture remains a dominant feature of Rockingham County's economy in the 21st century, it no longer holds the supreme position. Noting that the initial settlers in the Shenandoah Valley spent much time clearing the land and living self-sufficiently, historians Kenneth E. Koons and Warren R. Hofstra suggest that by the 19th century "the culture of wheat governed how farm families spent their time." This remained true into the early 20th century, but the agricultural base had begun to shift in the 1890s as developing markets encouraged farmers to move toward production of fruit, livestock, and poultry. By mid-century, innovations in the poultry industry—with Rockingham County leading the way—further transformed the agricultural landscape of the Shenandoah Valley. Today, significant portions of the county's farmlands are giving way to suburban "estates" and consumer-driven landscapes; however, agriculture continues to be the foundation of life in Rockingham County.

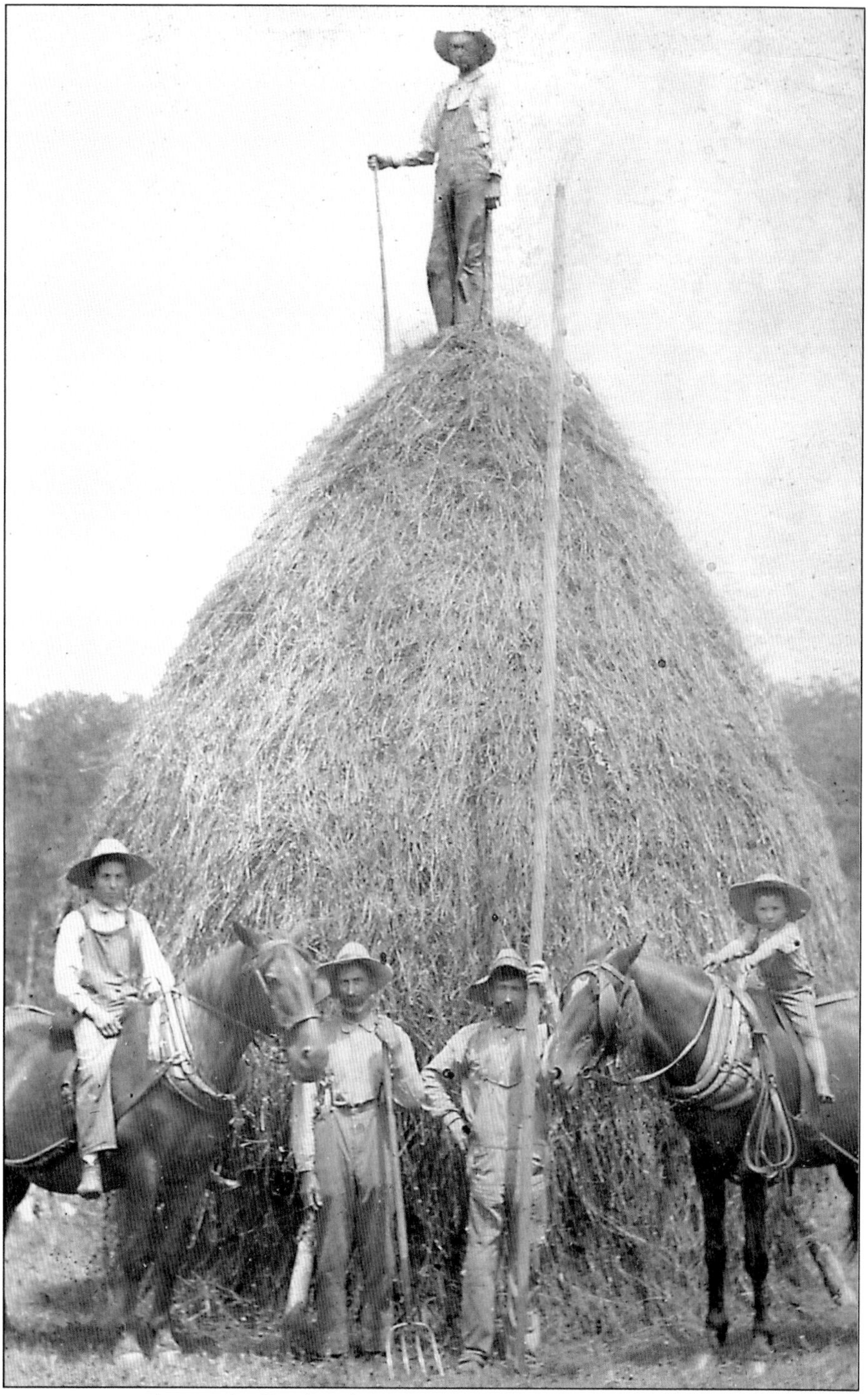

Once a common sight on the Rockingham County countryside, haystacks are seldom found today. For a stack this tall, farmers needed special tools such as the long hayfork held by the worker second from the right and possibly a hay derrick, a device for hoisting hay to the top of the pile. (Private collection.)

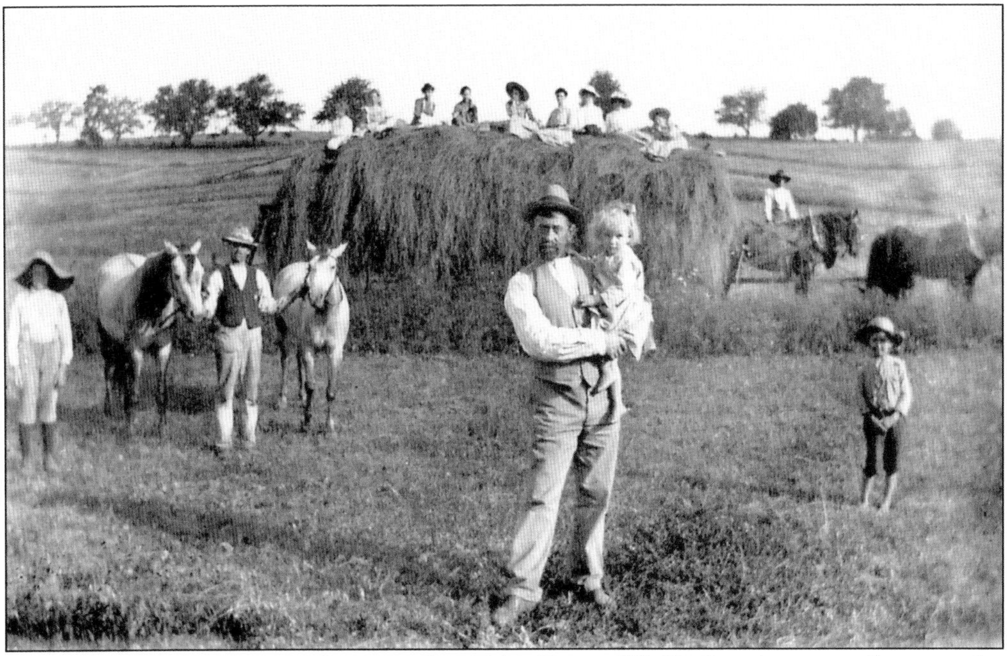

Photographed near Singers Glen around 1900 by George W. Shaffer, this scene illustrates the pride rural residents took in their hard work. Joseph Funk (center) poses contentedly with his daughter Josie and other family members by their annual hay crop. (Eastern Mennonite University Collection.)

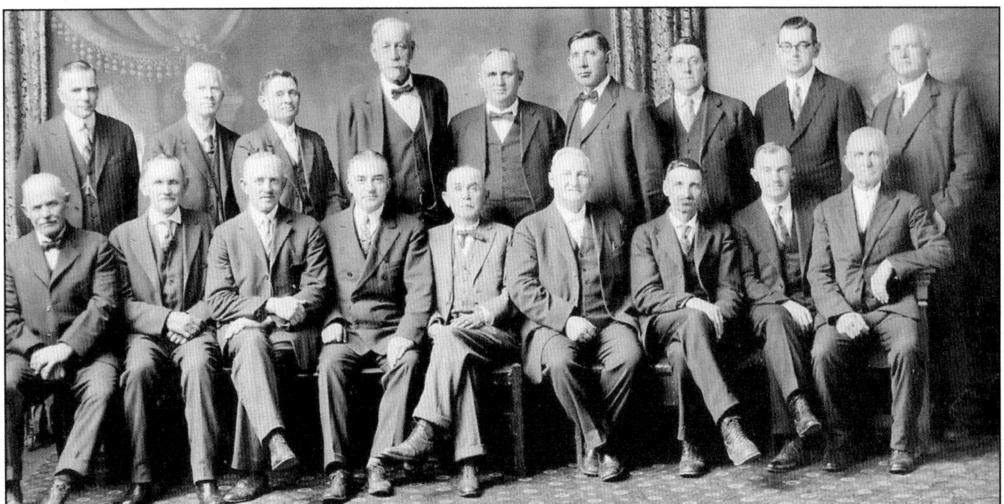

The importance of agriculture to Rockingham County's economy led to the creation of an Agricultural Advisory Board, which was responsible for extension work in the area. Chosen from each magisterial district and the city of Harrisonburg, the group included, from left to right: (front row) C.E. Long, L.E. Swank, W.R. Sellers, Col. T.P. Berry, M.M. Jarman, Dr. C.P. Harshberger, D.C. Acker, Dr. Gilbert Ralston, Eli Brunk; (back row) Emanuel Blosser, C.S. Craun, O.L. Burtner, Sen. George B. Keezle, John H. Hoover (chairman of the board), G.F. Holsinger, O.D. Garber, R.C. Dingledine, and C.M. Keezle. (Harrisonburg-Rockingham Historical Society Collection.)

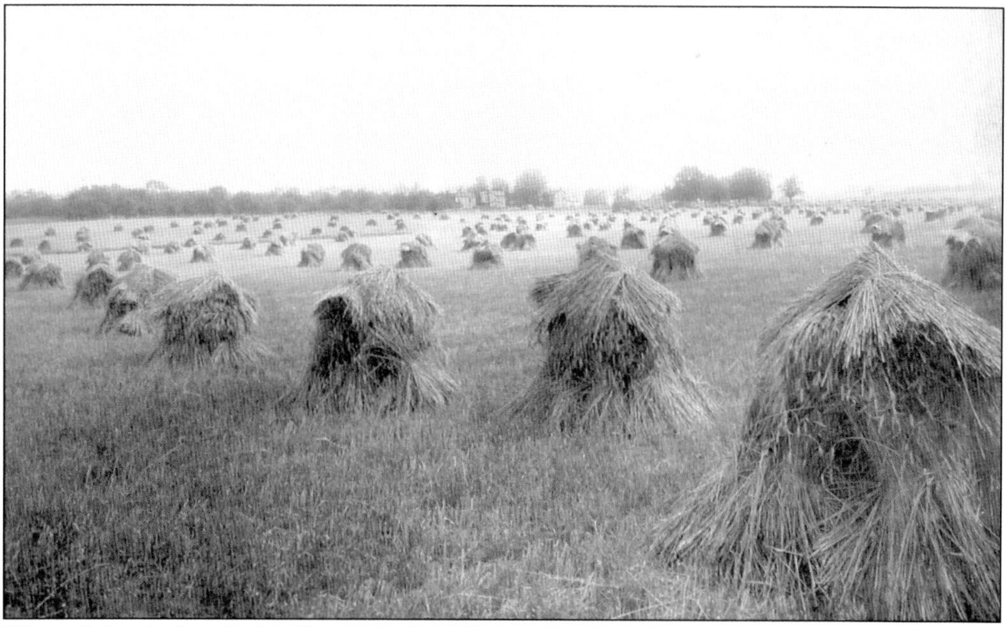

Wheat helped identify the Shenandoah Valley as the "bread basket of the South" during the Civil War. This artistic shot of Emanuel Suter's wheat field in the New Erection community testifies to the importance local farmers placed on a healthy harvest. (Harrisonburg-Rockingham Historical Society Collection.)

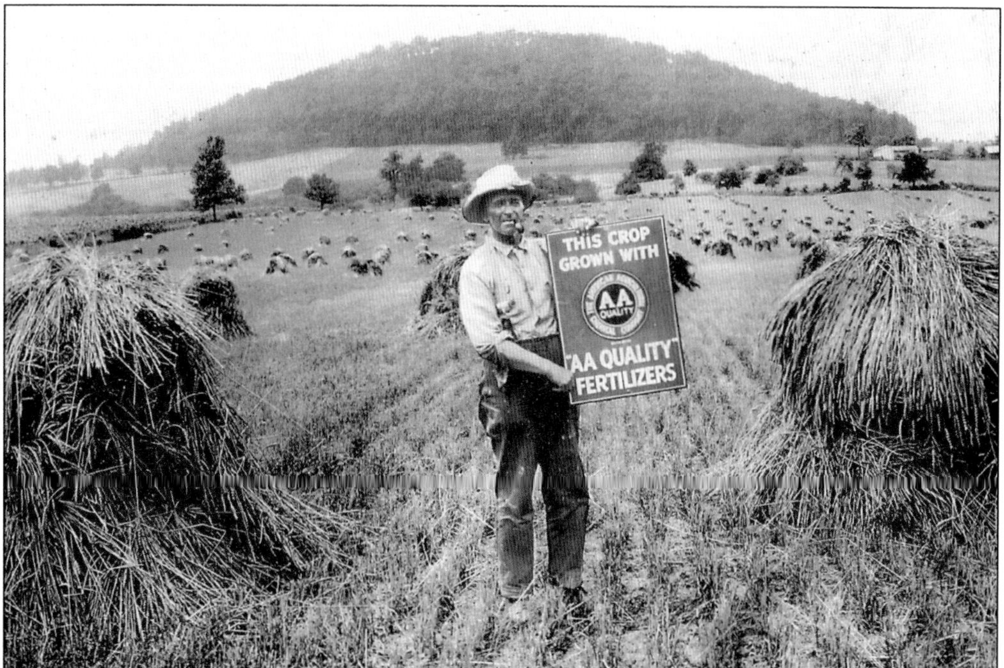

Wheat continued to be harvested in large amounts in the county through the middle of the 20th century, and farmers employed all means to raise a fine crop. Abram Daniel Heatwole, posing in his wheat field on the east side of Mole Hill, reveals one reason for his bumper crop. (Private collection.)

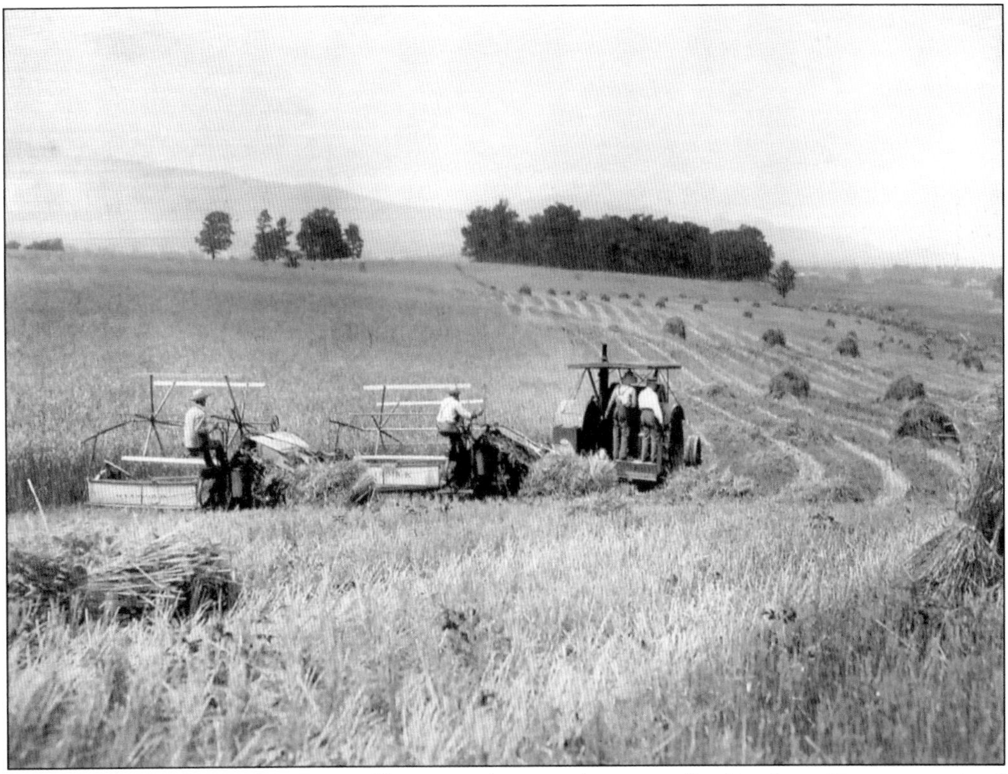

As the photographs on these pages illustrate, wheat production in Rockingham County remained strong despite the ravages of the Civil War years. In fact, growth increased dramatically in the final third of the 19th century and early years of the 20th century as farmers took advantage of new developments such as fertilizers, steam-powered engines, and new methods of harvesting the grain. (Harrisonburg-Rockingham Historical Society Collection.)

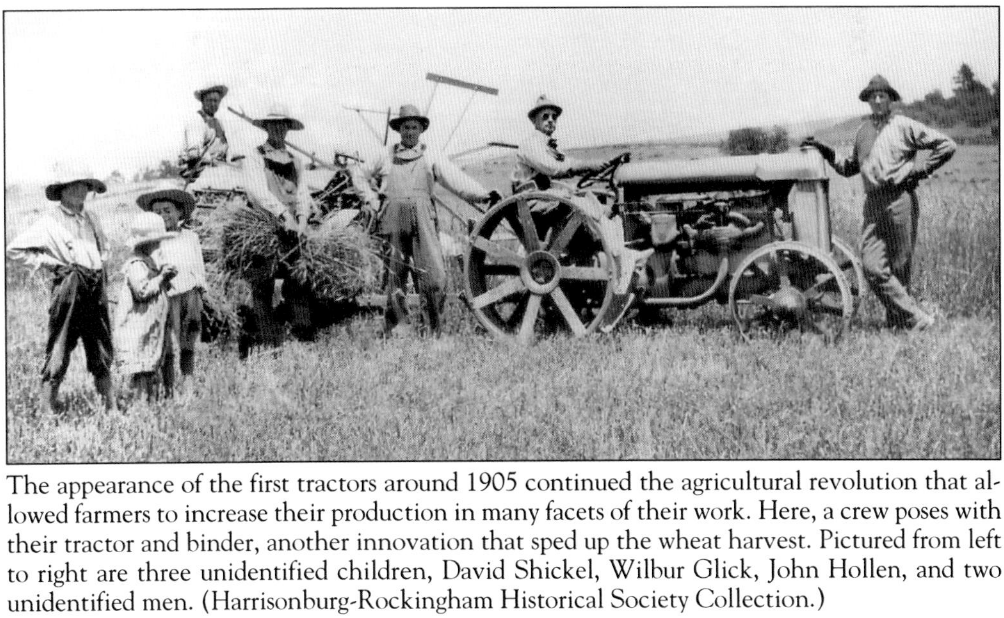

The appearance of the first tractors around 1905 continued the agricultural revolution that allowed farmers to increase their production in many facets of their work. Here, a crew poses with their tractor and binder, another innovation that sped up the wheat harvest. Pictured from left to right are three unidentified children, David Shickel, Wilbur Glick, John Hollen, and two unidentified men. (Harrisonburg-Rockingham Historical Society Collection.)

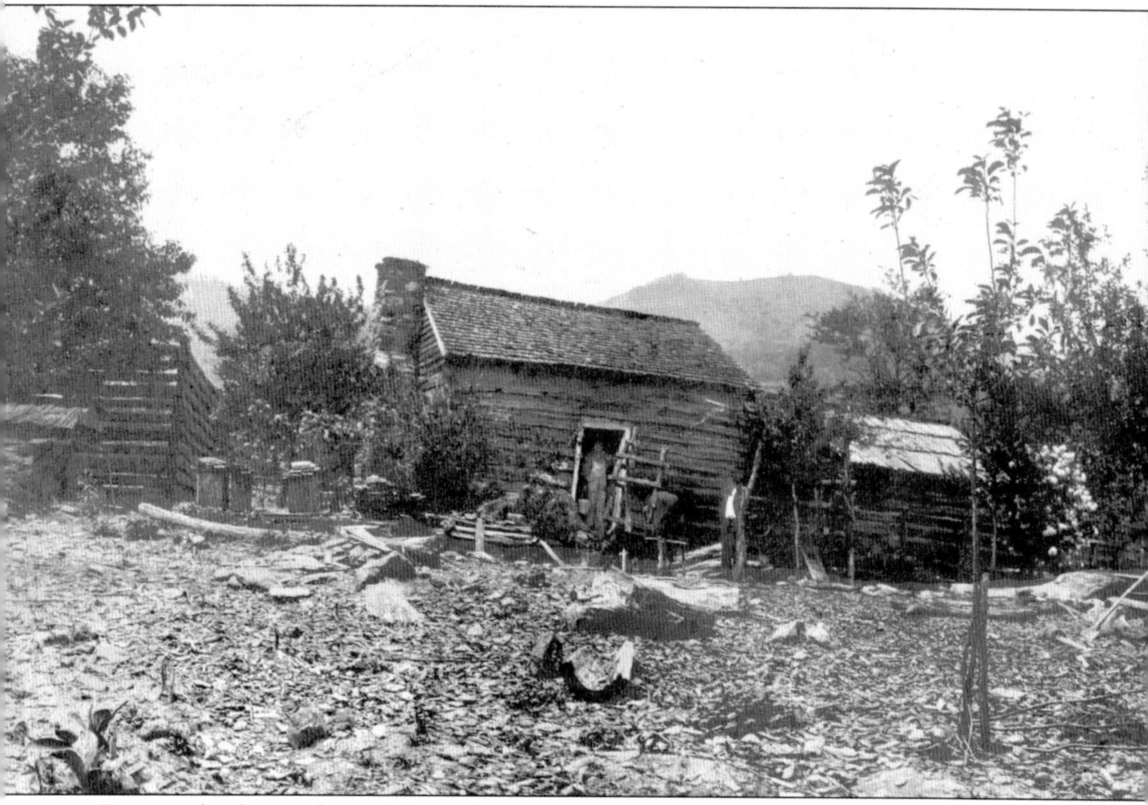

Farmsteads often took on different looks according to where they were located in the county. This image of a dwelling and outbuildings near the mountains in the west of the county suggests that its residents were subsistence farmers, growing what they needed to exist in the rocky

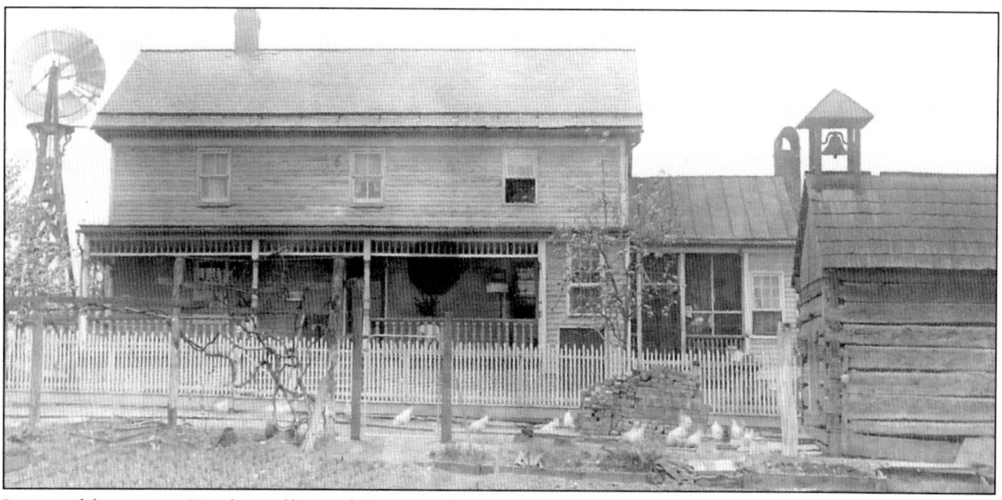

Located between Timberville and Forestville in the northern section of the county, the Houston Bowman house illustrates a typical two-story farmhouse with adjacent outbuildings for the activities of everyday life. The bell on the washhouse suggests that the Bowman farm was large enough to need a signal that could be heard in the distant fields. (Jeffrey S. Evans Collection.)

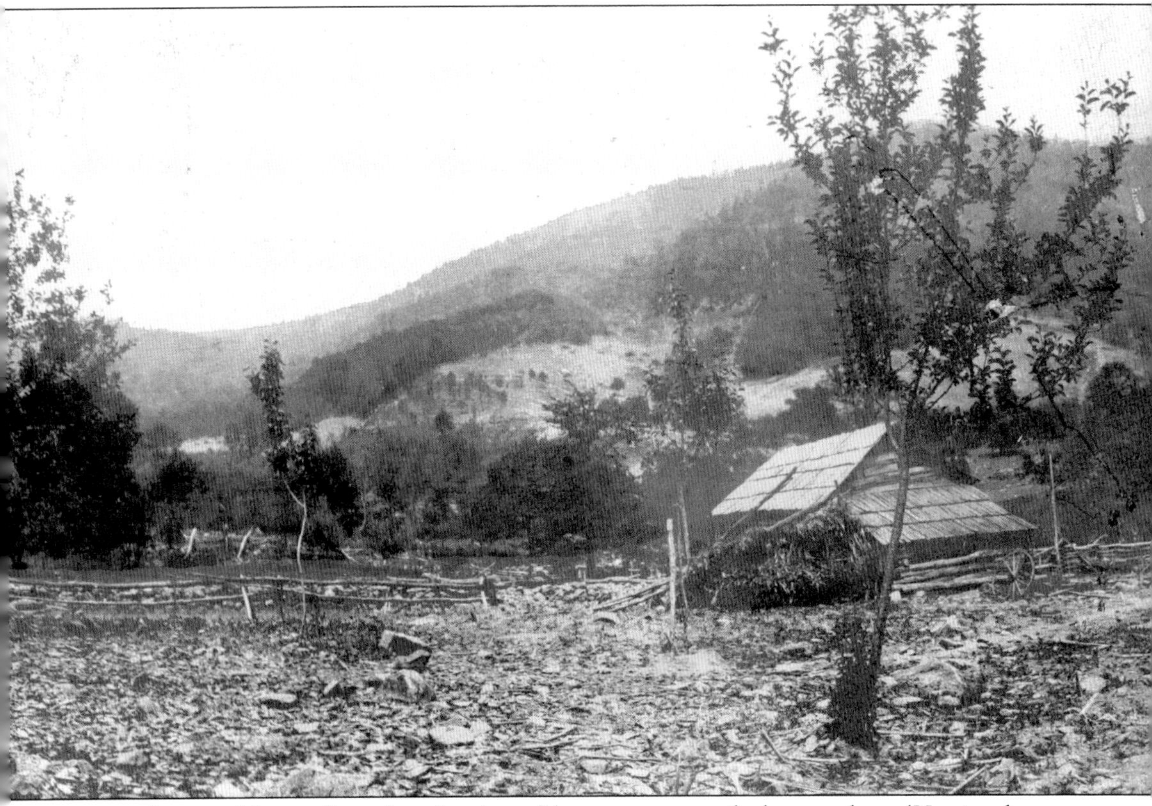

terrain that would not allow the planting of large expanses of wheat or hay. (Harrisonburg-Rockingham Historical Society Collection.)

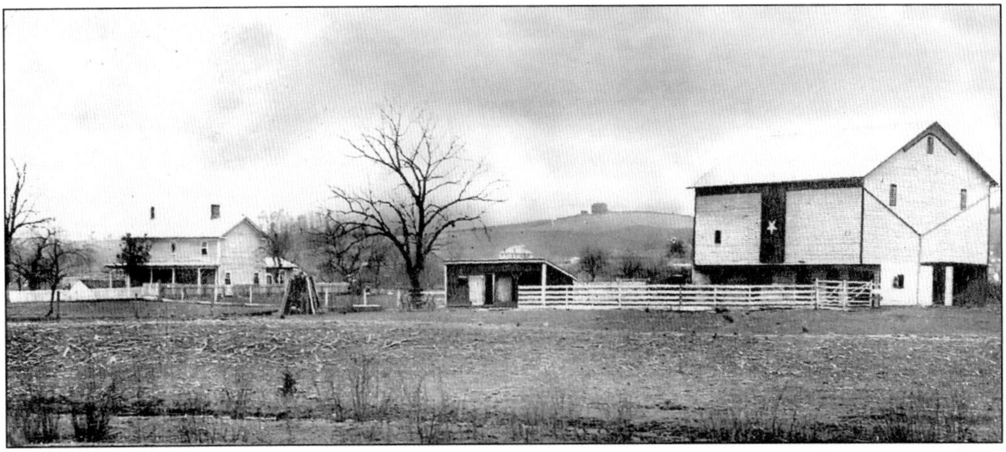

Located in Spring Creek near the county's southern boundary, this turn-of-the-century photo of the Frank Wine farm exemplifies another type of landscape. The large forebay barn, typical of the Shenandoah Valley, was located near the house, while crops and grazing pastures spread out from this family center. (Private collection.)

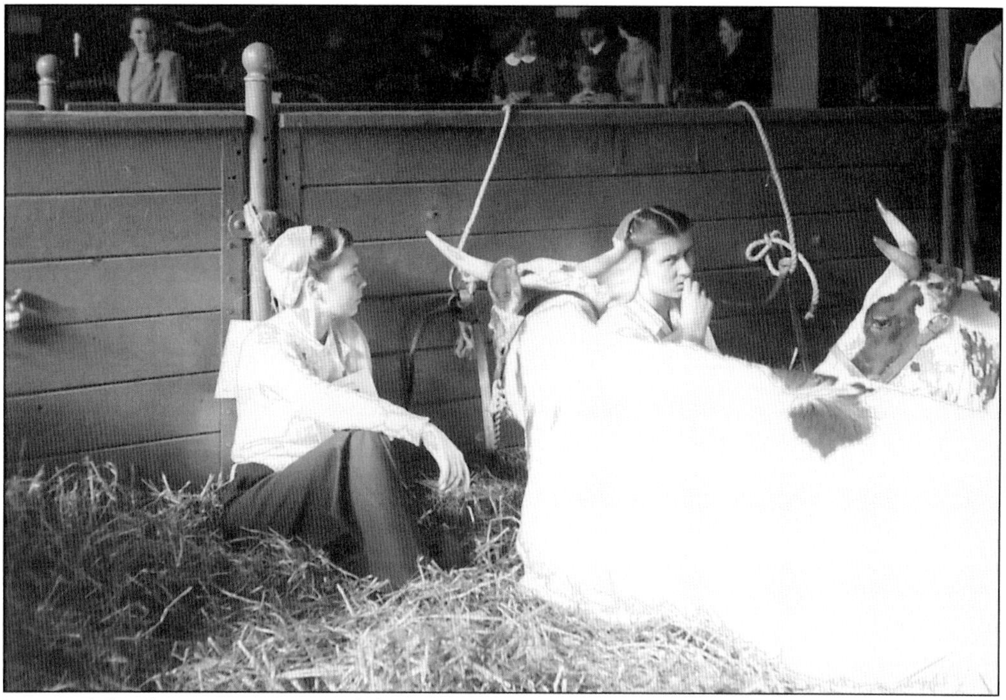

Livestock has been a major part of the county's economy since the 18th century, and the Rockingham County Fair was first organized as an agricultural event in the late 19th century. Here two unidentified youths relax with their cattle in a 1950s exhibit barn. (Private collection.)

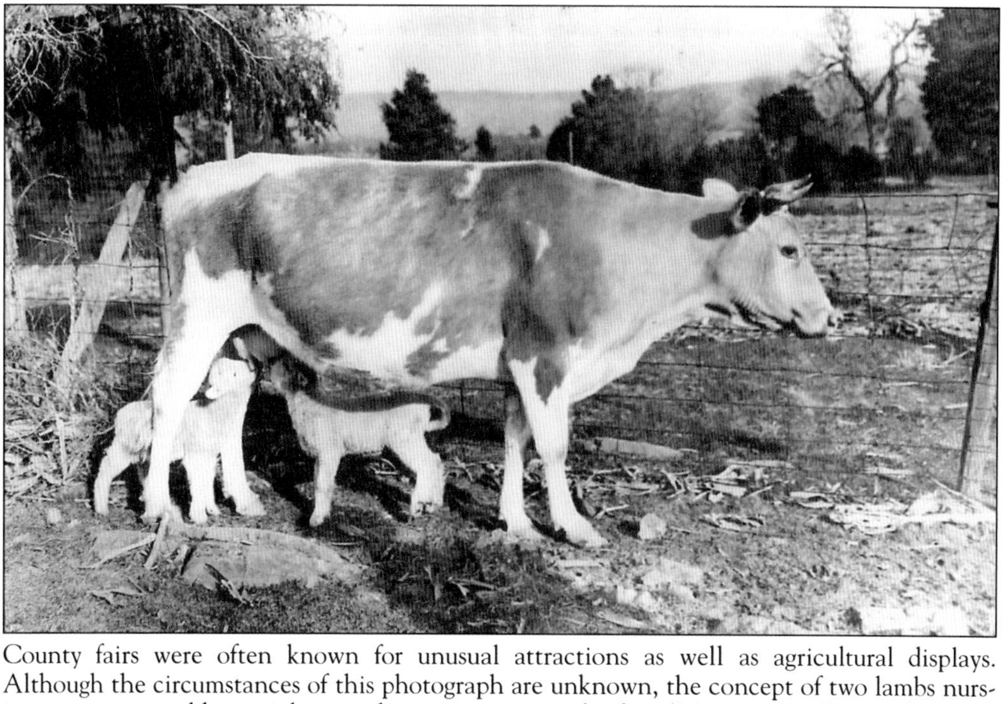

County fairs were often known for unusual attractions as well as agricultural displays. Although the circumstances of this photograph are unknown, the concept of two lambs nursing on a cow would certainly earn this team a spot at the fair. (Massanutten Regional Library Collection.)

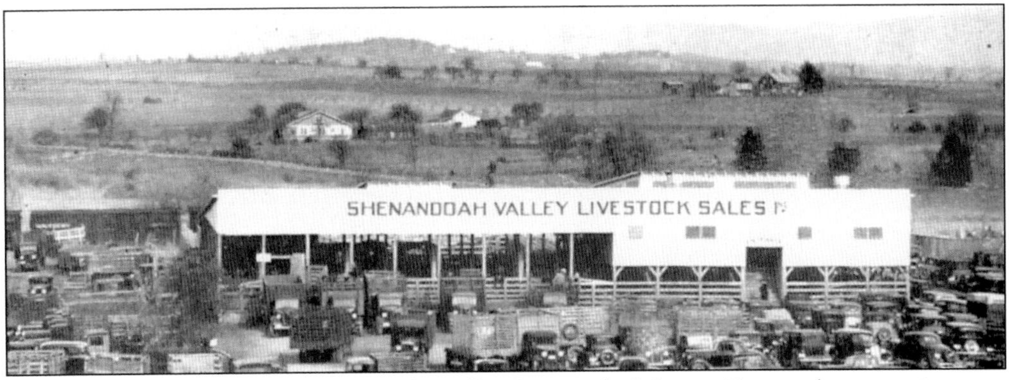

Chartered in April 1935, Shenandoah Valley Livestock Sales in Harrisonburg continues to operate, providing a market for the county's cattle raisers. Ironically, the grounds are located on property earmarked for industry by 19th-century developers. (Private collection.)

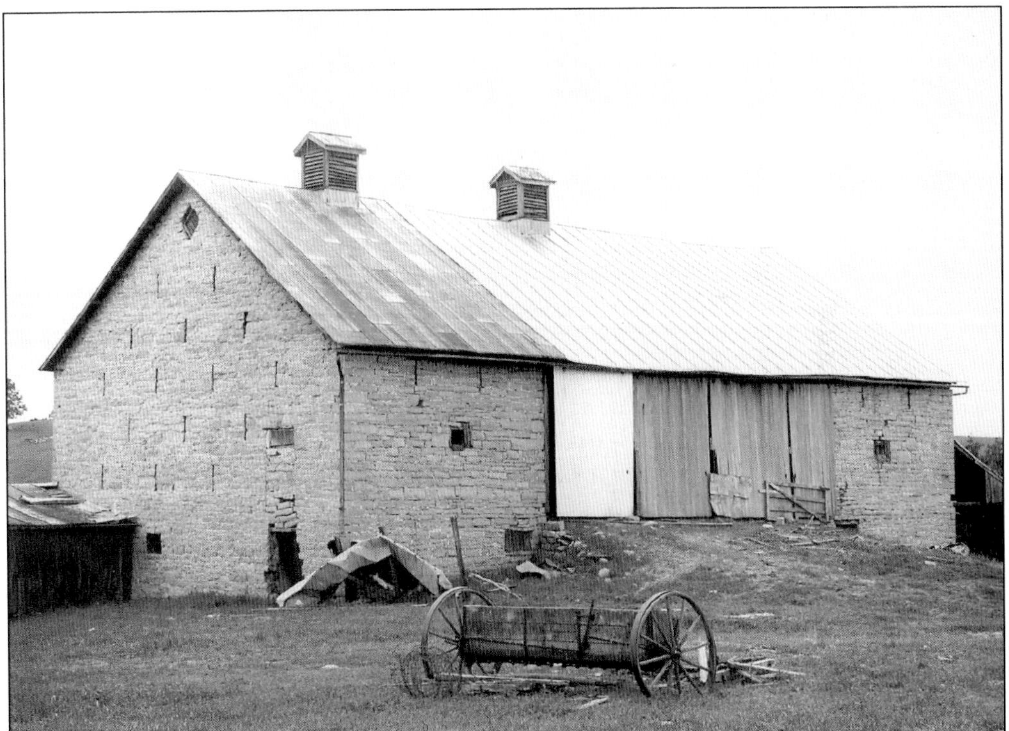

Most of the large barns that dot the county's landscape are frame structures covered with weatherboard; however, this impressive stone barn, built around 1838 near Edom, demonstrates that a tradition of building with stone also existed in the early years of the 19th century. Located on what was known as the Beery place, this barn and its solid appearance corroborate the adage, "A good barn will build a good house before a good house will build a good barn." (Eastern Mennonite University Collection.)

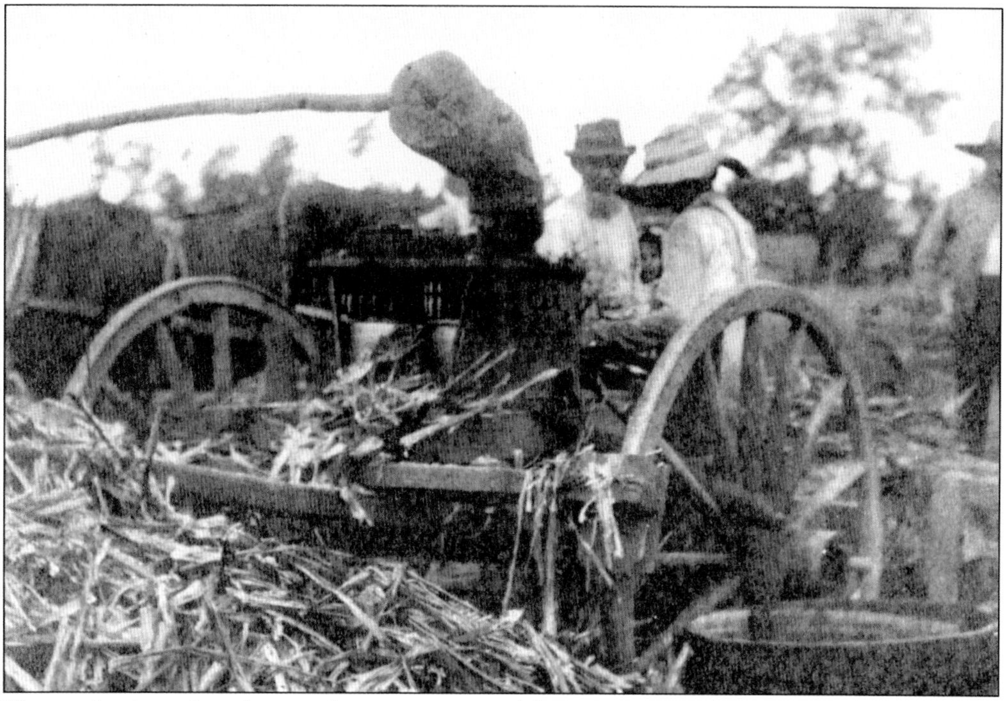

The production of sorghum molasses was once a laborious process that was an annual event as much as butchering or boiling apple butter. A mule or horse turned the sorghum mill pictured here. Sorghum was apparently so abundant in the area east of Mount Crawford that it became known as Sorghumville. (Harrisonburg-Rockingham Historical Society.)

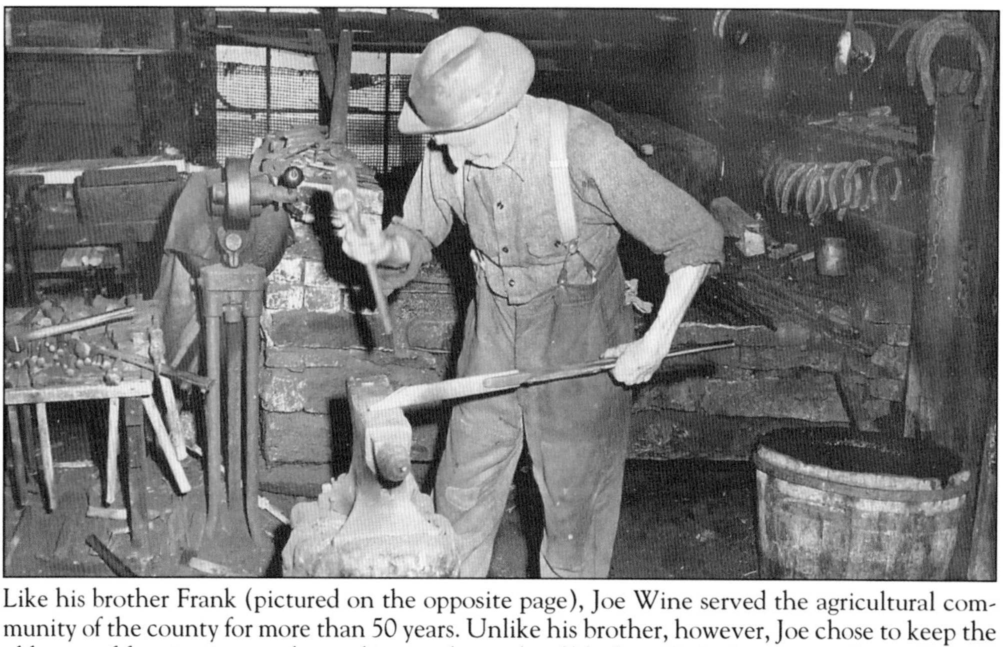

Like his brother Frank (pictured on the opposite page), Joe Wine served the agricultural community of the county for more than 50 years. Unlike his brother, however, Joe chose to keep the old ways of farming in tune by working at the trade of blacksmith. In his shop at Spring Creek, he shod horses, repaired machinery, and served the local farm community's needs well into the 1950s. (Private collection.)

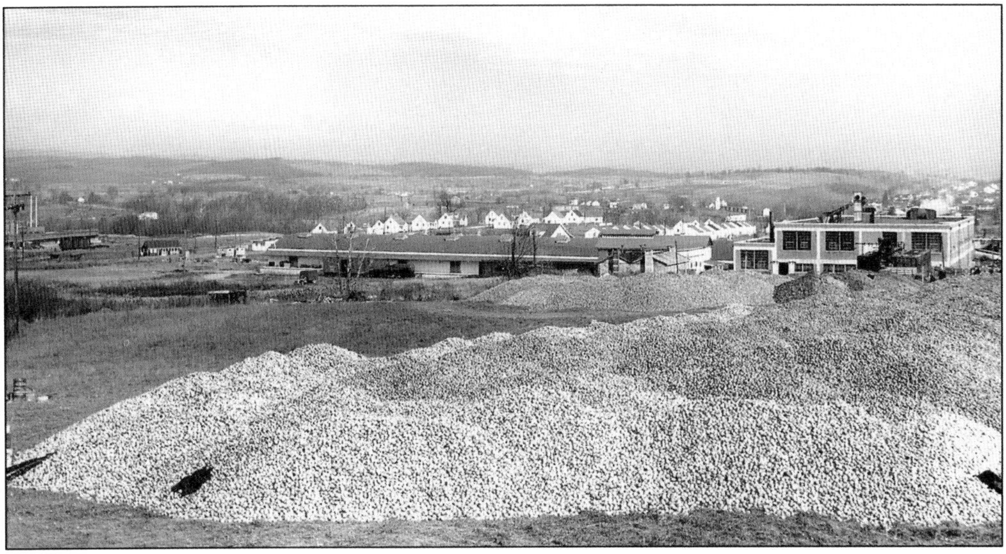

Commercial fruit production has been a part of Rockingham County's economy since the 19th century. This pile of apples at the Zigler Canning Company in Timberville attests to the large number of orchards on the fertile county landscape. The company canned both fruits and vegetables and, during World War II, prepared chicken and turkey for the U.S. Armed Forces. (Private collection.)

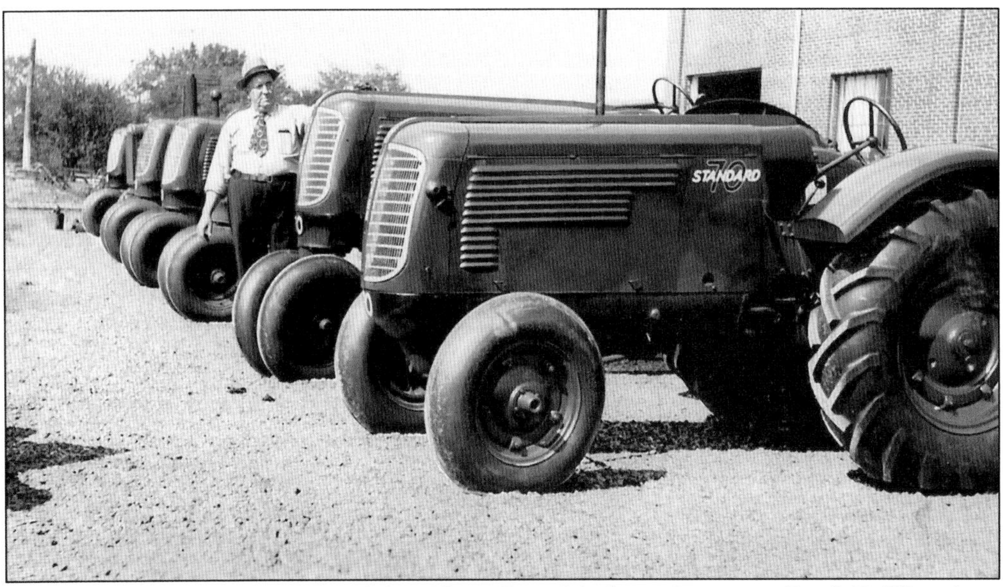

Well known as a district agent of the Oliver Farm Machine Company, Frank E. Wine later worked for Whitesel Brothers in Harrisonburg. He poses at the Whitesel Brothers lot in the 1940s with a fleet of Oliver tractors ready for sale to the county's farmers. (Private collection.)

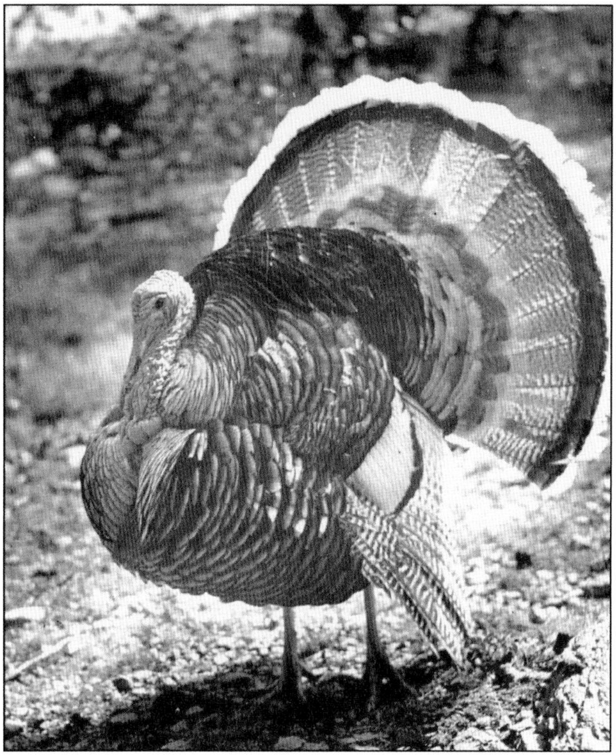

Developed by breeding wild turkeys with domesticated fowl, the Bronze turkey has long been a symbol of Rockingham County. Revolutionary innovations in the poultry business arose in the county as early as the 1880s, when Samuel Blosser developed the first commercial poultry incubator. Later, Charles Wampler Sr. experimented with raising large numbers of birds and started the county's poultry industry on its way to being one of the leaders in the nation. (Massanutten Regional Library Collection.)

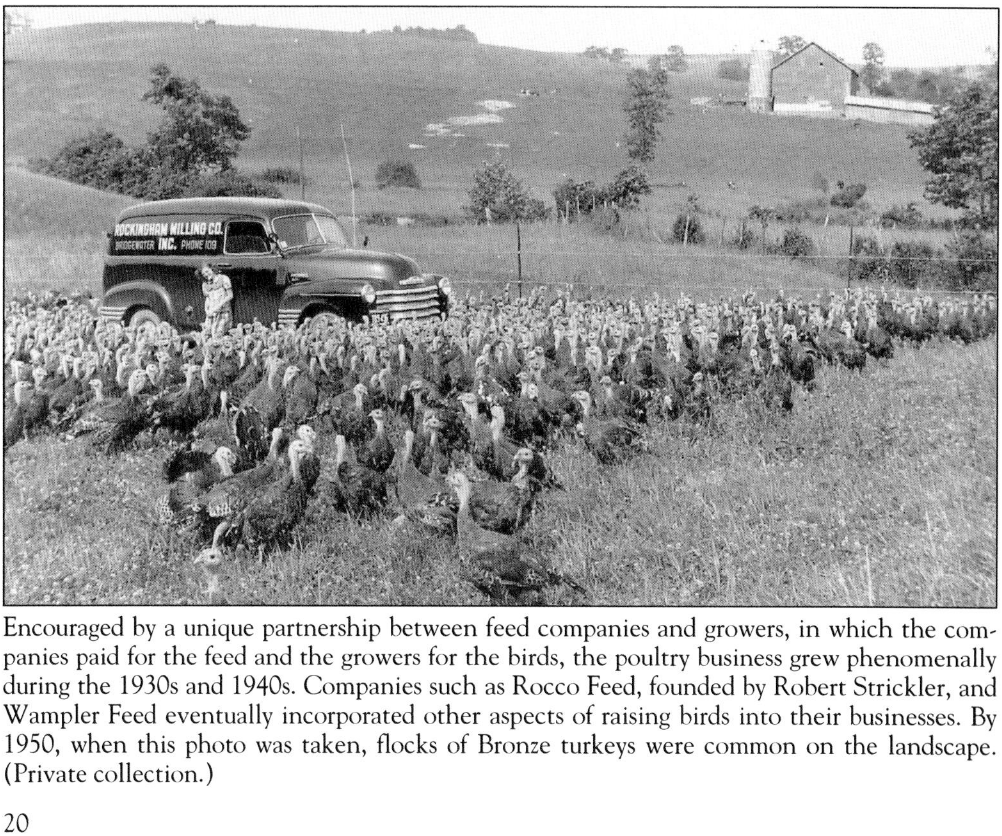

Encouraged by a unique partnership between feed companies and growers, in which the companies paid for the feed and the growers for the birds, the poultry business grew phenomenally during the 1930s and 1940s. Companies such as Rocco Feed, founded by Robert Strickler, and Wampler Feed eventually incorporated other aspects of raising birds into their businesses. By 1950, when this photo was taken, flocks of Bronze turkeys were common on the landscape. (Private collection.)

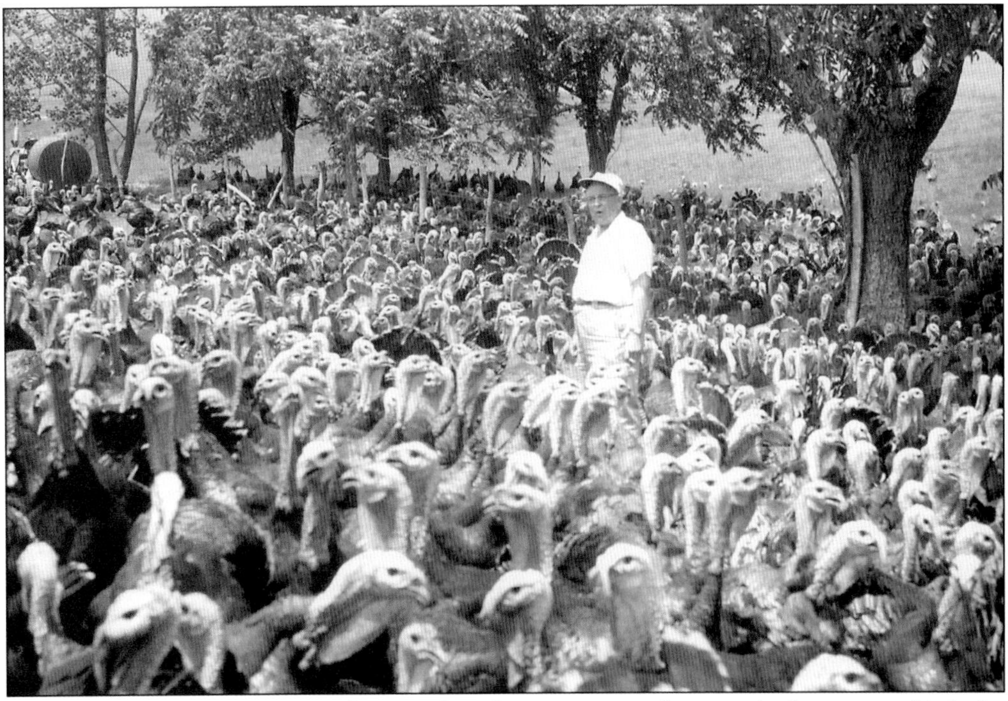

As poultry processing increased, many hands were required to catch the mature birds for transportation to the processing plants. By the 1940s, many teenagers and family members earned extra money by joining in this task. Here, a grower appears lost in a sea of bronze birds. (Private collection.)

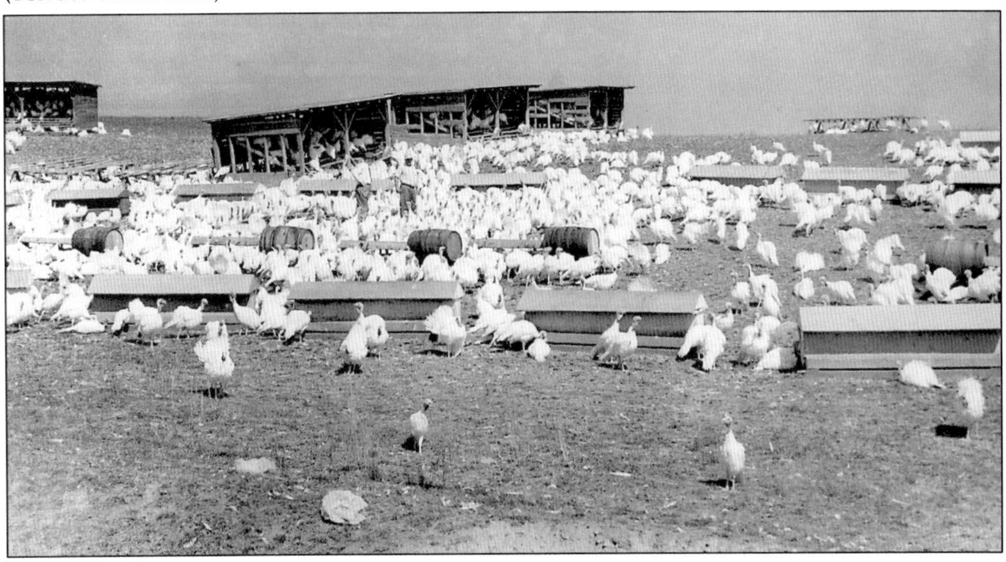

In 1938, the U.S. Department of Agriculture began to experiment with developing a new breed of turkey that would be more economical for small families. The result of this work forever changed the landscape of Rockingham County; in six years, the Beltsville White breed appeared. Laying heartier eggs and maturing with a plumper breast, this bird eventually replaced the Bronze, and today the Beltsville White breed is the standard in the industry. (Private collection.)

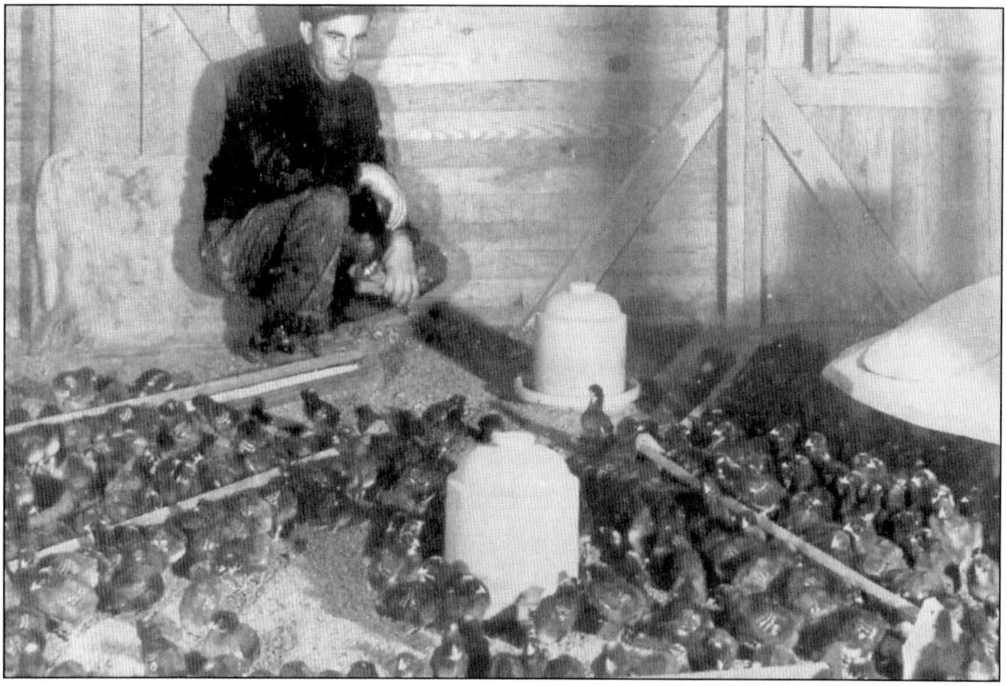

In this early promotional photograph, a "satisfied customer" observes the progress of his investment. The photo also illustrates one of the initial steps in the commercial poultry industry; birds were raised in a brooder house for about eight weeks. (Private collection.)

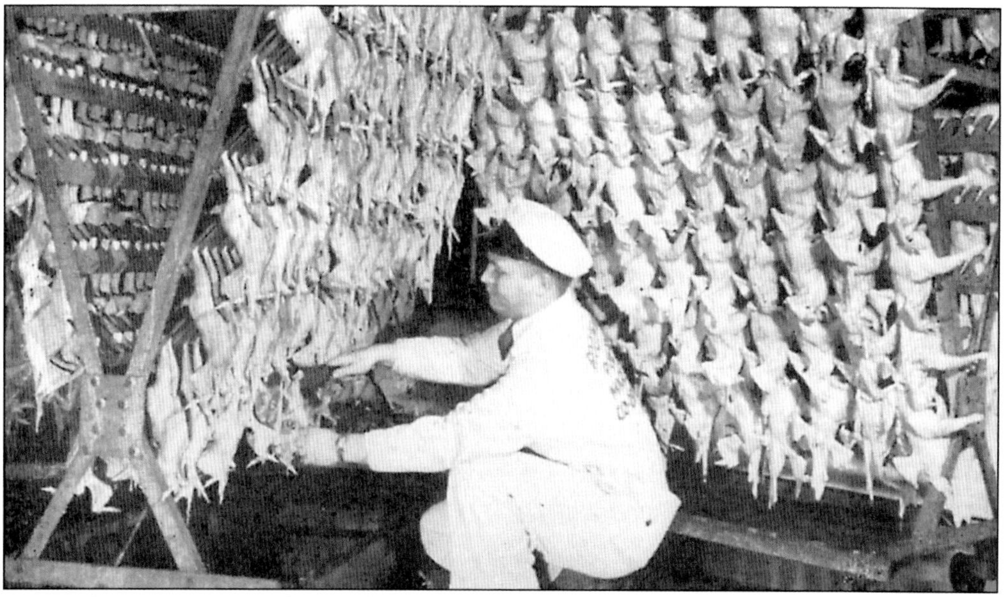

During the Depression, as farmers began raising more birds for city markets, prices fluctuated, forcing growers to pull together to form co-operatives to bring price stability. Formed in 1940, Rockingham Poultry Marketing Co-op of Broadway quickly added two new plants and, by 1944, brought its capacity to 35,000 chickens daily. Taken from an early advertisement, the caption for this photo encourages readers to "Note that entrails, head and feet have been removed." (Private collection.)

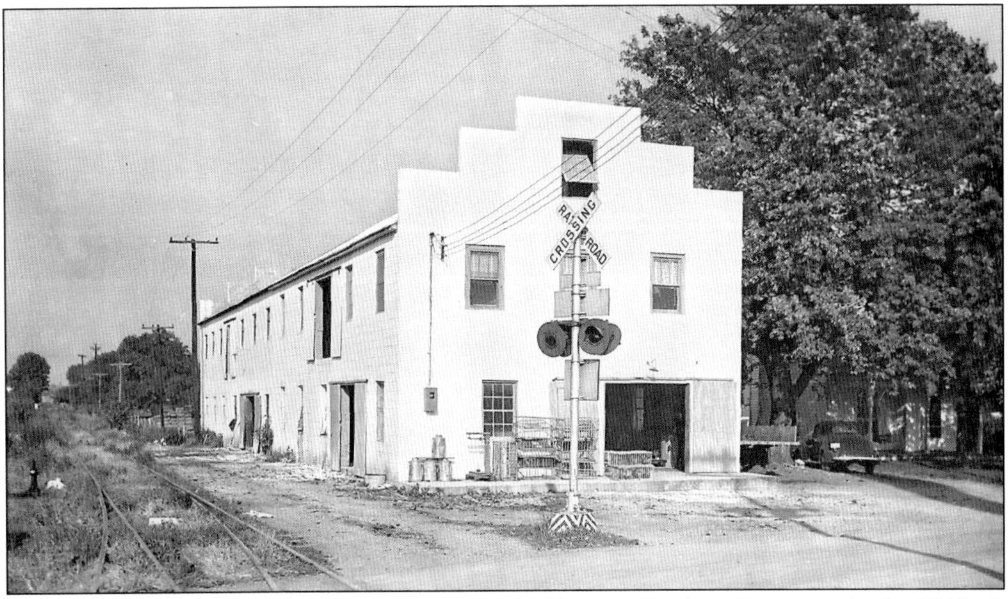

J.W. Spencer built this early eviscerating plant, the Spencer Produce Company, in the 1940s; it was located in Dayton along the Chesapeake and Western line. Later purchased by the Marval Poultry Company and then a part of the Rocco poultry conglomerate, the site continues to function as a poultry processing plant. (Jim Suter Collection.)

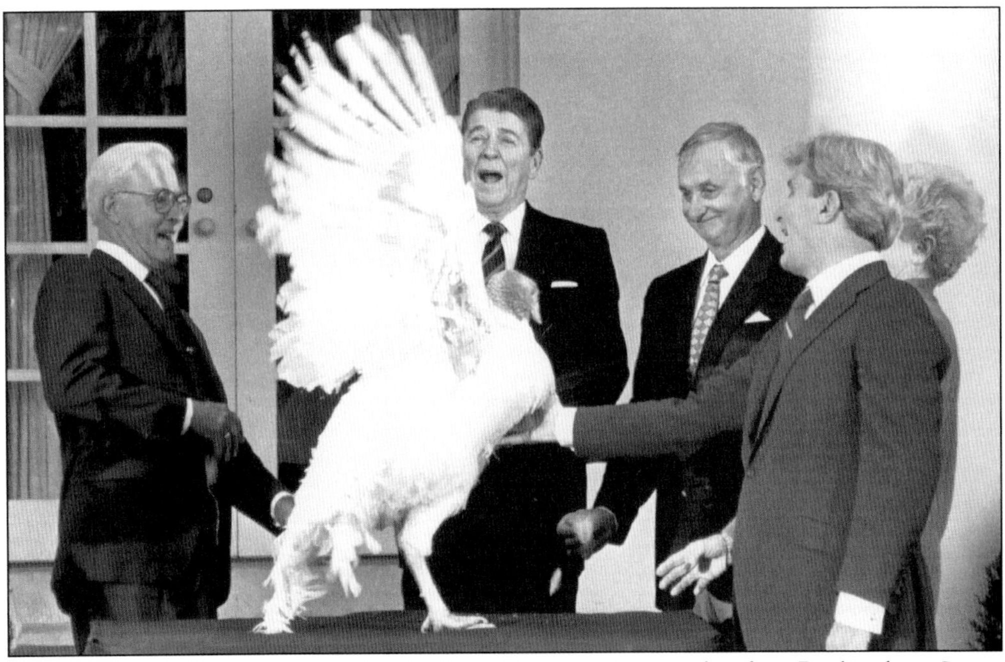

President Ronald Reagan appears shocked by this Thanksgiving turkey from Rockingham County. Pictured from left to right are Lou Watts, former director of the National Turkey Federation; President Reagan; Herman Mason, president of the National Turkey Federation; Louise Mason; and Sen. John Warner; at center is the turkey, Hawaiian Charley. (Harrisonburg-Rockingham Historical Society Collection.)

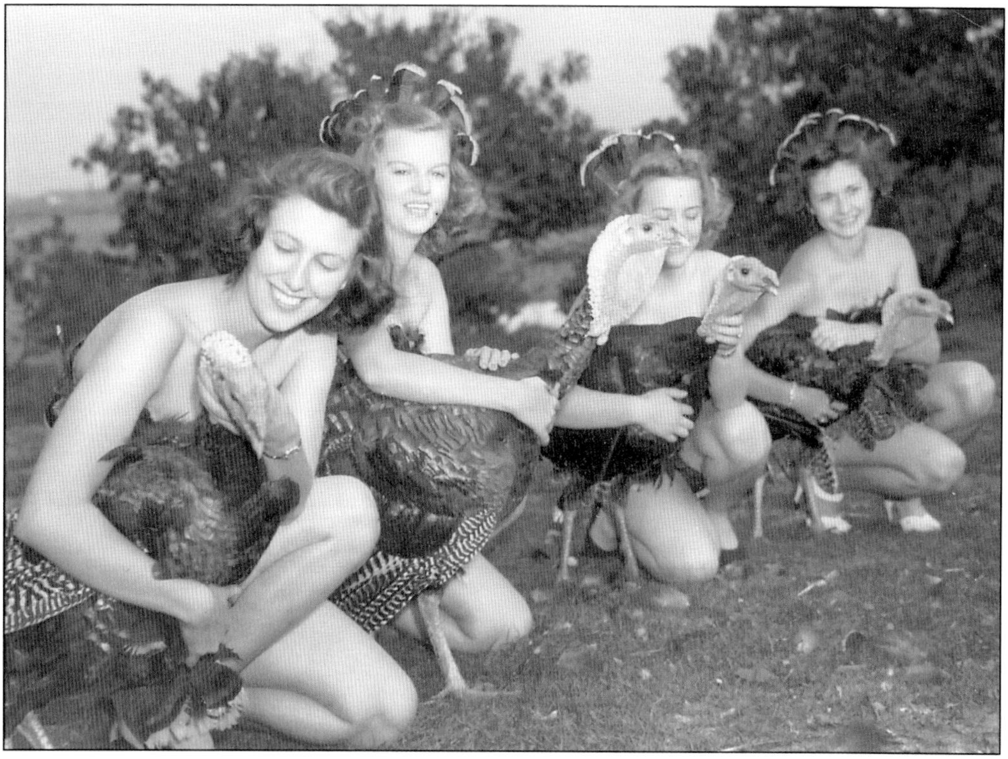

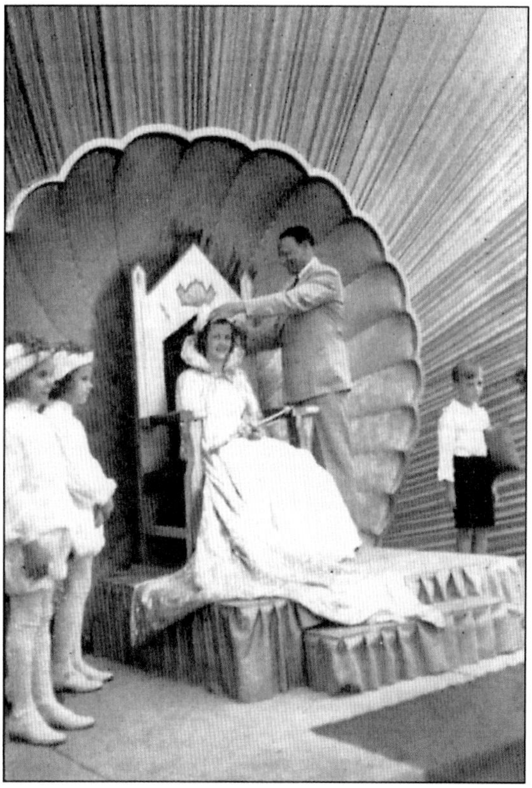

Encouraged by Shenandoah Valley Incorporated, a group formed to lure tourists to the valley, Rockingham County staged its first Turkey Festival in 1939. An attempt to complement Winchester's Apple Blossom Festival, the Rockingham event drew thousands of visitors to the county in its three years of existence. In this promotional photograph from 1940, appropriately dressed maidens happily corral the festival's guests of honor. (Harrisonburg-Rockingham Historical Society Collection.)

Ruth Wampler, daughter of poultry innovator Charles Wampler Sr., was crowned queen of the first Rockingham County Turkey Festival by Sen. Harry F. Byrd Sr. While viewed as a success on numerous levels, the festival was canceled during World War II and efforts to revive the event following the war failed to garner the enthusiasm of its initial years. (Private Collection.)

Two

Mechanization Takes Command

In his 1948 study Mechanization Takes Command, *historian Siegfried Giedion notes that the United States offered the best example of how "mechanization is inextricably woven into the pattern of thought and customs." His observation holds true in Rockingham County where, along with advances in the agricultural sphere, mechanization began to change the face of many aspects of life. Portable steam engines, for instance, made it possible to set up a sawmill at any site or even to quicken the pace of threshing wheat. Similarly, numerous mills throughout the county adopted the roller process. Three advances, however, have made the most impact on the visual landscape of the county: the automobile, the telephone, and the railroad. Today, car culture is omnipresent throughout the United States, and Rockingham County is no exception. Photographs in this section reveal the evolution of roads as the switch was made from horses to autos and local blacksmith shops to service stations. The telephone, along with electricity, has led to a web of phone and power lines crisscrossing the county. Railroads reached Rockingham County in the 19th century, but sights and sounds of trains increased in the 20th century as the Chesapeake and Western line stretched across the entire county, allowing more freedom of movement for people and products. The camera, undergoing many changes itself, recorded this evolution in the hands of professionals and amateurs.*

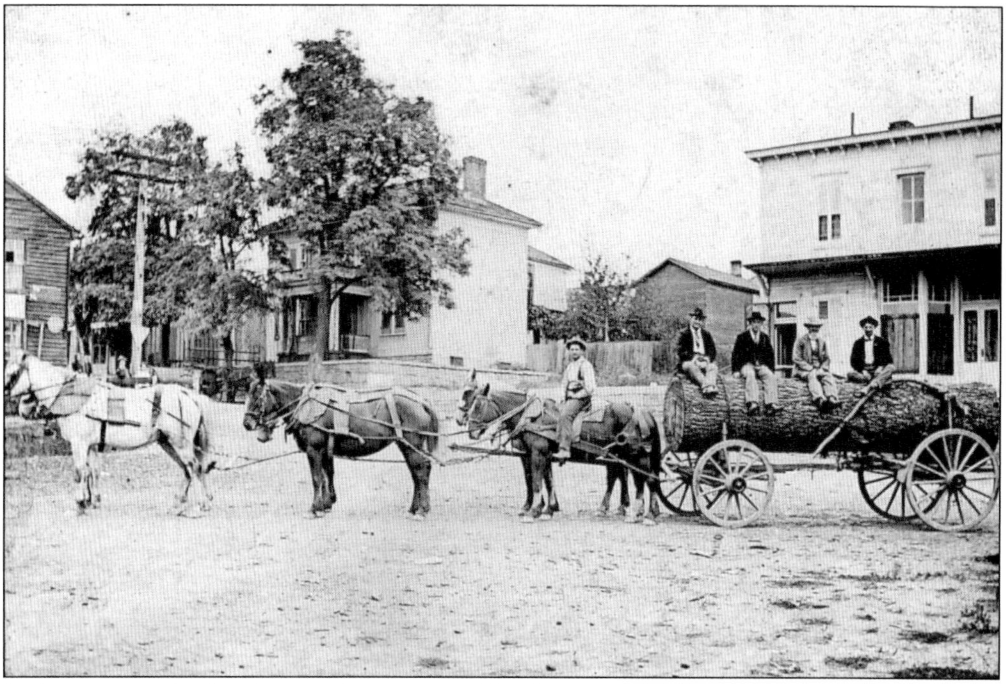

Perhaps astounded by their work, a group of lumbermen sit atop a massive timber that they harvested in the mountains of western Rockingham County. Photographed on Main Street of Timberville around 1890, the log was undoubtedly intended for the Zigler brothers, well-known dealers in lumber and noted as the largest sellers of walnut lumber in Virginia. (Jeffrey S. Evans Collection.)

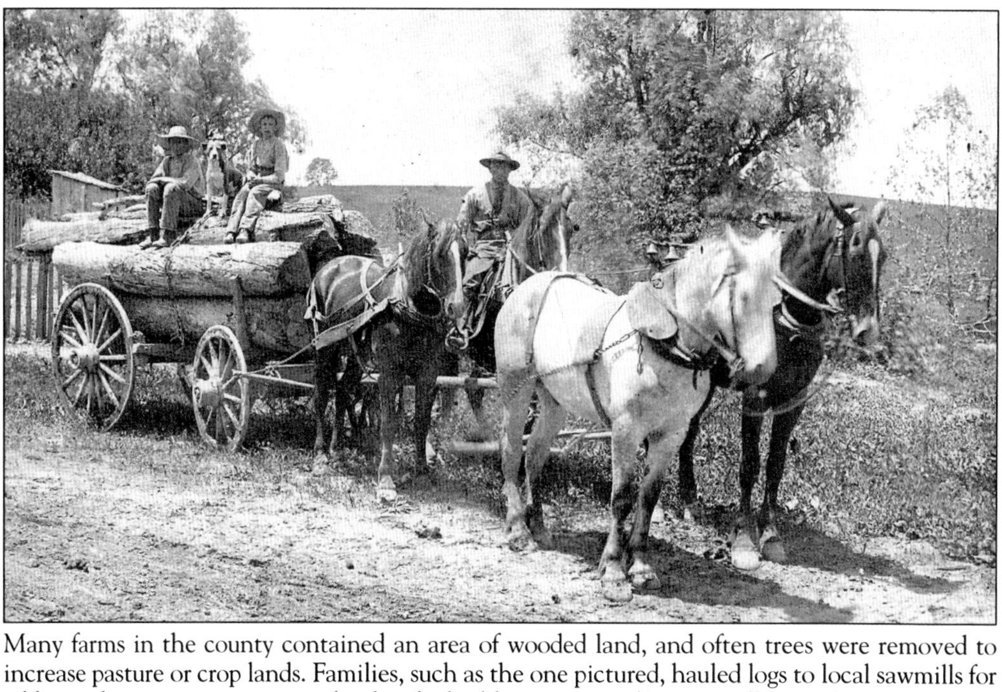

Many farms in the county contained an area of wooded land, and often trees were removed to increase pasture or crop lands. Families, such as the one pictured, hauled logs to local sawmills for additional income or to procure lumber for building projects. (Private collection.)

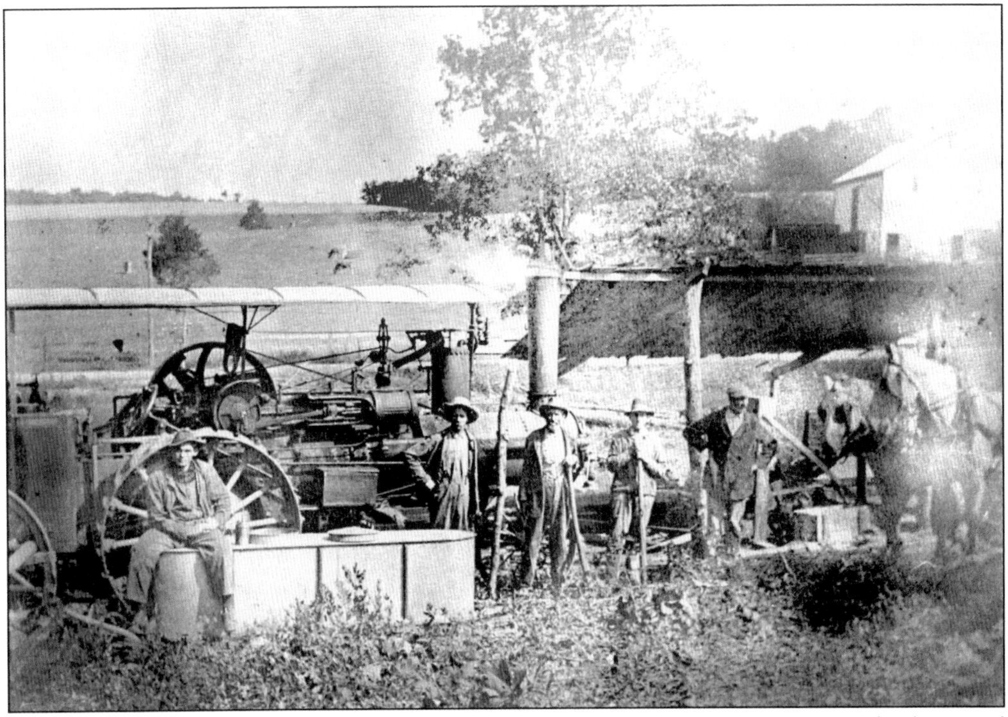

The application of portable steam engines as motive power for sawmills greatly decreased the amount of time and labor involved in preparing wood. These two photographs reveal that sawmills were often located at temporary sites, wherever there was work to be done. (Private collection.)

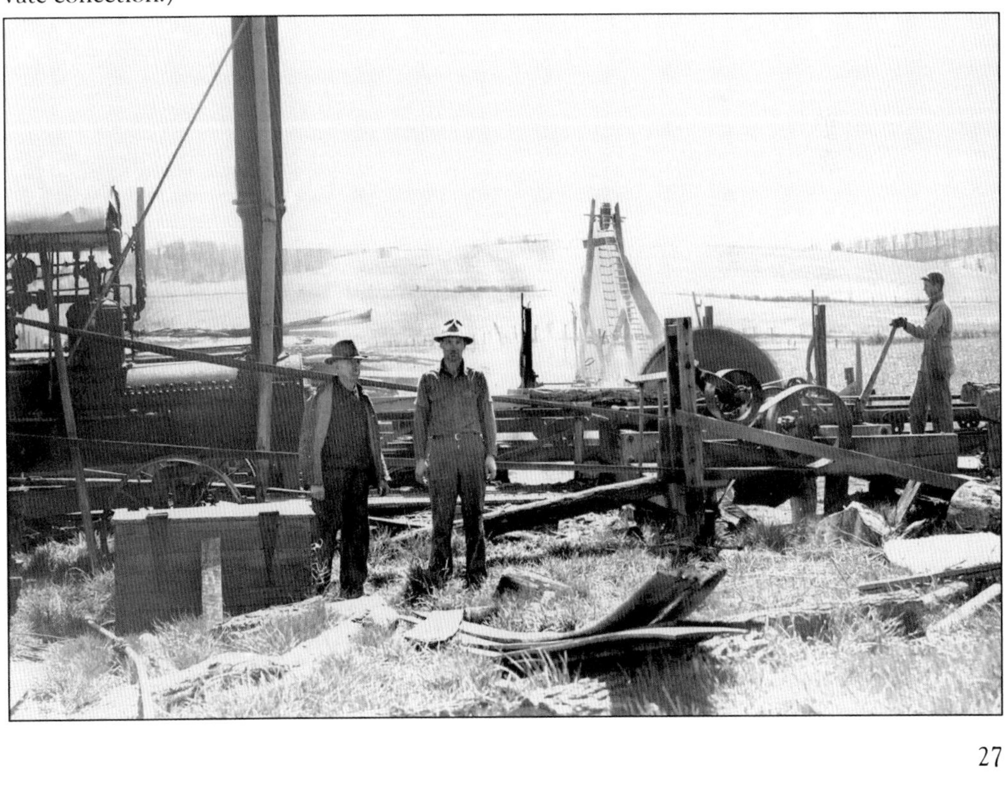

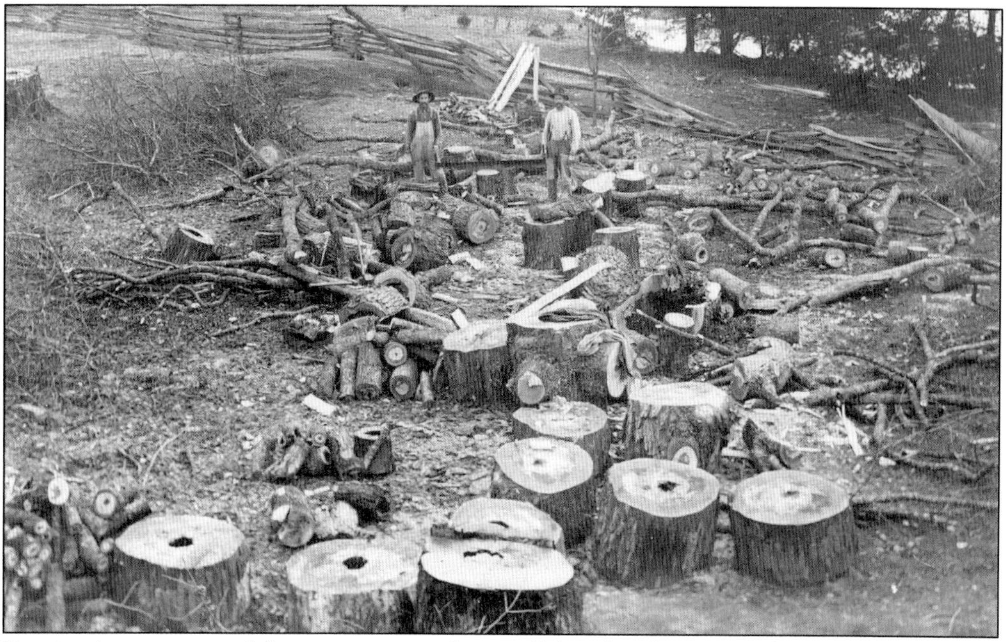

Despite the existence of the steam-powered sawmill, handwork continued to be necessary. The pair of sawyers in the center of this photograph is almost hidden by the expanse of timber that they cut using a two-man saw. The fence in the background attests to the labor involved with early techniques of splitting logs to make rails, a process that the sawmill rendered obsolete. (Private collection.)

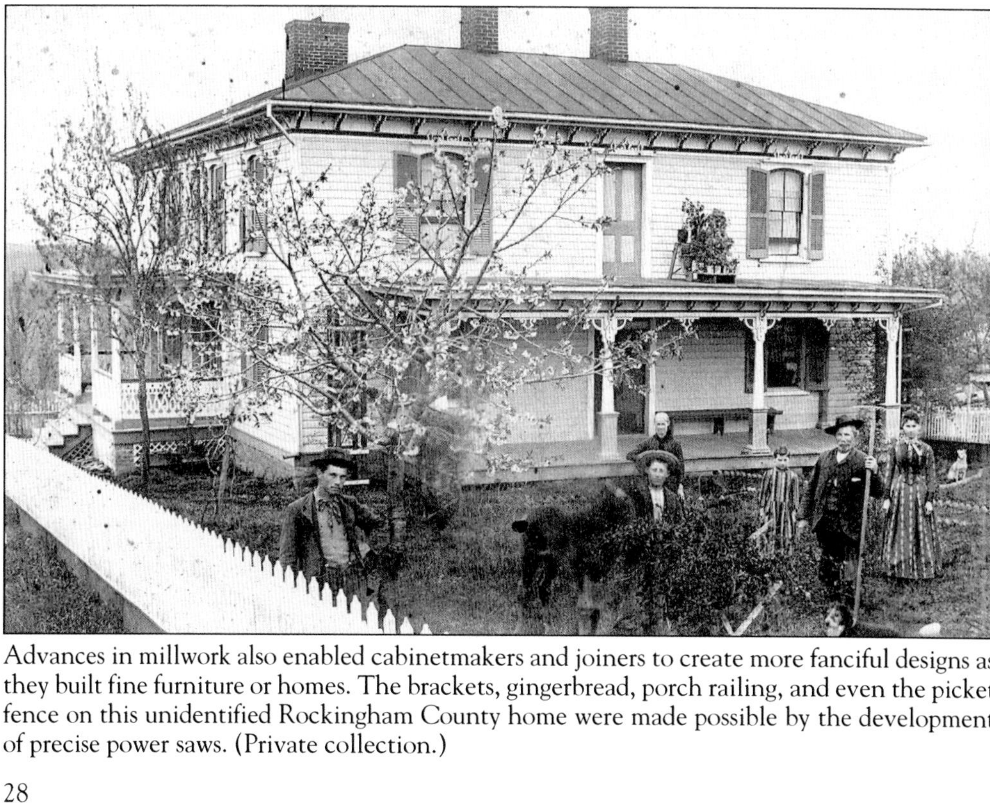

Advances in millwork also enabled cabinetmakers and joiners to create more fanciful designs as they built fine furniture or homes. The brackets, gingerbread, porch railing, and even the picket fence on this unidentified Rockingham County home were made possible by the development of precise power saws. (Private collection.)

Pottery production had a long history in Rockingham County when this photograph was taken at the Shenandoah Pottery in Broadway around 1927. The pottery had two kilns and manufactured porcelain and sanitary wares to be shipped throughout the East Coast. Pottery manager C.C. Wood and his son Harold stand in the left of the doorway. (Harold Wood Collection.)

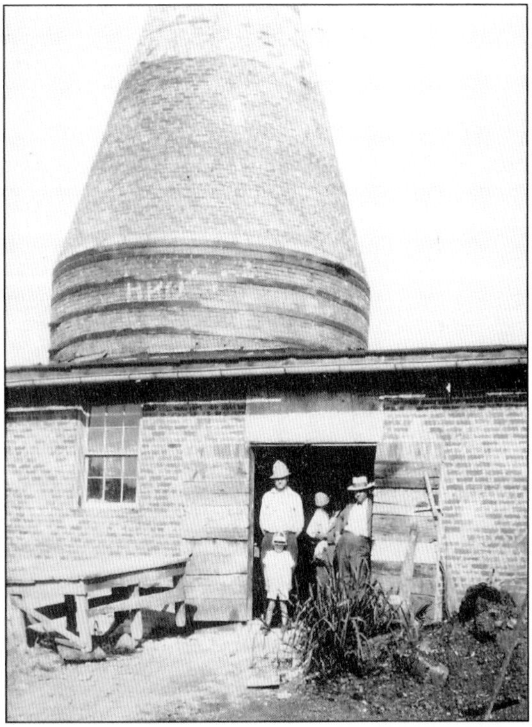

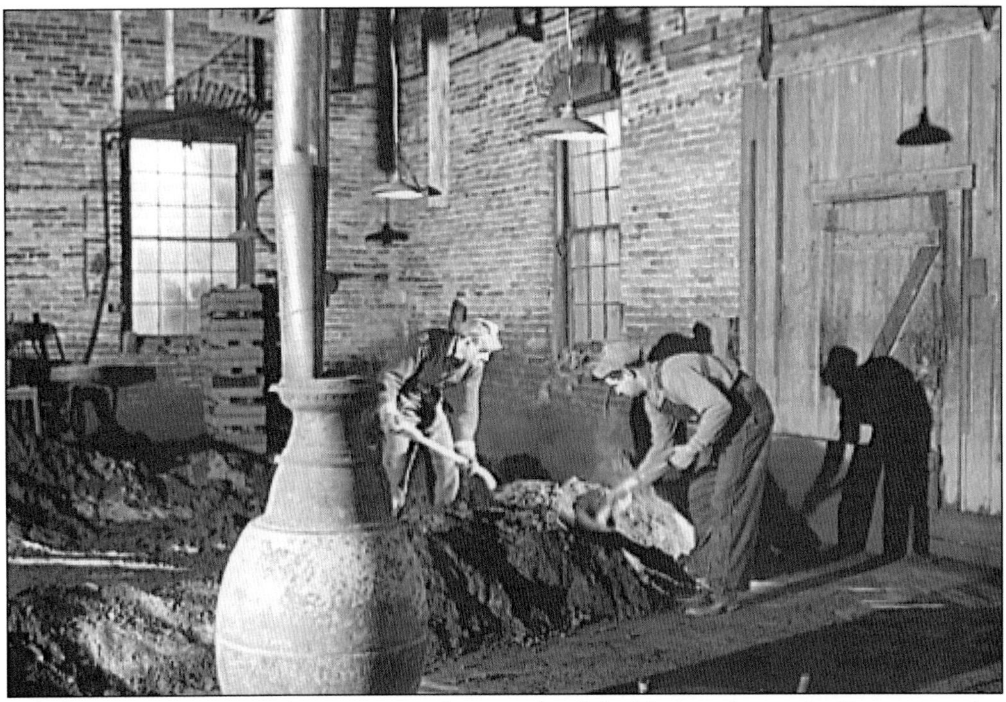

Taken by Farm Security Administration photographer John Vachon during the Depression, this photograph demonstrates the stark conditions in the Trumbo Foundry in Broadway. Trumbo's shop was typical of many in the county in the first half of the 20th century—"locally owned and operated." (Library of Congress Collection.)

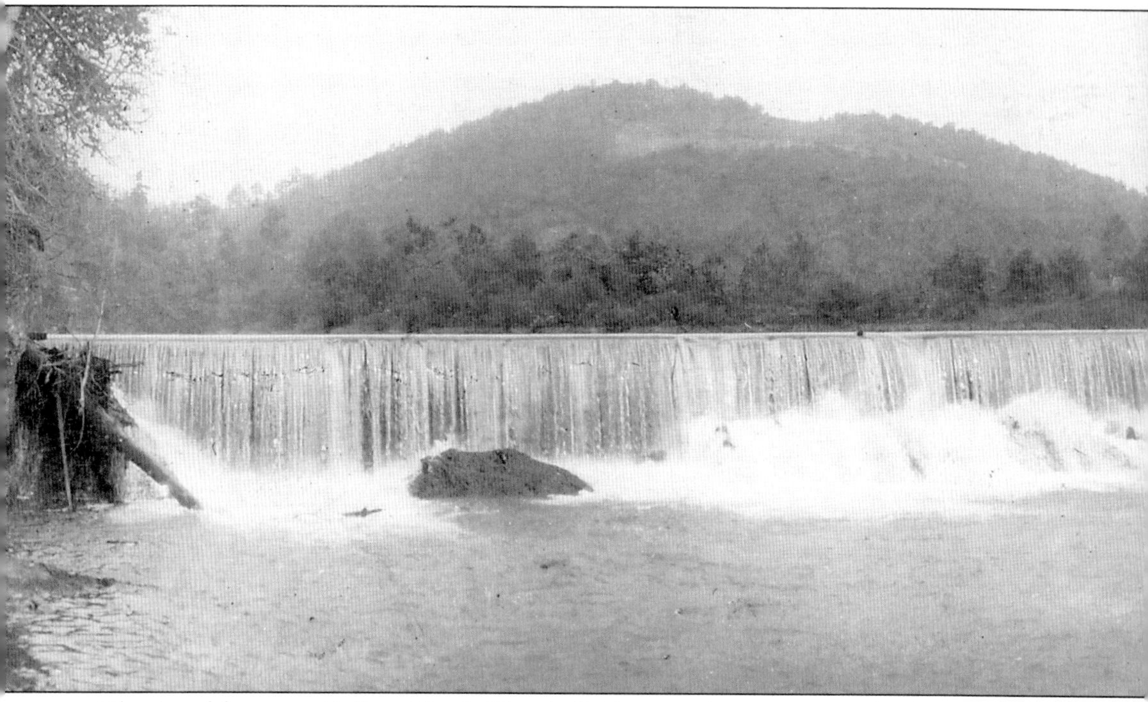

The site of the natural falls on North River in Bridgewater became a sort of industrial park of the 19th century. It boasted the Natural Falls Milling Company and, by 1872, the Farmers Milling Company. In 1877, the Bridgewater Manufacturing Company opened a woolen mill there along

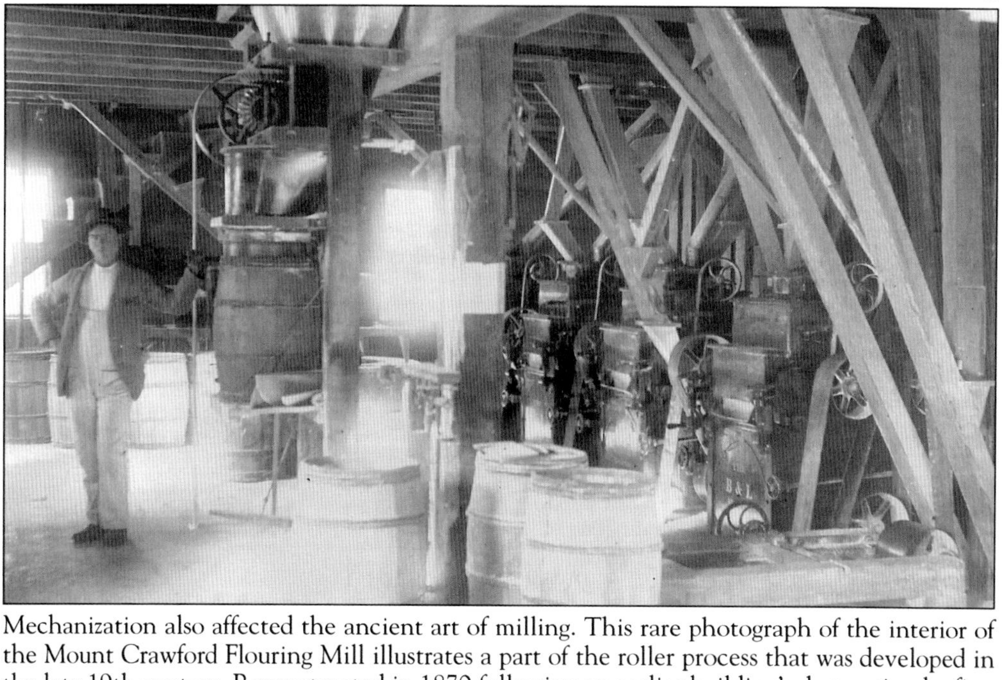

Mechanization also affected the ancient art of milling. This rare photograph of the interior of the Mount Crawford Flouring Mill illustrates a part of the roller process that was developed in the late 19th century. Reconstructed in 1870 following an earlier building's destruction by fire, the mill produced 60 barrels of flour per day by 1900. Unfortunately, the mill was once again destroyed by fire in 1962. (Kent Botkin Collection.)

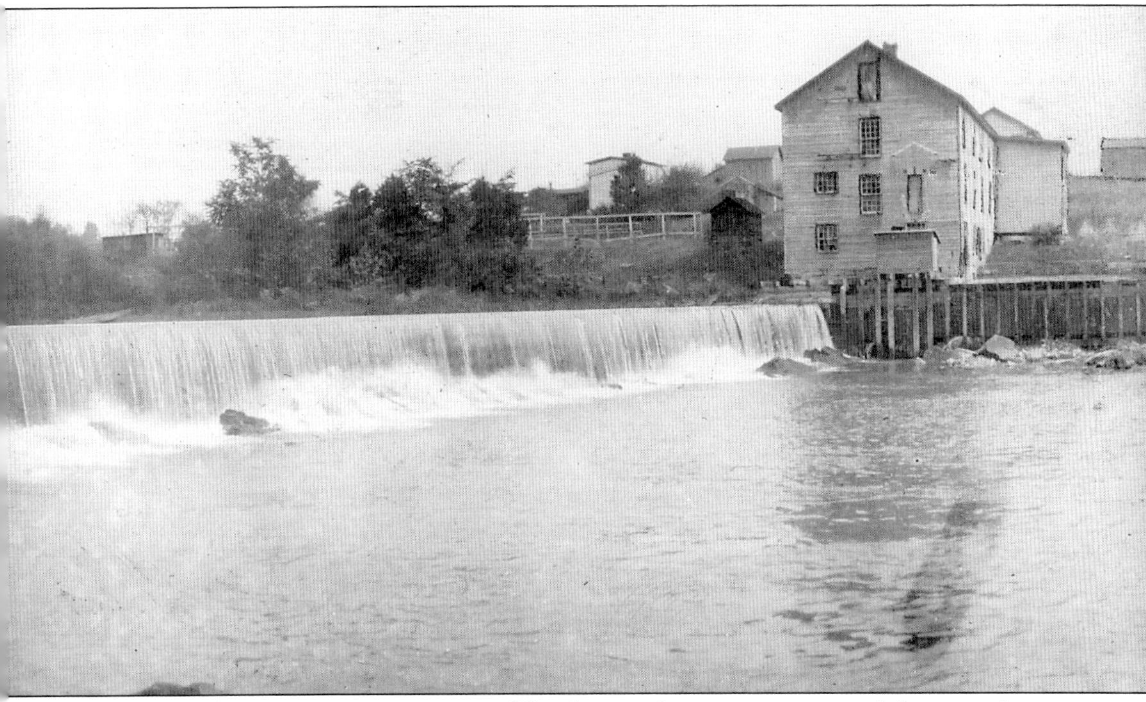

with a facility for repairing steam engines. The dam on the river remains, and the grounds are now a municipal park. (Bridgewater College Collection.)

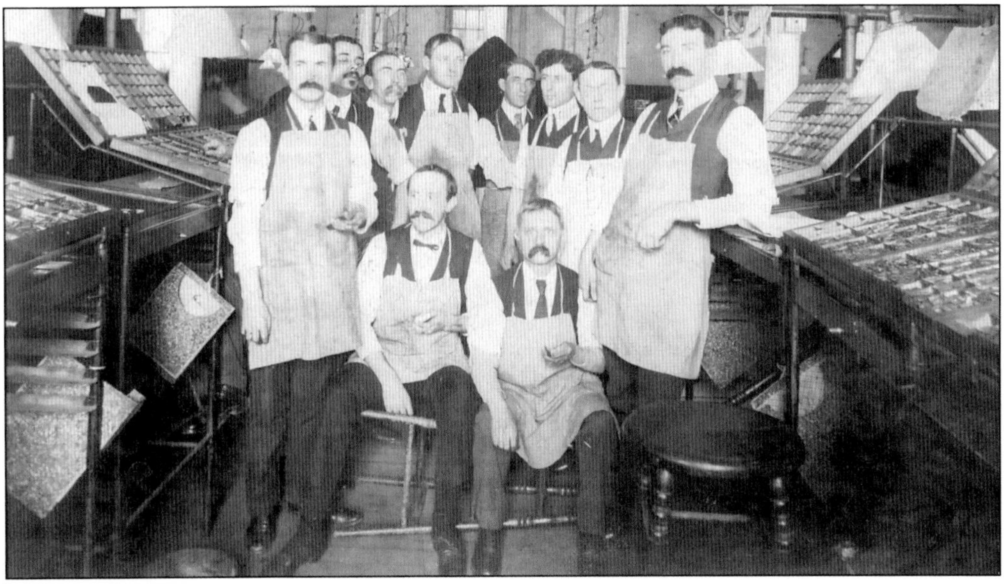

By the turn of the 20th century, the printing process had undergone dramatic changes from the early days of the Ruebush-Kieffer Company in the 1870s. Employees of the company pose with type, which was then still set by hand, in their Dayton building. The following employees are pictured from left to right: (front row, seated) Mark B. "Hack" Ibach and George B. Roberts; (back row) S.K. Kieffer, Alfred Fisher, ? Goshorn, Evan T. Sheerer, Dale Sheriff, William Gardner, and William B. Meyers. (Eastern Mennonite University Collection.)

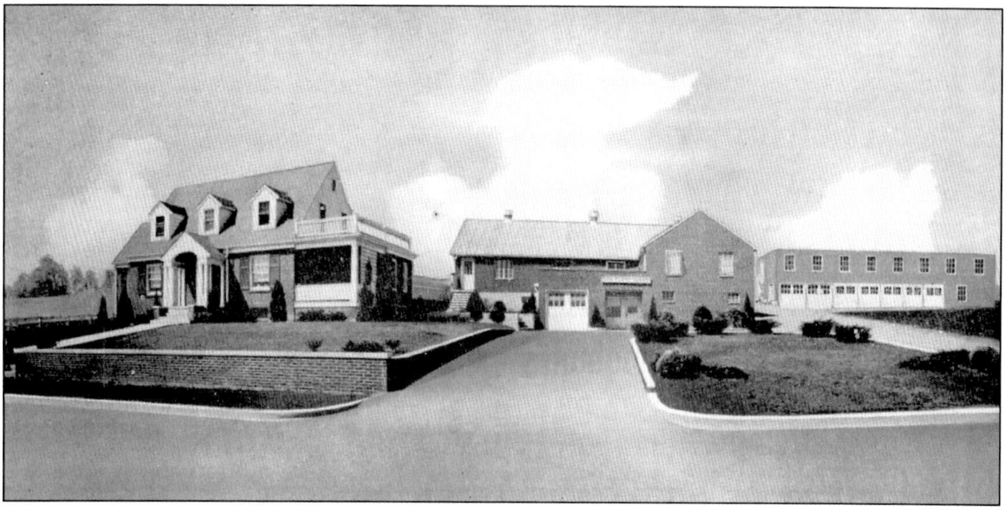

Obviously important to Rockingham County, the poultry industry continued to advance technologically. In 1944, the Shenk Electric Hatchery, operated by Mr. and Mrs. Jacob Shenk, had a capacity of over one million eggs at one setting, enabling the company to produce nearly six million chicks per year. (Private collection.)

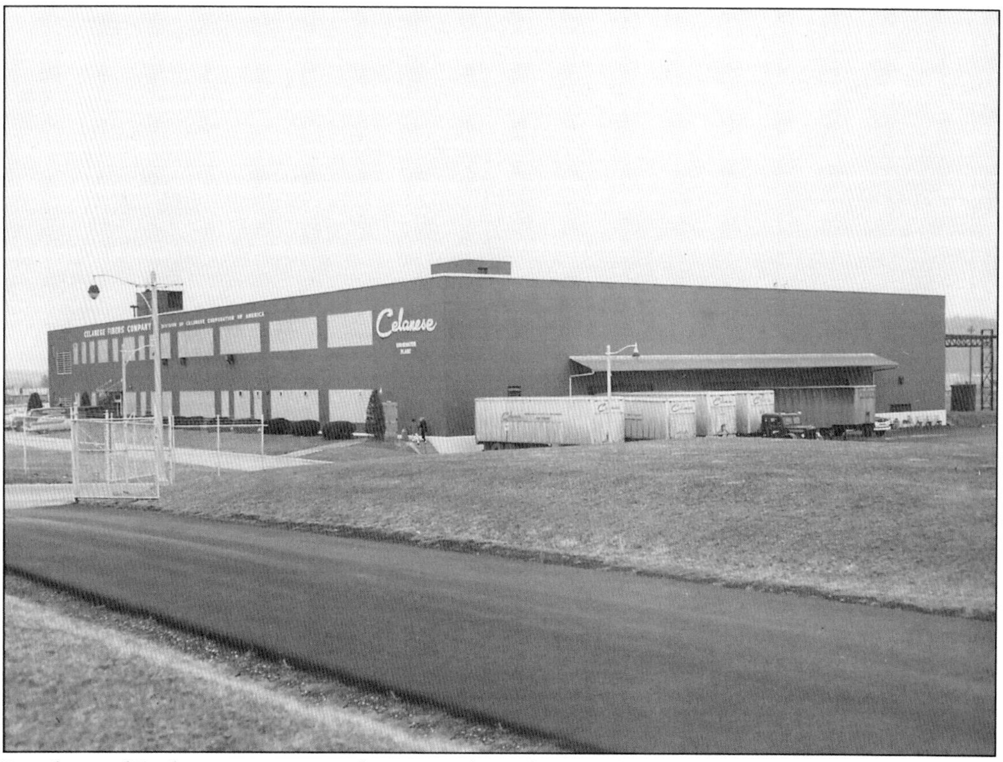

Residents of Bridgewater witnessed a tremendous change when Celanese Corporation of America located a knitting mill on the town's northern boundary in 1946. Operating until 1971, the company knitted acetate and arnel fabric. Several generations of Bridgewater's youth recall playing Little League baseball at the park located behind the plant. (Harrisonburg-Rockingham Historical Society Collection.)

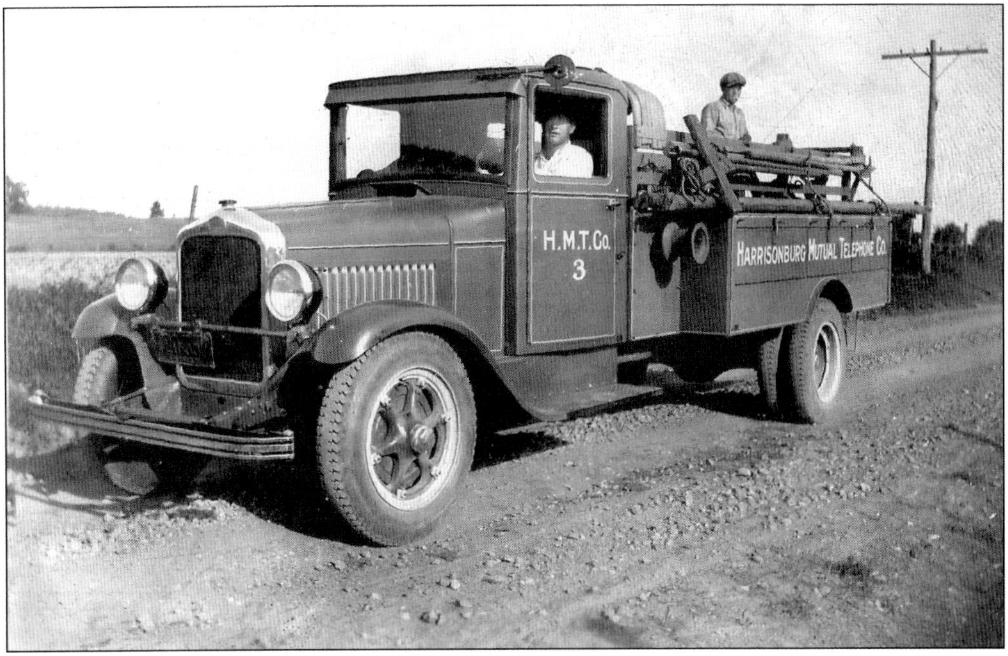

The first telephone in Rockingham County was installed in 1879 when the telegraph operator for the Baltimore and Ohio Railroad connected a line between the passenger depot and the freight station, a distance of nearly 100 yards. By 1902, Walter Switzer had organized the Harrisonburg Telephone Company, which evolved into the Harrisonburg Mutual Telephone Company. Above, the company's truck hauls materials to a rural site where two workers (below) use the derrick to plant a pole for the company's expansion into the county around 1930. (Massanutten Regional Library Collection.)

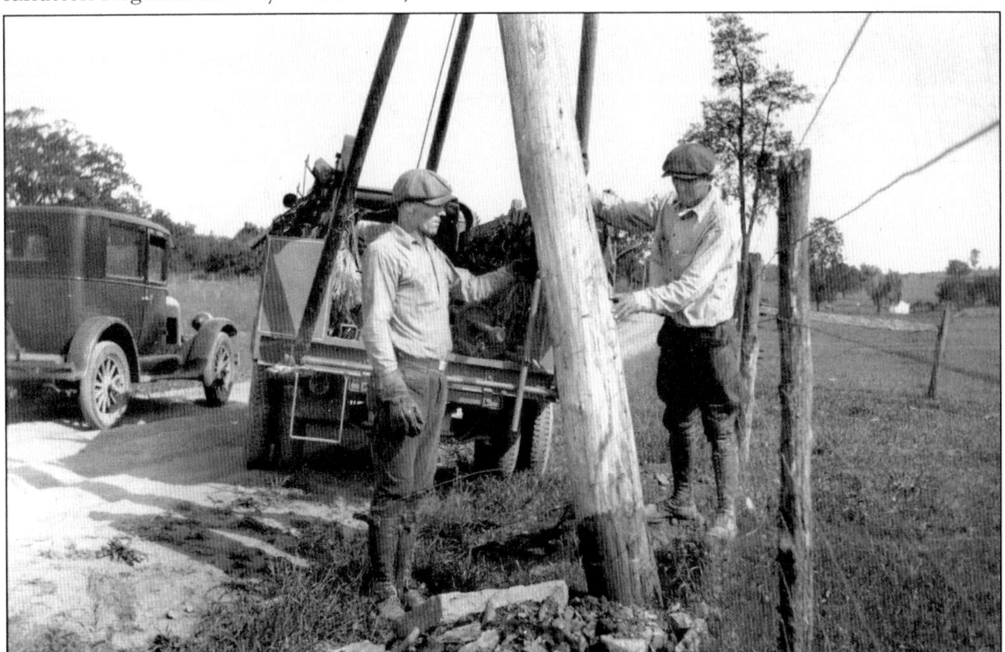

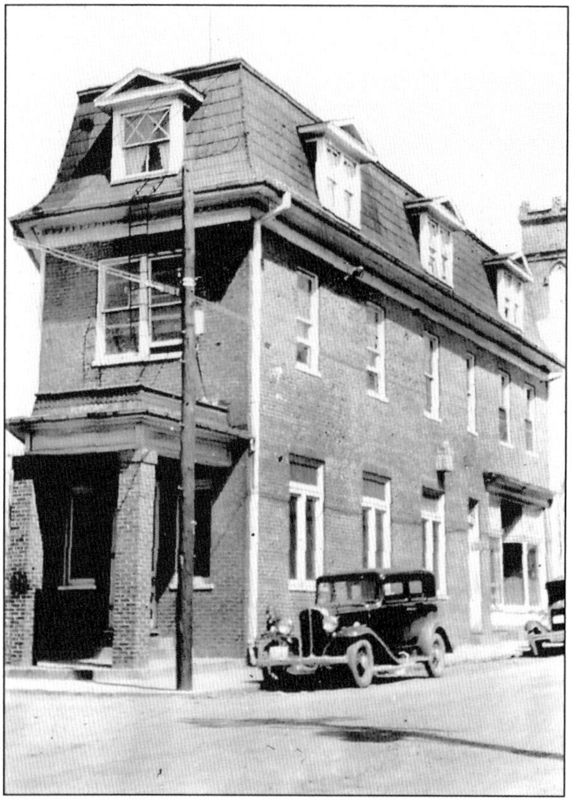

The Harrisonburg Mutual Telephone Company's central office in Dayton was located in the 1911 bank building at the intersection of Main and College Streets. By 1934, the time of this photograph, the telephone was in wide use throughout Rockingham County. (Massanutten Regional Library Collection.)

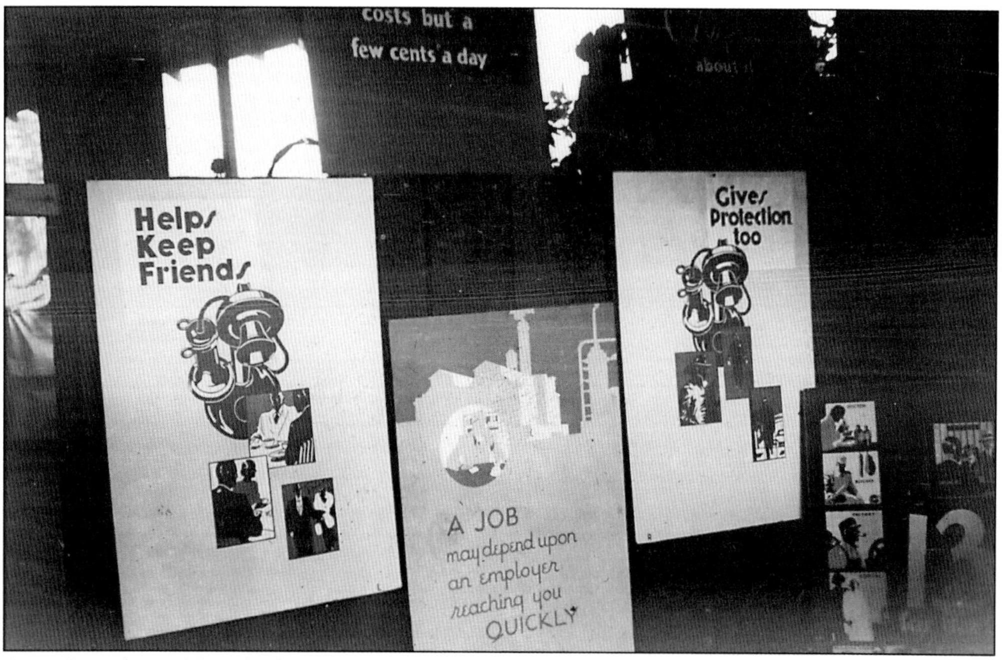

As early as the 1930s, telephone companies understood the importance of their product to adolescents. These posters were part of a Harrisonburg Mutual Telephone Company display at the 4-H Club fair held at Ed's Park in Rawley Springs. (Massanutten Regional Library Collection.)

Phone company employees ? Black and ? Wenger splice a spider web of cables in Dayton's central office. By 1935, the telephone was transforming communications in the county's rural towns. (Massanutten Regional Library Collection.)

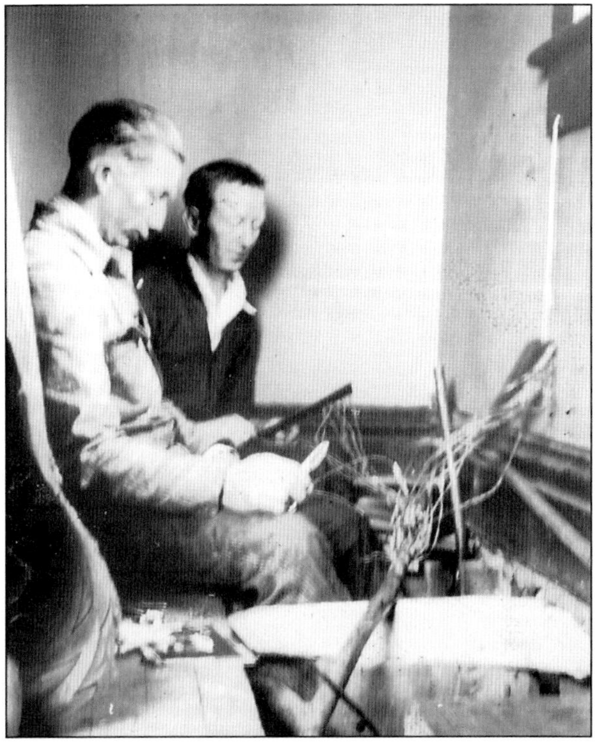

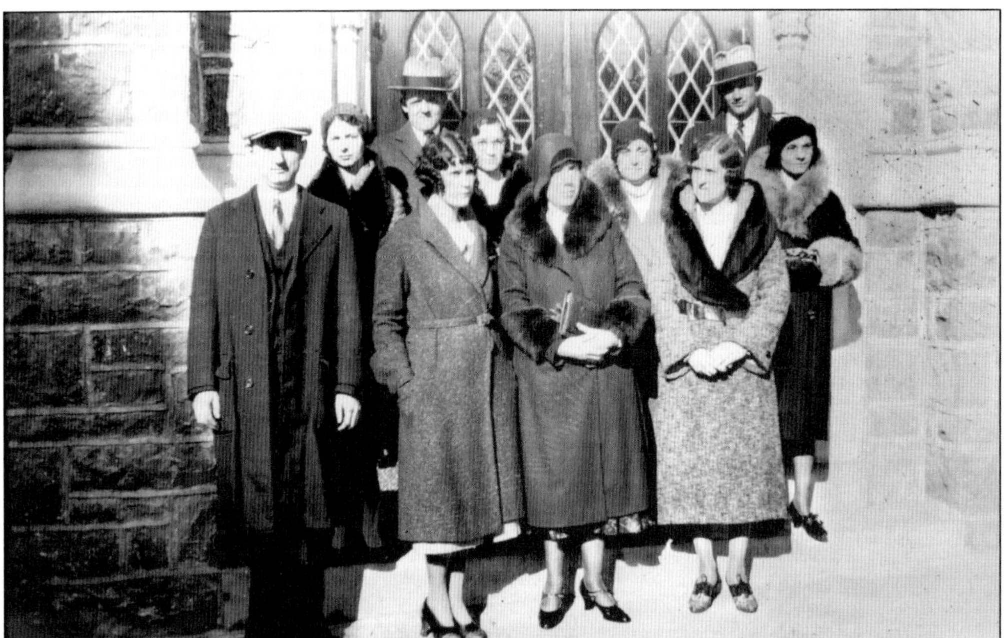

The telephone company's chief operators pose together at their conference in 1932. The following employees are pictured from left to right: B. Frank Wingard (Elkton), Mabel Saufley (Weyers Cave), unidentified, Miss Young (Harrisonburg), Beulah Neff (Timberville), Blanche Hartman (Dayton), Mattie Miller (Bridgewater), L.C. Knicely (assistant at Harrisonburg), unidentified, and Anna M. Pence (Broadway). (Massanutten Regional Library Collection.)

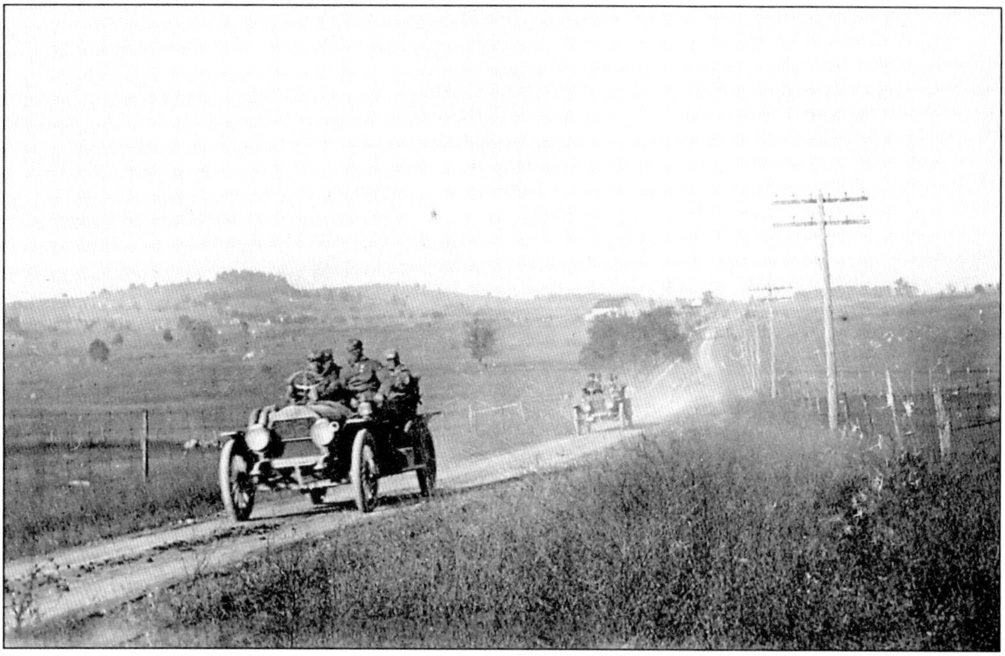

The advent of affordable automobiles meant fewer horses and more traffic even in the 1920s. Here, two autos travel down the unpaved, one-lane Valley Pike between Harrisonburg and Mount Crawford. This landscape is currently covered with dealers offering new and used automobiles. (Kermit Early Collection.)

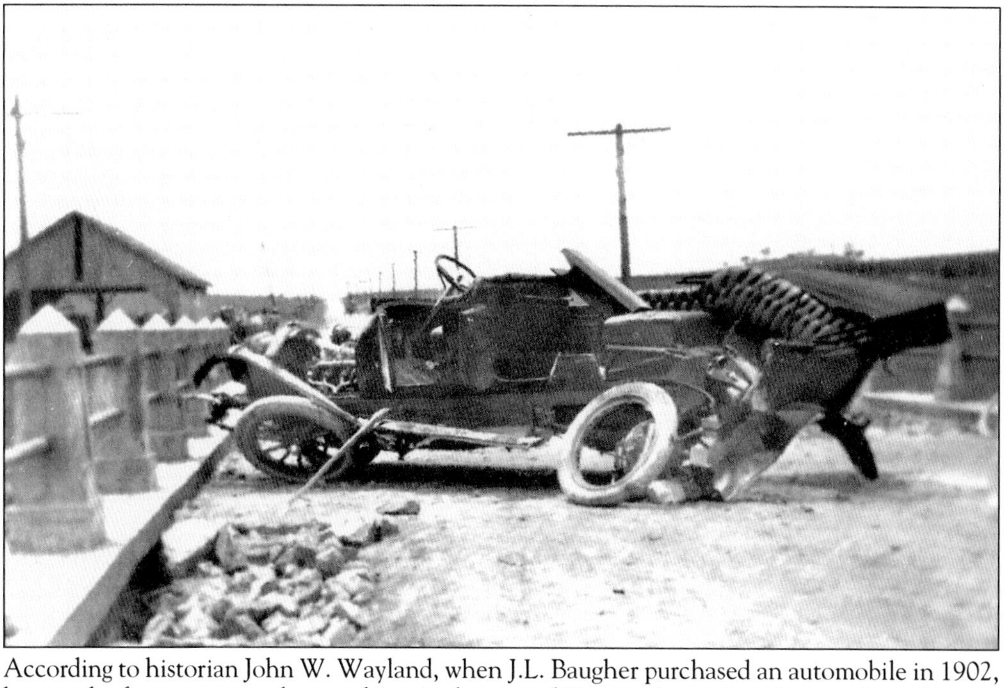

According to historian John W. Wayland, when J.L. Baugher purchased an automobile in 1902, he was the first to own such a machine in the city of Harrisonburg. Accidents such as this one near Tenth Legion in 1920 undoubtedly became more frequent as the number of automobiles on county roads increased. (Kermit Early Collection.)

The need for automobile service increased as the 20th century progressed. During his trip through the region in the early 1940s, Farm Security Administration photographer John Vachon took this photograph of a mechanic at Spitzer's Garage in Grottoes, noting that this was "one of the flourishing shops" in the Shenandoah Valley. (Library of Congress Collection.)

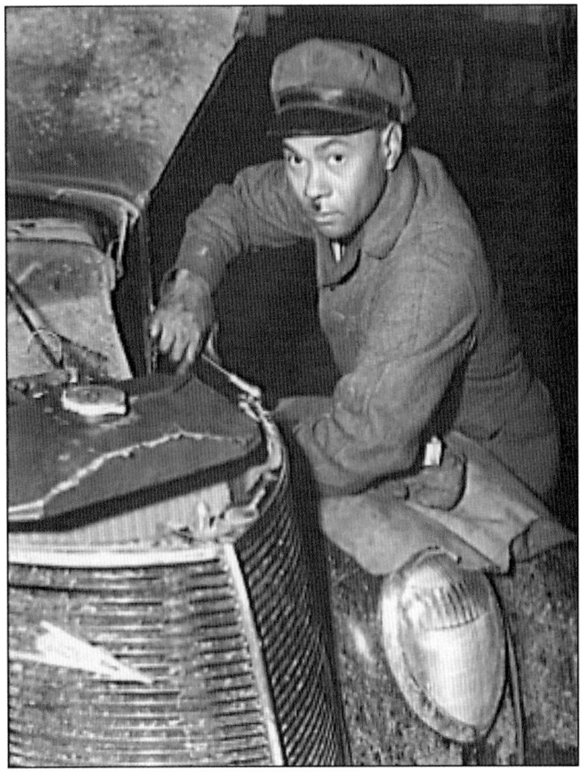

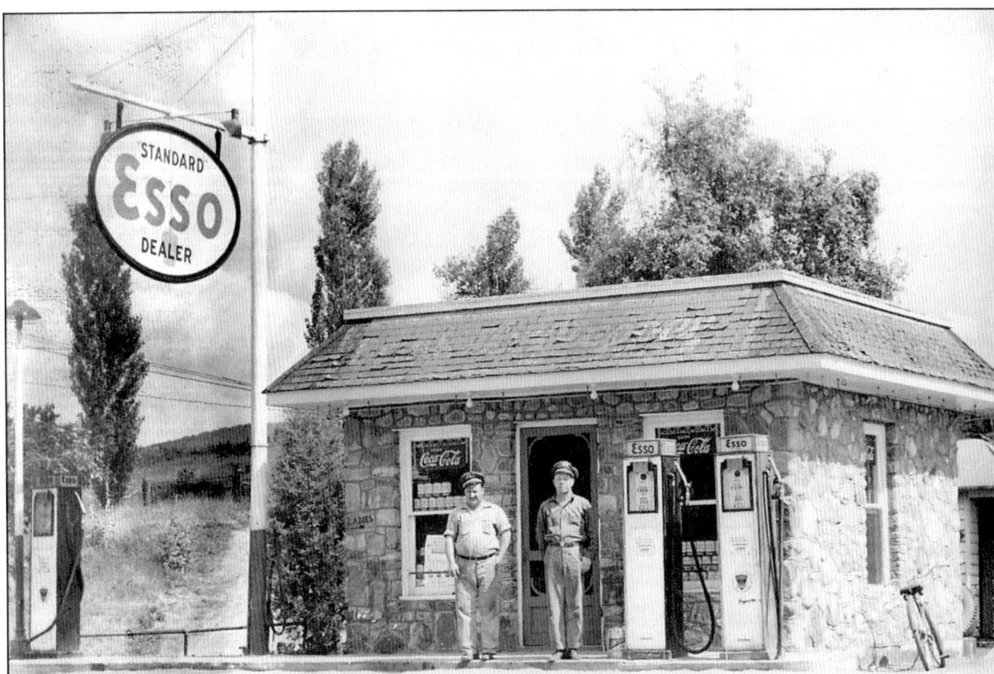

Gasoline stations became more common on the county's landscape as motorists needed access to quick fuel and service. Wesley Shifflett and Lloyd Monger pose at the Blue and Gray Service Station in Elkton. (Harrisonburg-Rockingham Historical Society Collection.)

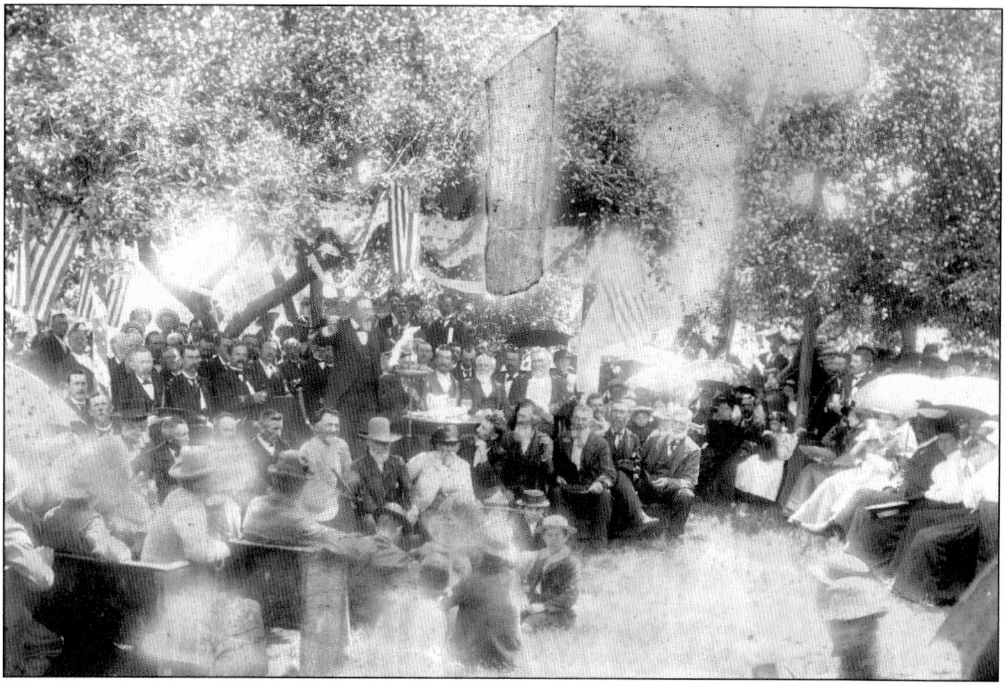

The Chesapeake and Western Railroad, well known in the county for many years, seemed a dream come true in 1895. After years of anticipating a railroad linking the east and west portions of the county, residents of Dayton held an unprecedented celebration when the rails reached their town on July 31, 1895. Col. E.C. Machen, a proponent of the rail line, rode the first train from Harrisonburg that day with the featured speaker Judge John Paul, shown here addressing the crowd of nearly 5,000. (Massanutten Regional Library Collection.)

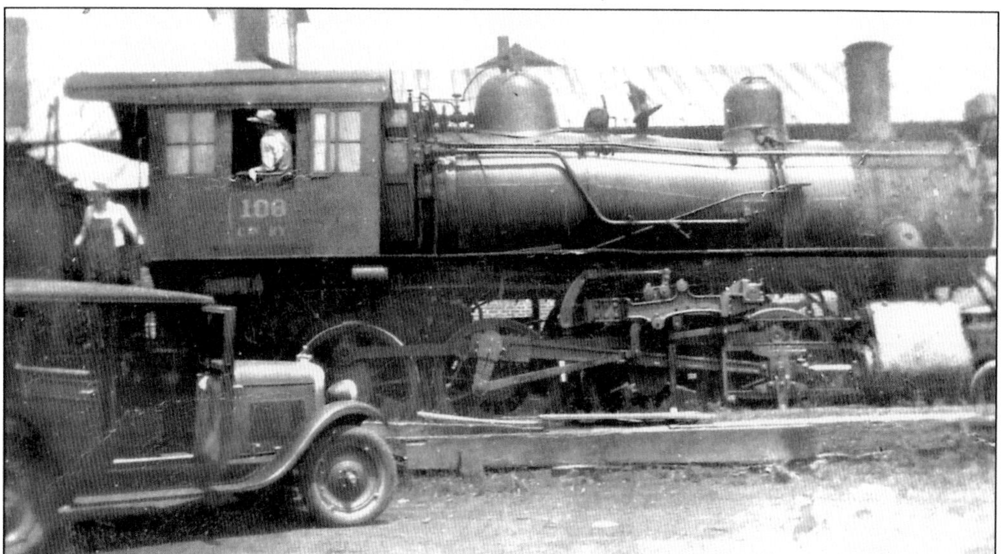

Chesapeake and Western Engine 108 sits outside of the Elkton shop in the late 1930s. Built in 1899 by the Baldwin Company, the engine was purchased from the Norfolk and Western Railroad in 1929. By 1941, engine 108 had been scrapped. (Harrisonburg-Rockingham Historical Society Collection.)

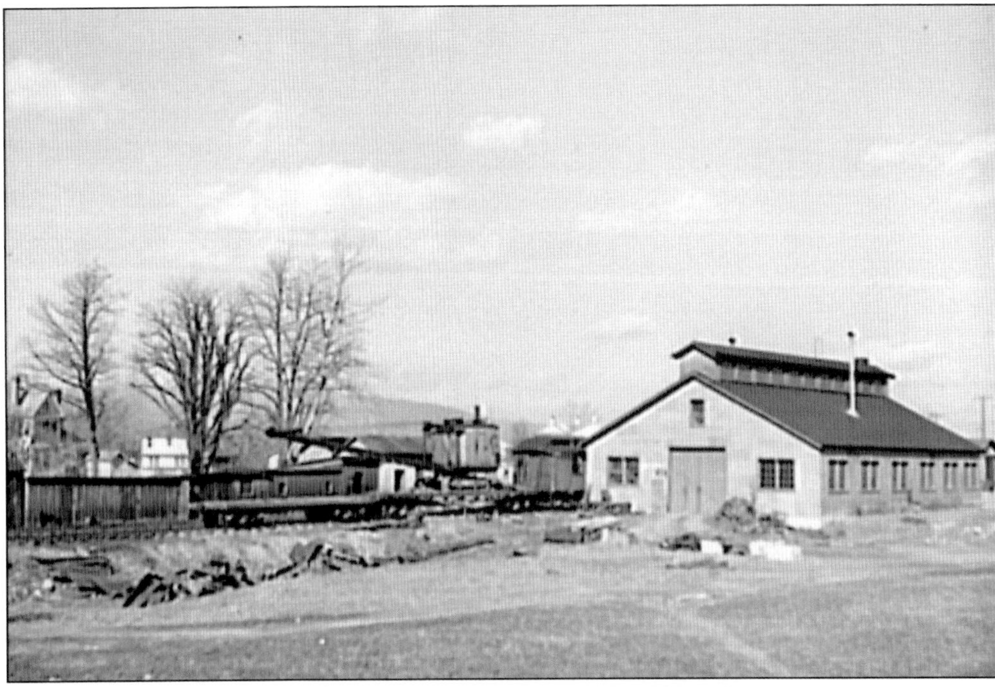

Always finding an artistic angle, photographer John Vachon of the Farm Security Administration captured these views of the Chesapeake and Western Railroad in the late 1930s. The car shop and maintenance building (above) were located in Elkton. At right, Engine 108 pulls out of the shop. (Library of Congress Collection.)

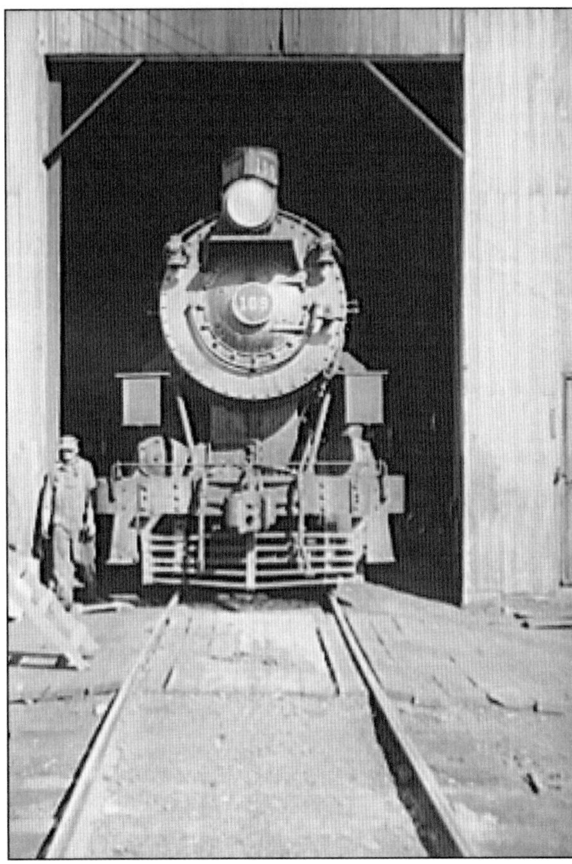

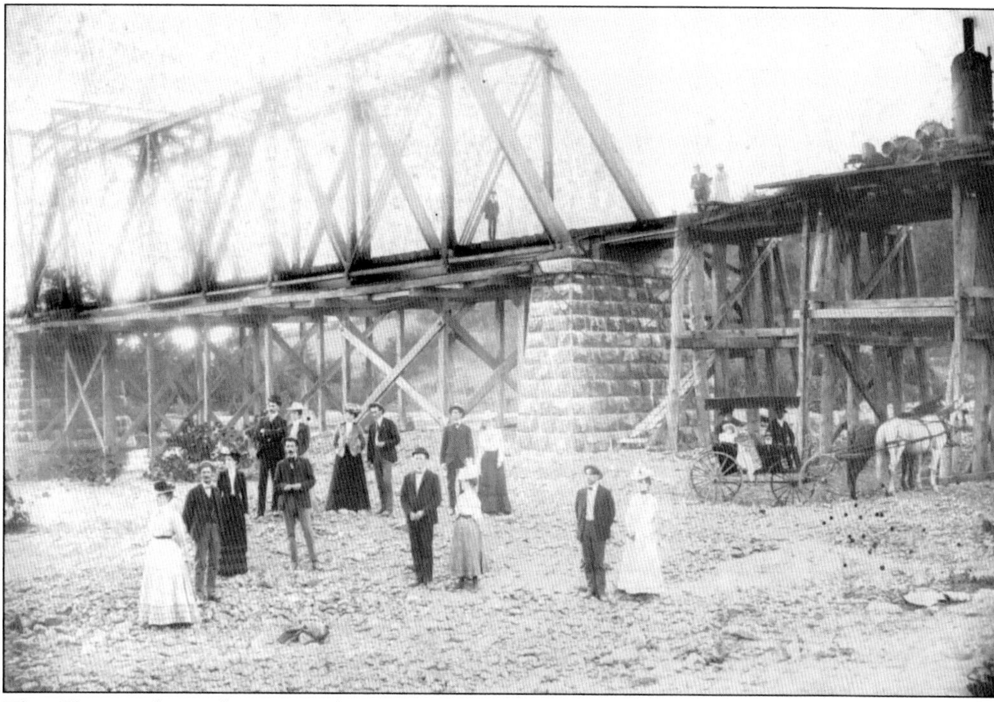

The Chesapeake and Western line ran into a number of natural barriers as it lumbered west toward its goal of the Ohio River. Notably, just west of Bridgewater the line encountered the confluence of Dry River and North River. Undaunted, the company constructed a bridge over the water in 1901. The construction site was the destination of sightseers even before its completion. (Jeffrey S. Evans Collection.)

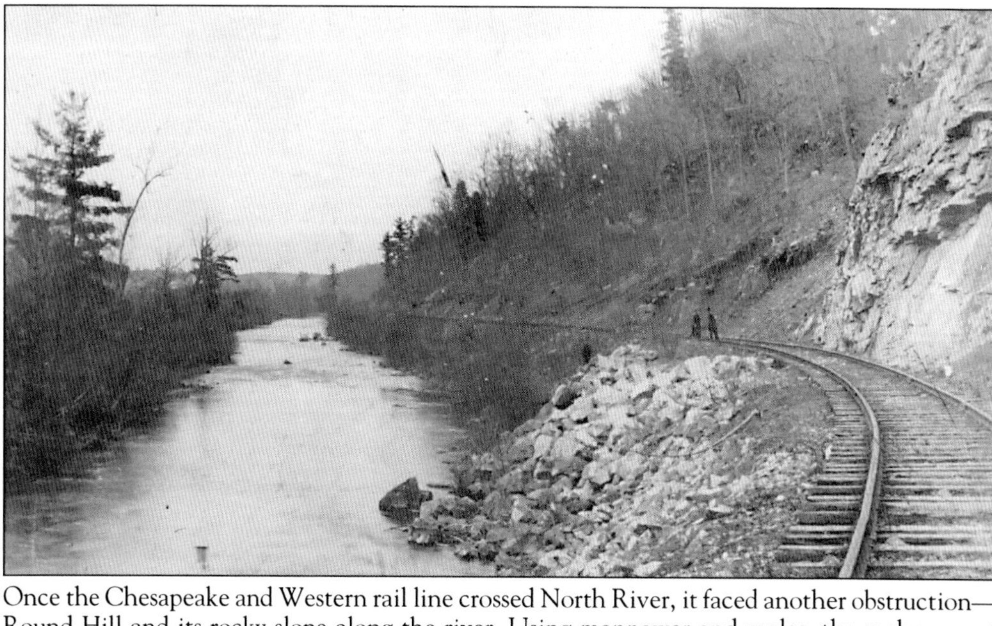

Once the Chesapeake and Western rail line crossed North River, it faced another obstruction—Round Hill and its rocky slope along the river. Using manpower and mules, the rock was cut away to enable the line to proceed. By 1902, it had reached Stokesville in Augusta County, the line's western terminus. (Private collection.)

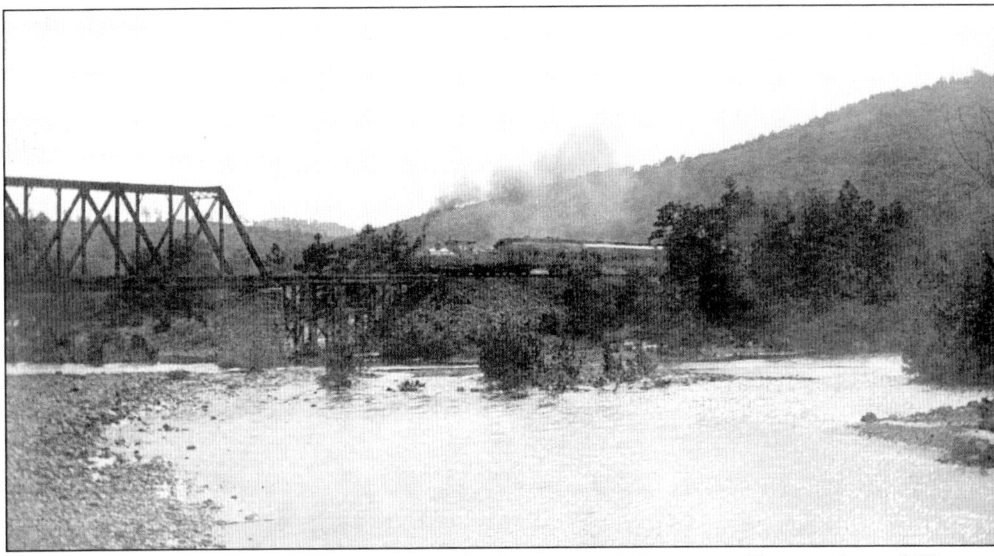

Pictured in 1903, shortly after the line stretched to Augusta County, a Chesapeake and Western engine hauls passengers across the North River bridge toward their destinations. From this point westward, travelers could disembark at Mossy Creek, Mt. Solon, or Stokesville, an industrial complex on the edge of the North River Gap. (Bridgewater College Collection.)

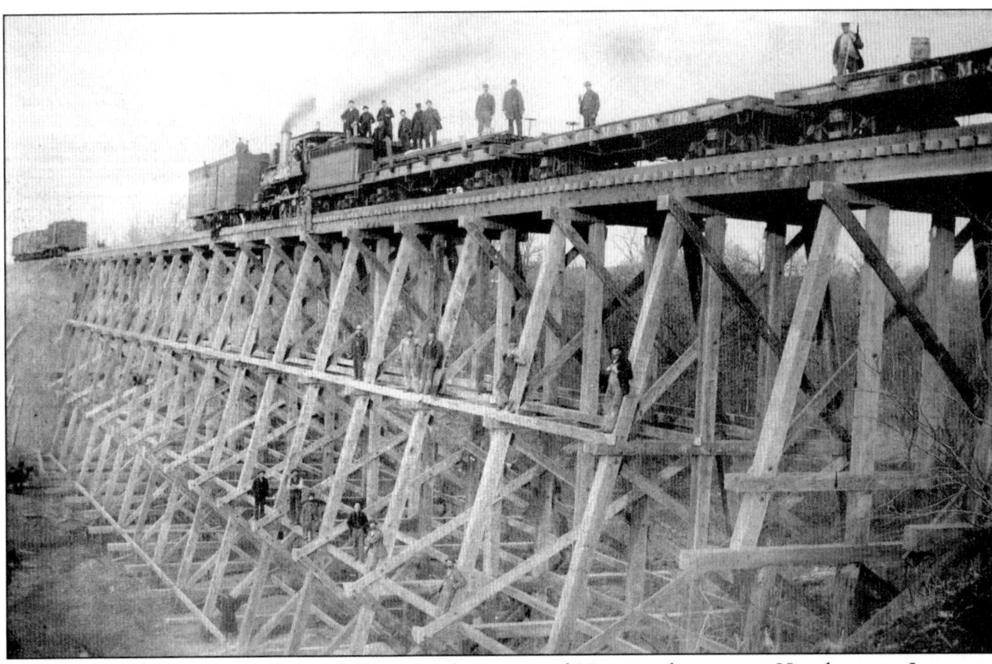

Located on the Chesapeake and Western line east of Harrisonburg near Keezletown, Laymans trestle was a treacherous wooden crossing 1,024 feet long with an average height of 40 feet. Under the direction of general manager Don Thomas, the dangerous trestle was filled in with earth beginning in 1929; the project was not completed until 1931. (Greg Evans Collection.)

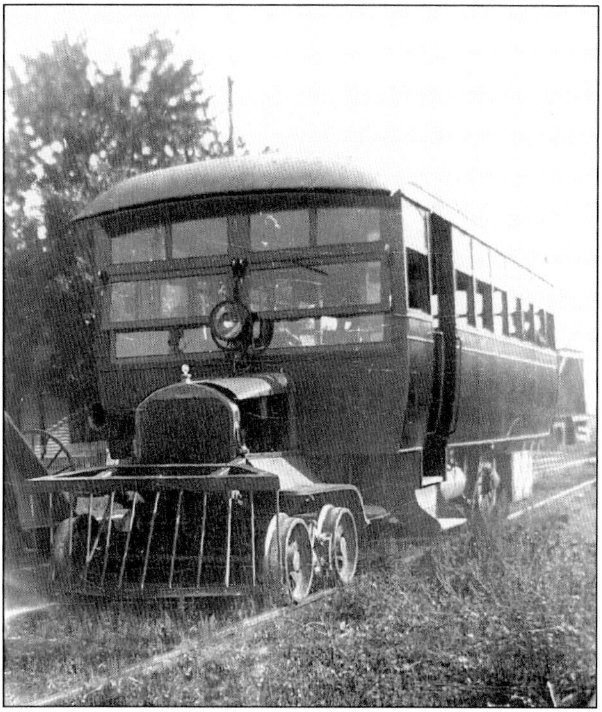

Facing declining traffic in the late 1910s and early 1920s, the Chesapeake and Western's general manager, W.E.D. Stokes, purchased a motor bus fitted for running on rails from the Mack Motor Truck Company in 1921 and began running two extra passenger routes daily. Operated by a crew of only one, the gas powered "Mack" ran more economically than a steam engine. This innovative form of transportation met its demise in 1938, when it collided with a locomotive at Laymans. (Private collection.)

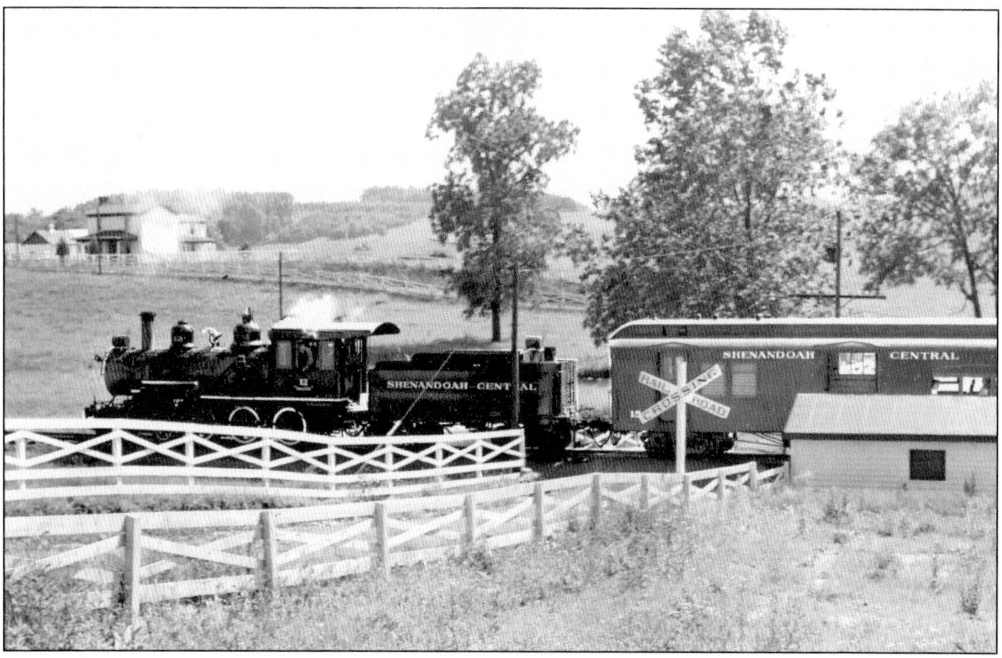

Originally in operation in Western North Carolina from 1917 to 1950, the train that became the Shenandoah Central was moved to Dr. Paul S. Hill's Penn Laird farm in 1953. Running on a narrow gauge track, "Tweetsie" operated as a recreational short line until Hurricane Hazel irreparably damaged the track in 1954. By 1955, Gene Autry had purchased the railroad for use in Hollywood, but the train ultimately returned to Blowing Rock, North Carolina, where it continues to operate as a tourist attraction. (Private collection.)

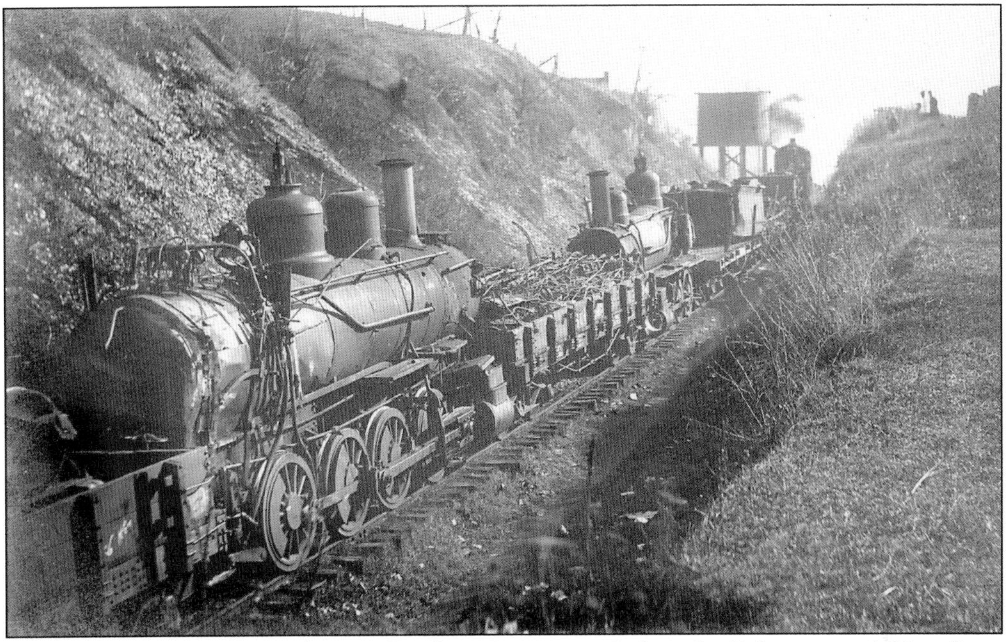

Other railroad lines operated in Rockingham County, including the Baltimore and Ohio (later the Southern) and the Norfolk and Western. In this photograph, several engines steam along the tracks near Timberville. (Jeffrey S. Evans Collection.)

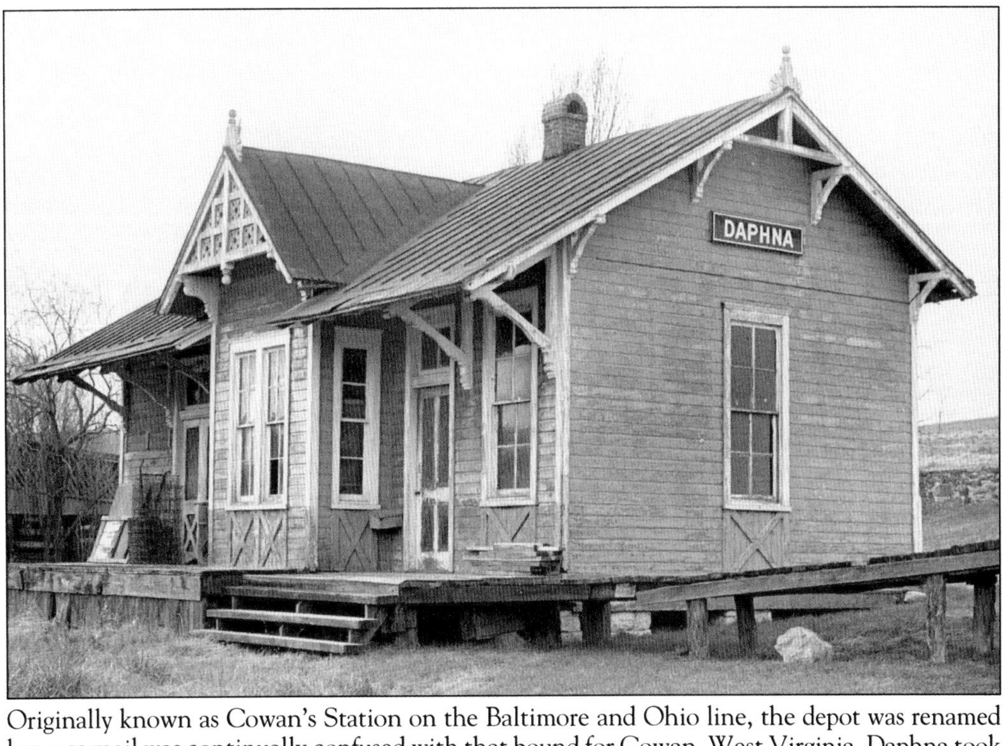

Originally known as Cowan's Station on the Baltimore and Ohio line, the depot was renamed because mail was continually confused with that bound for Cowan, West Virginia. Daphna took its name from the daughter of the stationmaster and postmaster at the time. (Eastern Mennonite University Collection.)

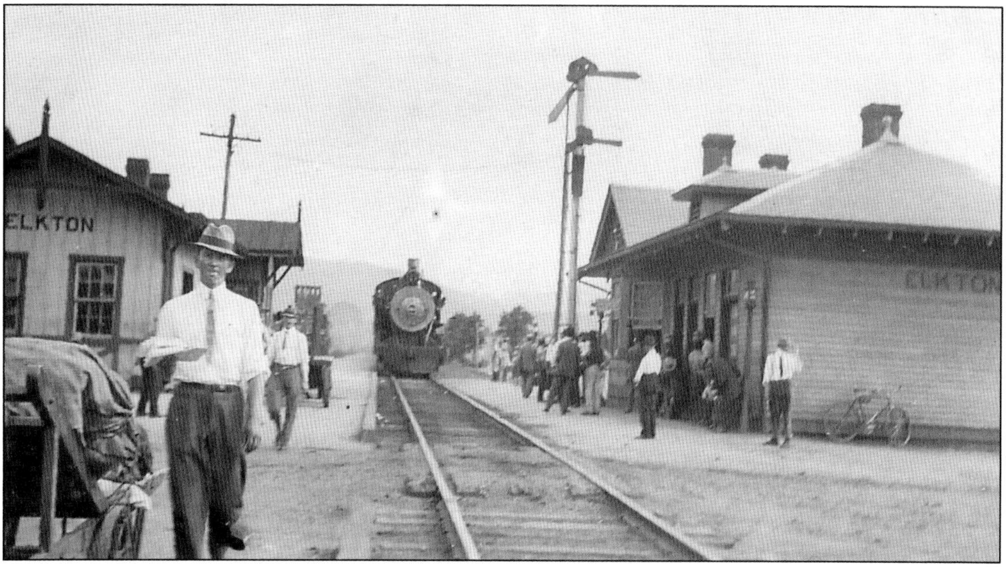

Located on the Norfolk and Western line, the town of Elkton had the unique distinction of having a station each for northbound and southbound trains. Elkton was also the eastern terminus of the Chesapeake and Western Railroad. A July 1911 note on the back of this photo states that it was "taken with a number 3A Folding Brownie Kodak." (Jeffrey S. Evans Collection.)

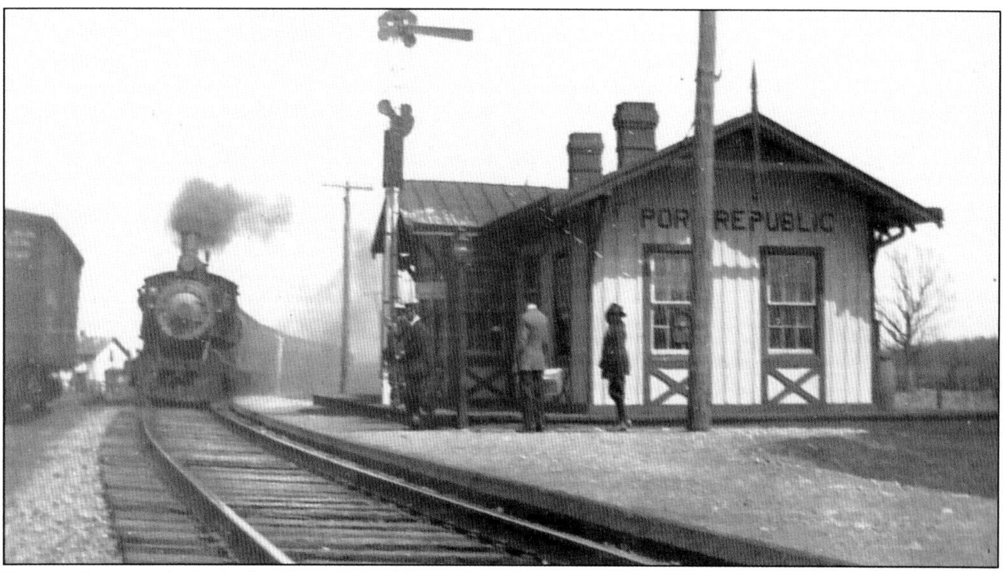

Pictured around 1900, the Port Republic station was once one of the busiest freight depots on the Norfolk and Western line. Six passenger trains a day once passed through the station. The building was razed in the 1950s. (Jeffrey S. Evans Collection.)

Three

SLICE OF LIFE

While photographic collections from the past and present often document the extraordinary events of a region, they also frequently include images of everyday life. Looking through a compilation of these photos often reveals the finer points that mold lives together to form a community. This section pulls together photographs that reflect the places where Rockingham County residents spent their time, along with how they presented themselves to one another, whether in church, school, or neighborhood. The photos are of streets, homes, businesses, and groups—each image revealing something about life in Rockingham County. As you browse through this collection, look for friends, relatives, and ancestors, and consider how life has at once changed and yet remained the same.

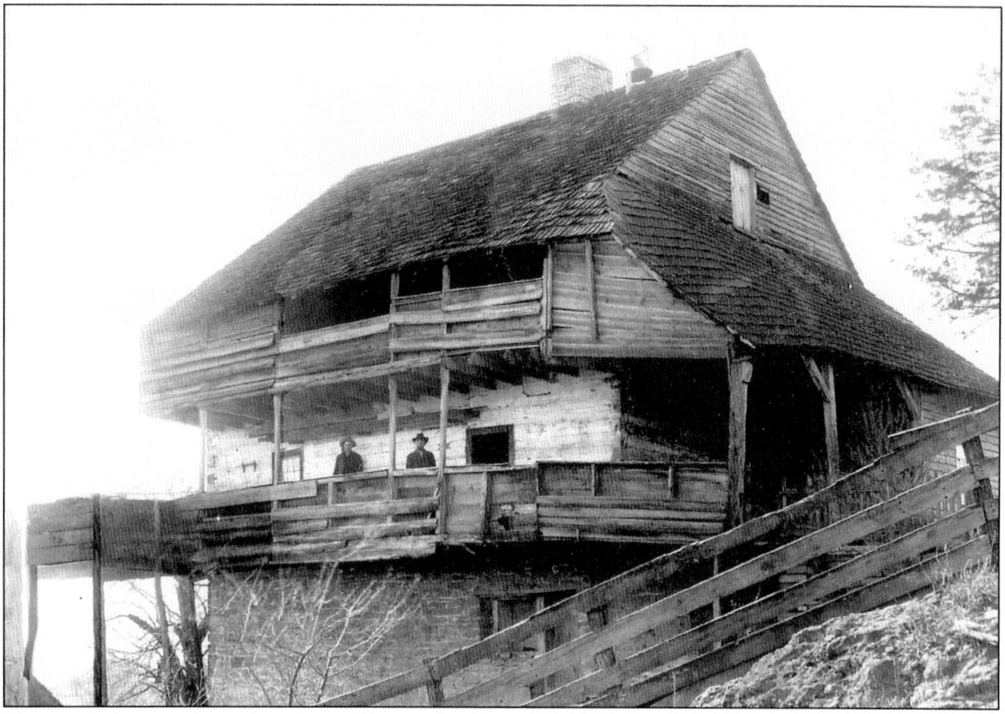

This early home along the Great Wagon Road south of Harrisonburg is atypical of those found in Rockingham County. It is, however, typical of the "bank" houses of Switzerland, so-called because they were built into a hillside, not unlike a "bank barn." It is not surprising that the Wenger family built such an ethnically influenced house when they arrived in the Shenandoah Valley from Switzerland. (Kermit Early Collection.)

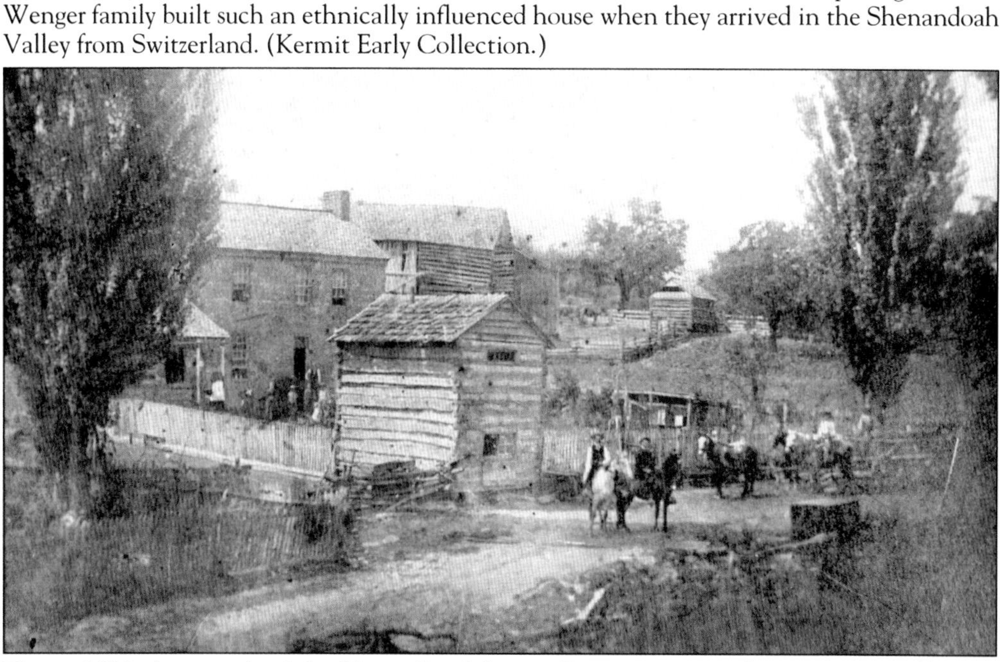

This *c.* 1880 photograph of the Henry Frank home illustrates a typical organization of houses and necessary outbuildings. A log barn, springhouse, and smokehouse are all within easy access to the main house. (Harrisonburg-Rockingham Historical Society Collection.)

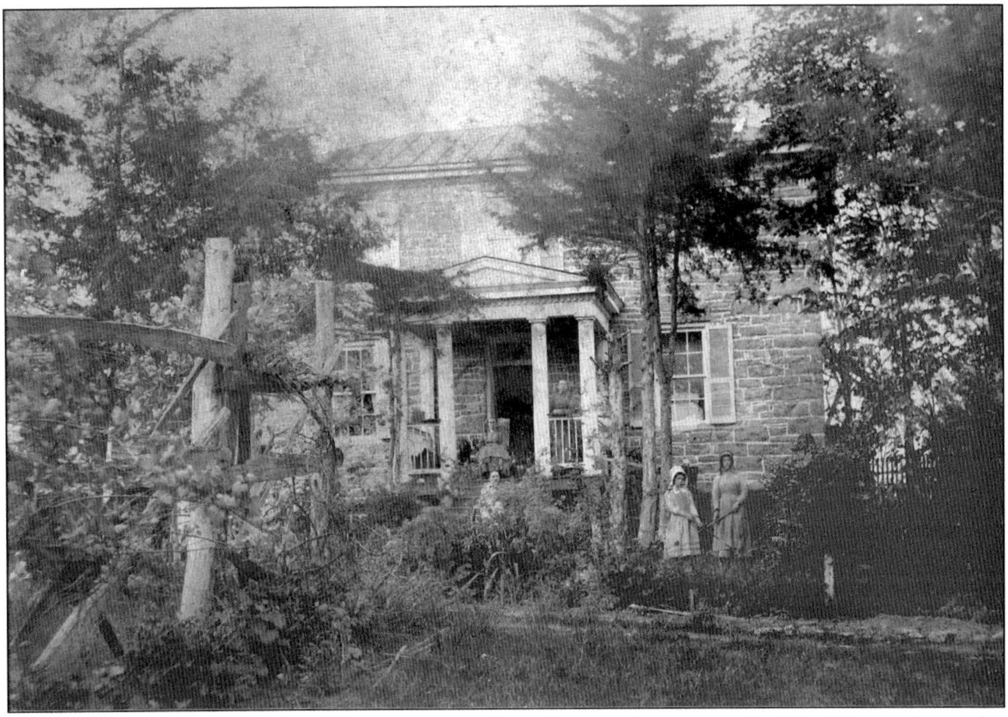

Located not far from the Frank home pictured on the previous page, the Funk house is on the southern edge of Singers Glen. The home is an excellent example of the stone architecture of the early 19th century. This 1890s photograph captures members of Solomon Funk's family. (Harrisonburg-Rockingham Historical Society Collection.)

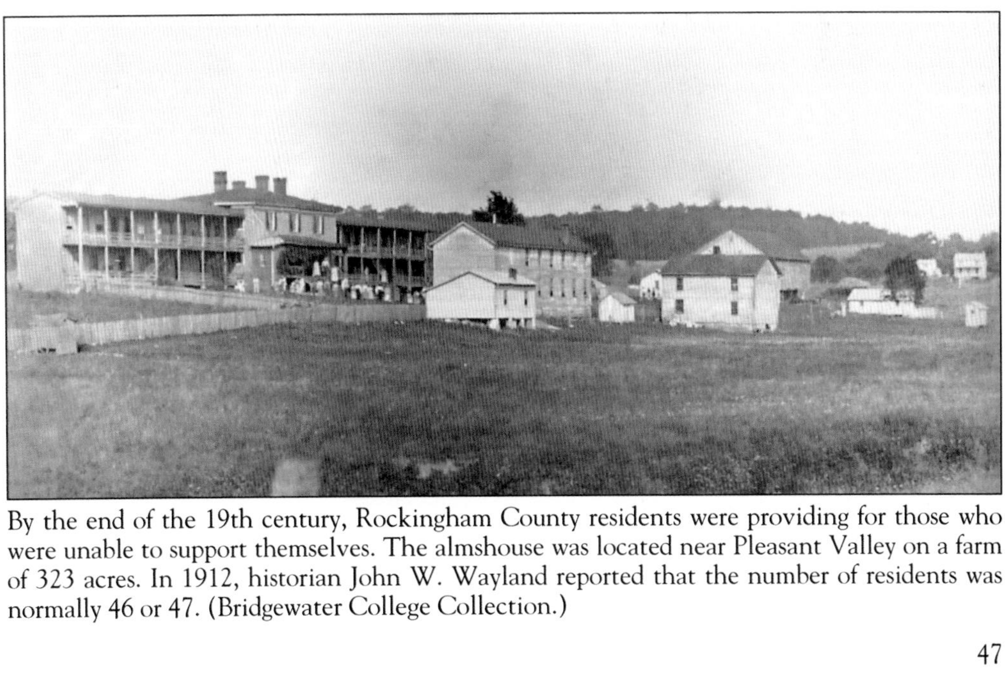

By the end of the 19th century, Rockingham County residents were providing for those who were unable to support themselves. The almshouse was located near Pleasant Valley on a farm of 323 acres. In 1912, historian John W. Wayland reported that the number of residents was normally 46 or 47. (Bridgewater College Collection.)

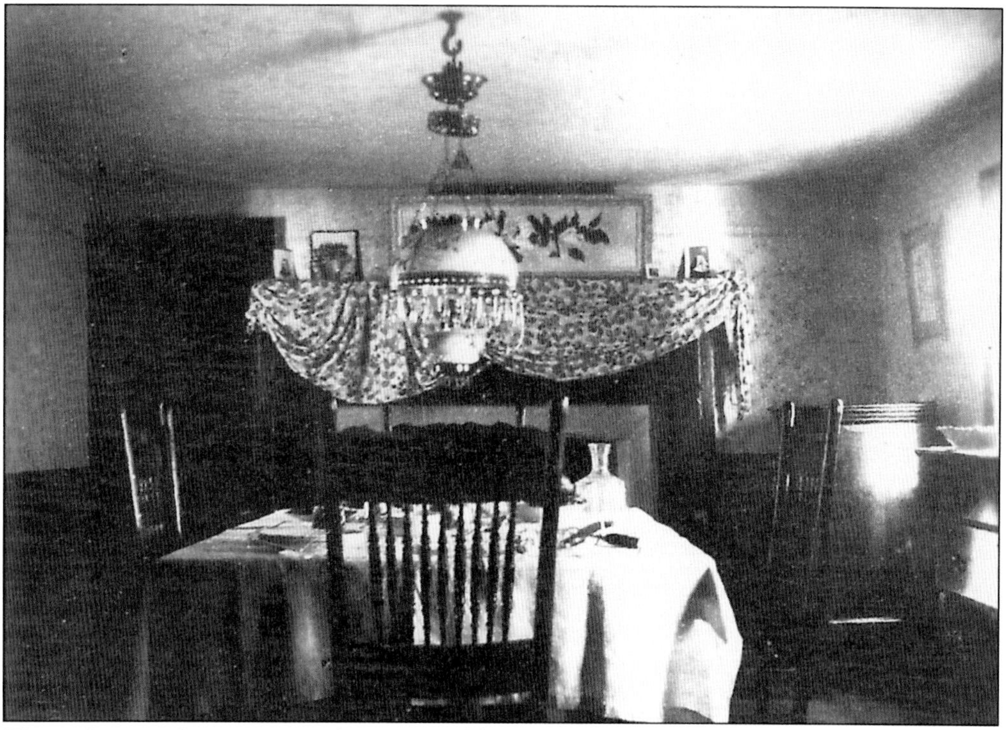

These photographs represent what a typical home in a county town might look like. Photographed in Mount Crawford around 1900, these views reveal the pressed-back chairs and hanging light of the dining room, as well as the more private bedroom space. The playbill hanging in the bedroom is for a performance of *Carolina Knights*. (Jeffrey S. Evans Collection.)

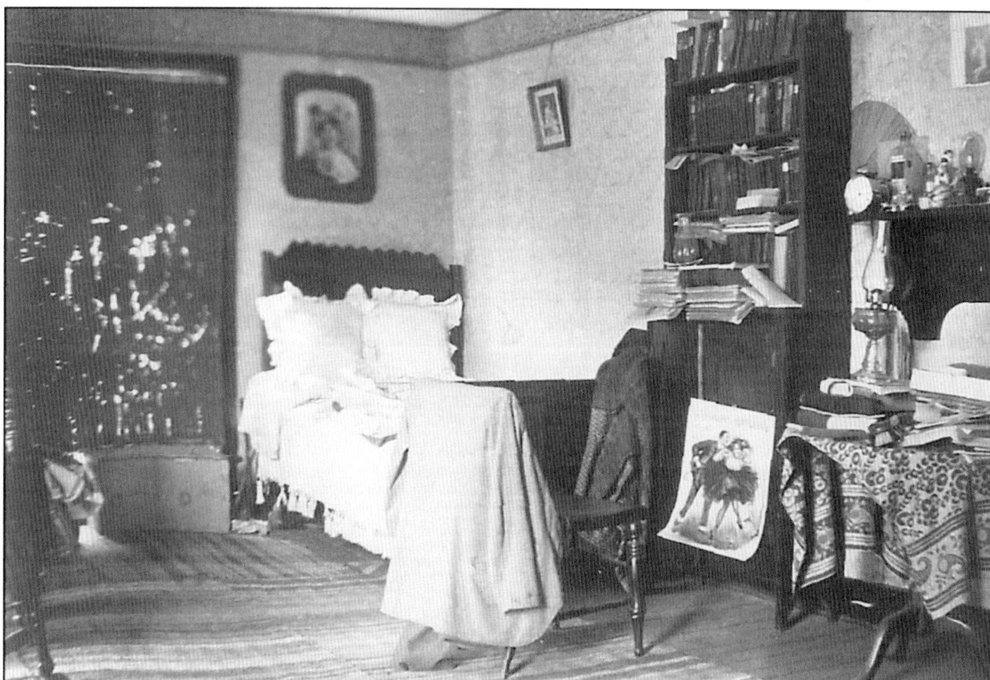

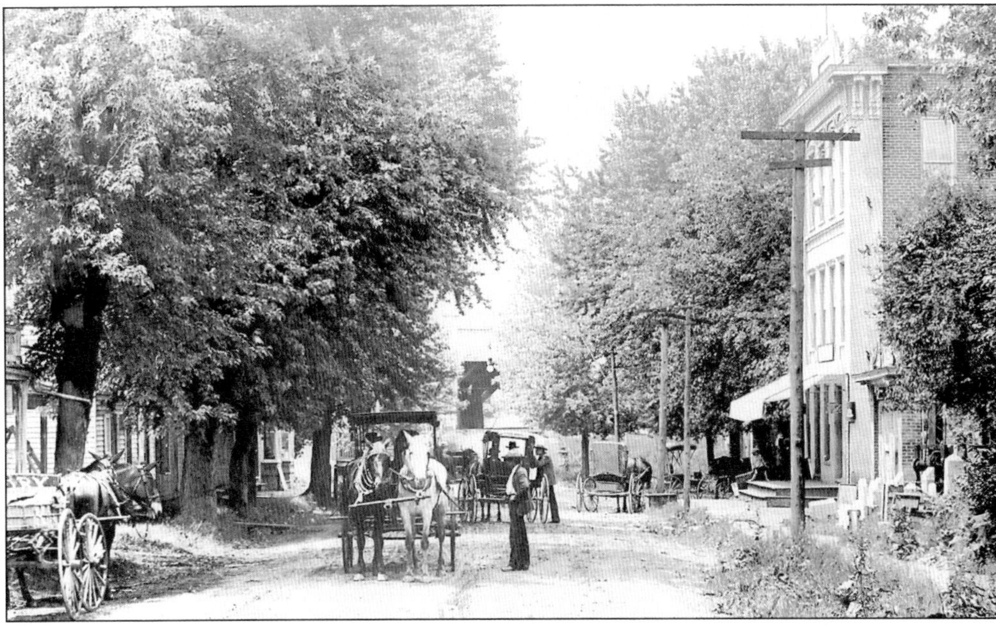

This c. 1900 view of Bridgewater's south Main Street presents typical activities on the street. Horse-drawn vehicles traverse the street in front of the long-established three-story mercantile building on the street's west side. Originally managed by J.W.F. Allemong, the business passed into the hands of J.W. Click in 1890, and by the turn of the century, the Robson brothers were the proprietors. Long known as the Robson building, the structure still stands on the south end of town. (Massanutten Regional Library Collection.)

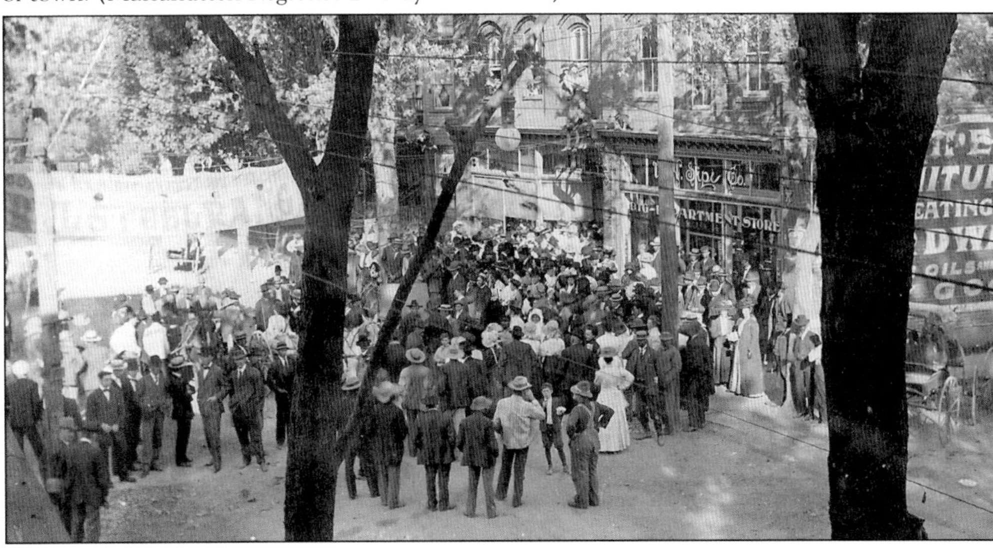

Clearly, W.H. Sipe was unveiling something spectacular at his "Big Department Store" located on the northeast corner of Main and College Streets in Bridgewater. Before opening this enterprise in 1900, Sipe had managed a successful mercantile business in the village of Lilly since 1882. After purchasing the Arey building on the corner and adding a second building to the north, Sipe and his investors boasted that they filled both floors of the two buildings, each offering 50 by 110 feet of space. By 1909, this was the largest mercantile establishment in the county outside of Harrisonburg. (Jeffrey S. Evans Collection.)

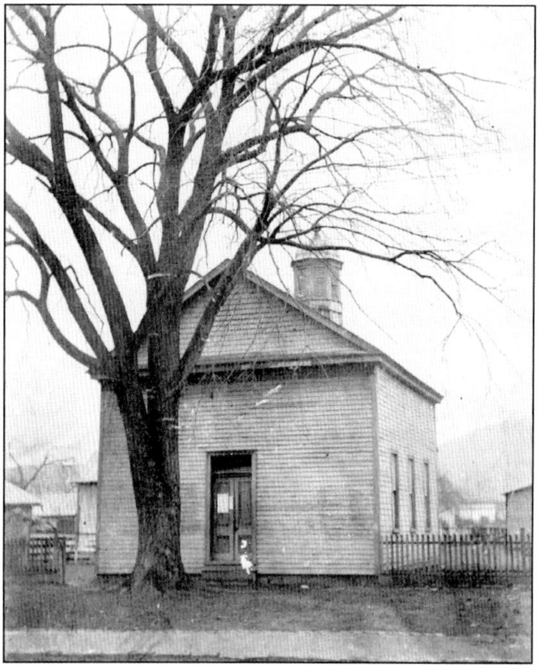

Reflecting the changing needs of a growing town of the mid-19th century, this building served as a church for numerous denominations after it was erected around 1820. By 1856, the Town of Bridgewater purchased the building for its town hall. The *Bridgewater Times* reported in 1925 that the structure was being refurbished; it noted, "Notwithstanding the inevitable corrosion of a century or more the Hall is now in good condition with an apparent possibility of rounding out another hundred years." The building continues to stand. (Bridgewater College Collection.)

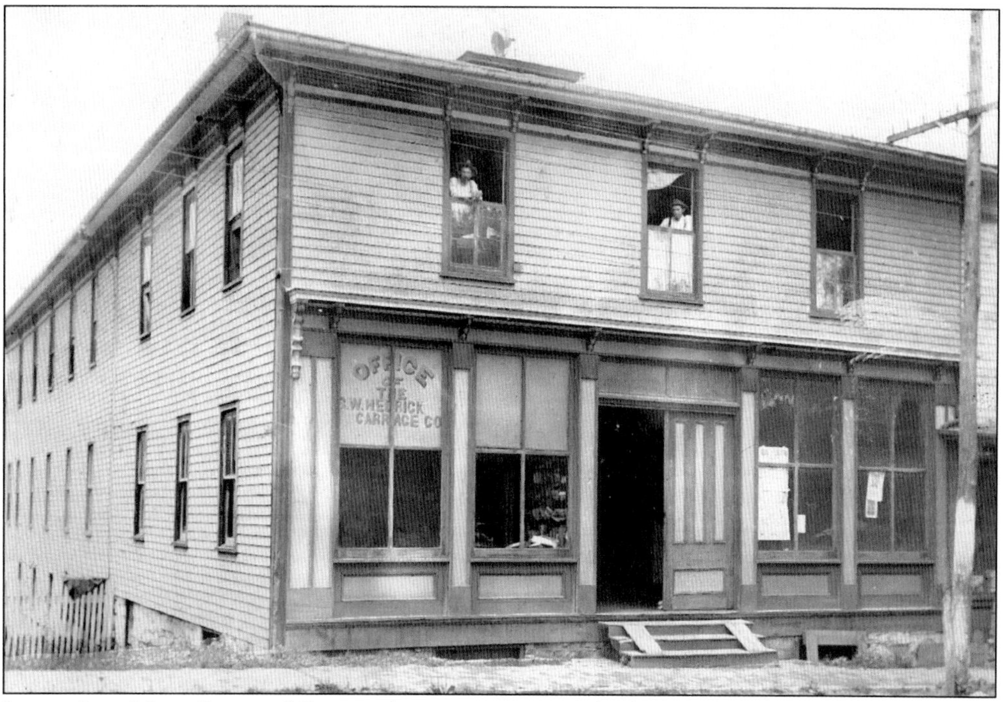

Located on Main Street of Dayton for many years in the late 19th century, the George W. Hedrick Carriage Company employed 16 to 20 men. In the 1890s, their catalogs illustrated the numerous styles of buggies, phaetons, surreys, and wagons that the company produced. While it reportedly built 500 carriages a year and grossed $20,000 annually, the company never reopened after a downtown fire destroyed the building in 1911. (Eastern Mennonite University Collection.)

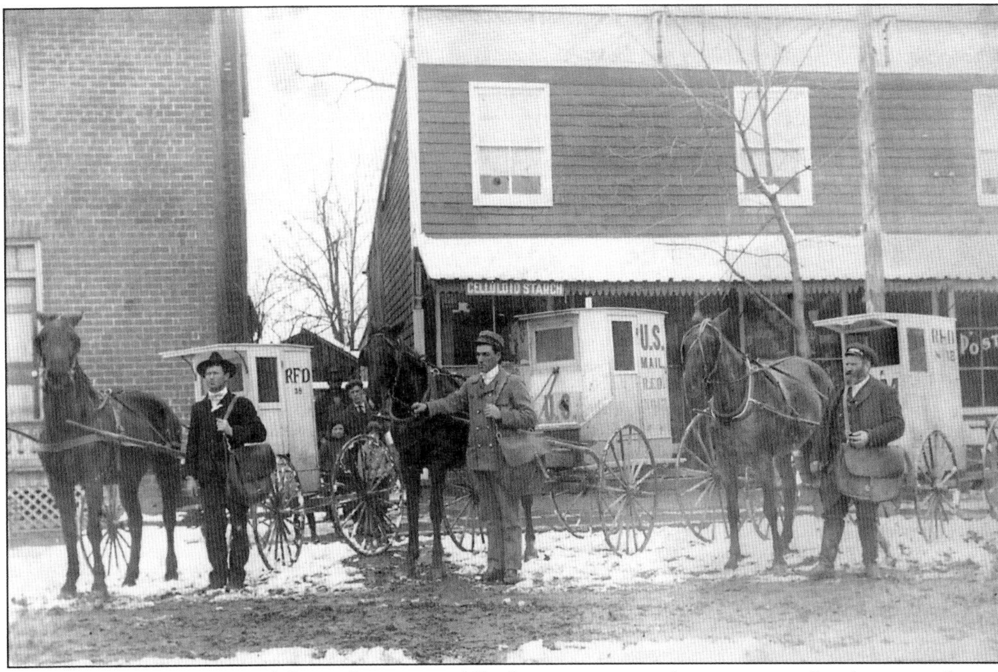

By 1900, mail was carried from the town of Bridgewater to outlying regions by three rural mail carriers. Posing with their carriages above are (left to right) John Dovel, John Click, and Gabe Miller. (Jeffrey S. Evans Collection.)

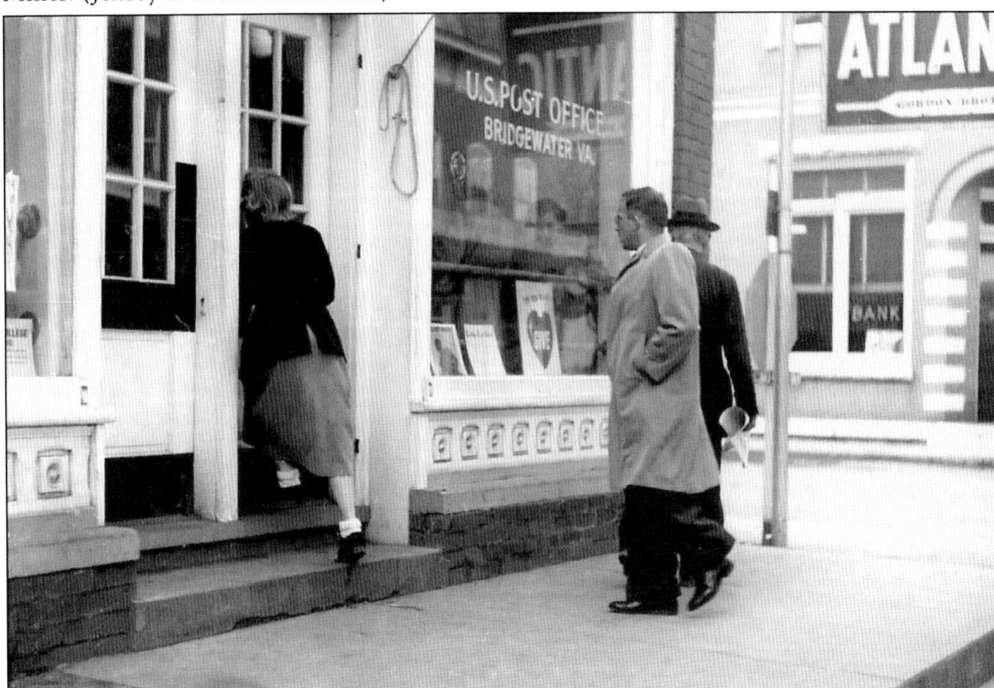

Bridgewater's post office has been located in numerous buildings throughout the years. In the 1950s, the post office was moved into the former site of W.H. Sipe's department store on the corner of Main and College Streets. (Private collection.)

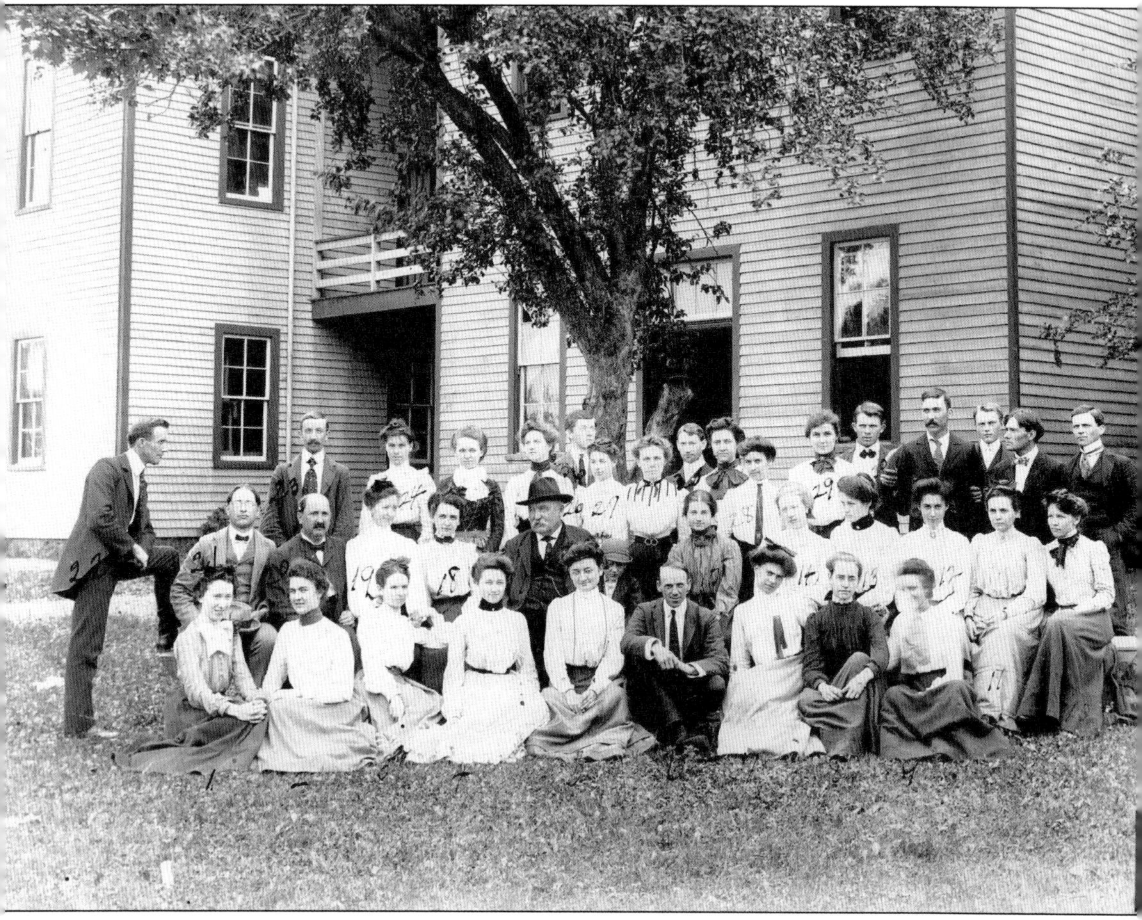

The West Central Academy in Mt. Clinton operated as a public and private institution under the guidance of Prof. I.S. Wampler from 1892 to 1903, when it closed its doors for a variety of reasons. The following are pictured from left to right: (front row) Mary Sheldon Rice, Annie Leap, Elvie Andes, Florence Koontz, Nannie Rutherford, Prof. D.I. Suter, Edith Ruebush, Georgie Wolfrey, and Kate Donivan; (middle row) Prof. ? Dingus, Prof. I.S. Wampler, Mrs. I.S. Wampler, Mary Zirkle, Prof. ? Hulvey, ? Hulvey Jr., Ray Bishop, Leona Harmon, Ella Heatwole, Lena Brown, and Emma Wright; (back row) Arthur Miller, ? Showalter, ? Turner, Nellie Lineweaver, Elsie Batterman, Pierce Heatwole, Emma Bishop, unidentified, ? Flick, unidentified, Elizabeth Hopkins, Mary Fauver, Walter Scothern, ? Lineweaver, Irvine Heatwole, M.G. Lilly, and Otis Landis; (inset) Homer F. Thomas, photographer. (Massanutten Regional Library Collection.)

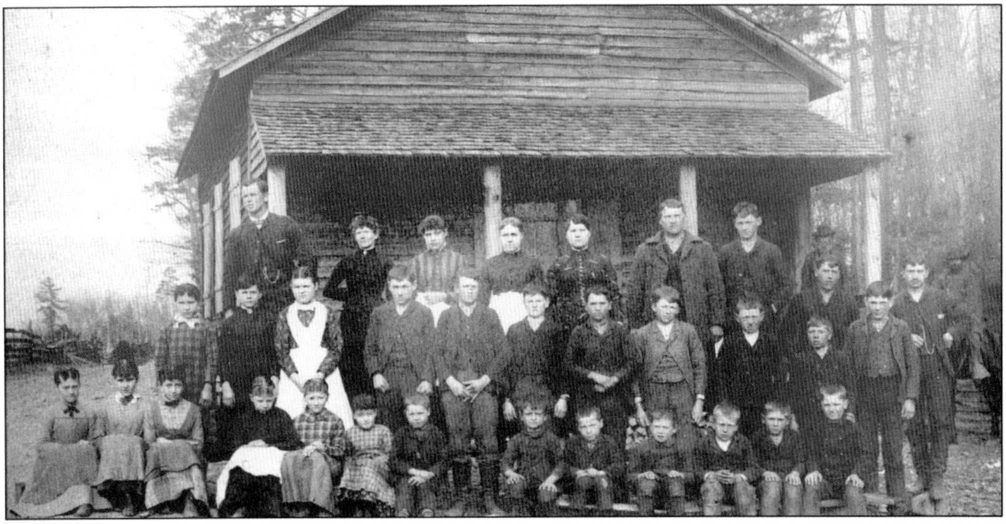

Although children often had other responsibilities along with their school attendance, life in the schoolhouse must have occupied a significant amount of their energy. The students at the Rushville School (above) remain unidentified; however, those attending the Spring Creek School around the turn of the 20th century are pictured below from left to right: (first row) Owen Swecker, Hugh Good, Harry Spitler, Bill Whissen, Odes Swecker, Edward Wright, Carl Gentry, Claude Swecker, Nona Swecker, ? Dodson, Mary Swecker (on Dodson's lap), Lydia Swecker, Willie Swecker, Mollie Miller, Ella Woods, Hazel Heatwole, Wilbur Thomas, Roy Heatwole, Clyde Heatwole, Ned Swecker, Harry Simmons, and Wilmer Simmons; (second row) Elmer Eavers, John Miller, Josh Philllips, Herschel Ringgold, Boyd Spitler, Jasper Swecker, Roy Blakemore, Roger Wine, William Woods, Charles Simmons, Ora Swecker, Barbara Ringgold, Ruth Heatwole, Sue Miller, Leon Gentry, Walter Swecker, Jake Miller, Warren Beard, Elmer Miller, and Lloyd Wright; (third row) Walker Miller, Dan Miller, Mary Miller, Johnnie Swartz, Grover Coakley, Mary Thomas, Lizzie Swecker, Katie Thomas, Vernie Ringgold, Lizzie Hopkins, Hattie Ringgold, Mary Miller, Leona Gentry, Carl Beard, and Hershel Wright; (fourth row) Charles Spitler, Will Phillips, Victor Miller, Elmer Ringgold, Cora Ringgold, Maude Spitler, Bessie Miller, Dalphia Skyles, Effie Thomas, Elsie Ringgold, Clara Simmons, Effie Miller, Hattie Miller, Margaret Beard, and Sallie Miller. (Private collection.)

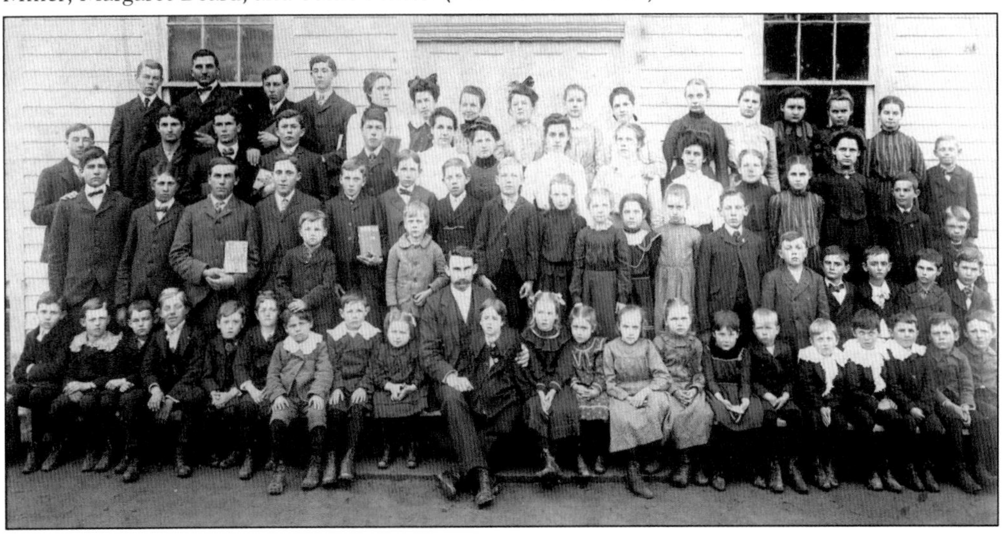

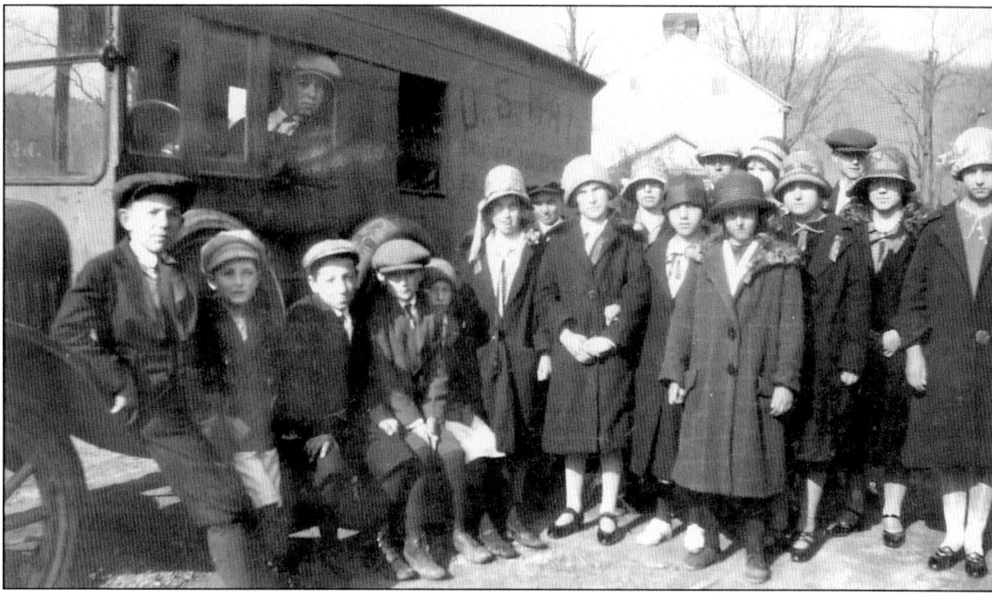

Often the community mail truck served more than one purpose. In this early 20th-century photograph, students from northwest Rockingham County pose with the mail carrier on the Broadway, Cootes Store, and Fulks Run route. (Harrisonburg-Rockingham Historical Society.)

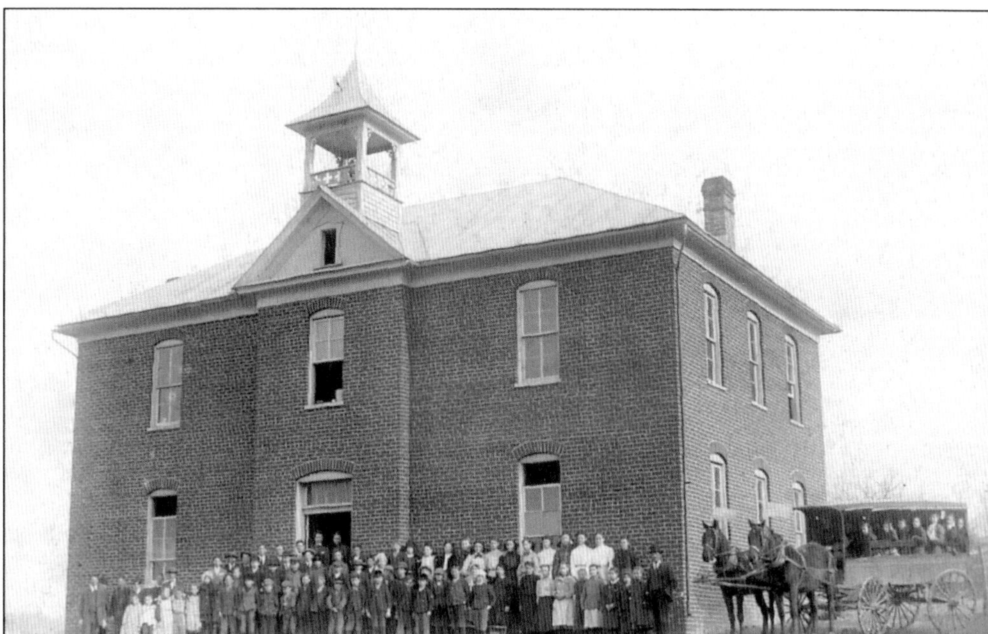

The third school to stand in Singers Glen, this building was constructed after the Commonwealth of Virginia mandated in 1902 that each magisterial district should have at least one high school. This photograph, taken by Bridgewater photographer J.M. Hill around 1905, shows the omnibus that transported students. (Jeffrey S. Evans Collection.)

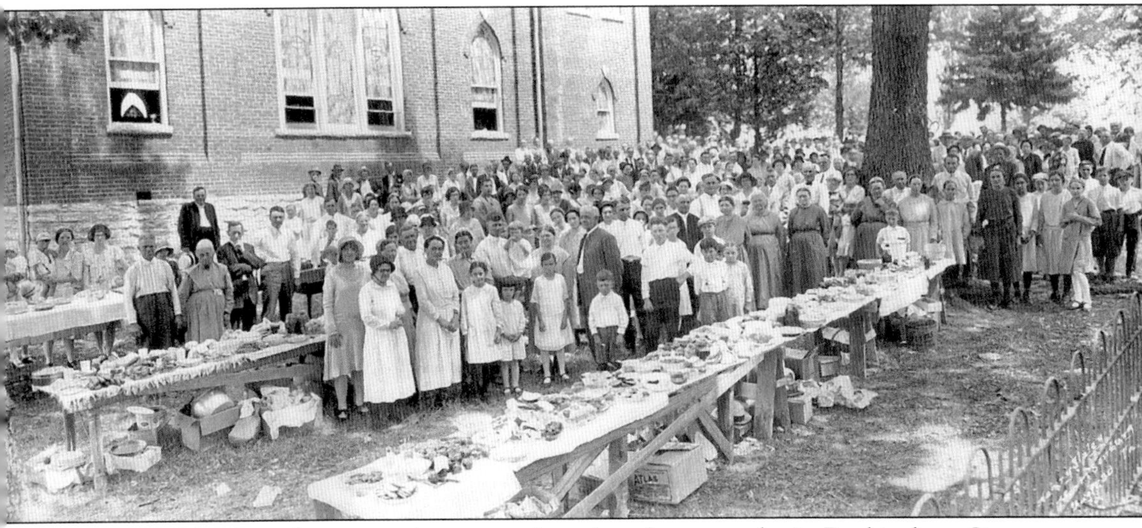

Reunions of family and various other groups have long been popular in Rockingham County. This Harry Staley photograph features the reunion of students of the New Erection School held on August 8, 1930. The school operated near the Cooks Creek Presbyterian Church from 1871 to 1935. The size of the crowd pictured here indicates the enduring importance of the local schools to neighborhood residents. (Jim Suter Collection.)

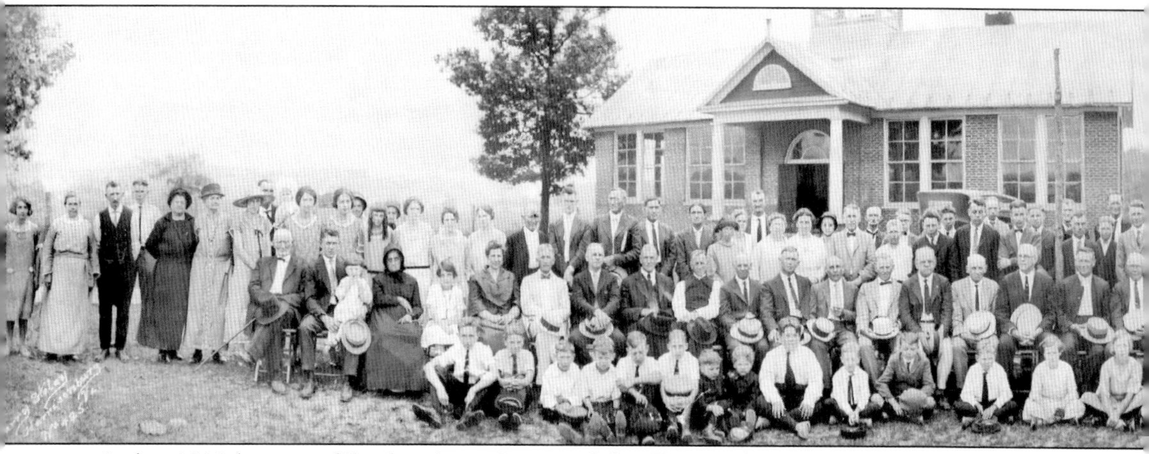

In his 1912 history of Rockingham County, John W. Wayland reported the formation of a group of young men who were anxious to discuss books and ideas. He wrote of this assembly: "In 1885, one evening in the dark, eight young men met in a fence corner, near Dale Enterprise, and sat on a log. They were tired but not exhausted; they were in the dark, but were seeking light. They organized a society for mutual improvement: They decided to buy books and read them, and to talk together of what they read" (436). This group came to be known as the Dale Enterprise Literary Society, and over the next 20 years, it expanded rapidly. The original members were Timothy O. Heatwole, Frank A. Heatwole, C.J. Heatwole, Aldine Heatwole, John J. Heatwole, John R. Swartz, William T. Swartz, and L.F. Ritchie. In 1924, a reunion was held for all who had participated in the society. The following people who attended the reunion are pictured from left to right: (front row) John Whitmore, Roy A. Heatwole, Weldon Coakley, George R. Heatwole, Harry Burkholder, unidentified, Wilson Robinson, Raymond Robinson, Mike Whitmore, Harry Showalter, Charles Suter, Richard Showalter, Naomi Heatwole, Charlene Coakley, Josie Heatwole, Virginia Senger, Harlin Senger, Dan Heatwole, Edward Heatwole, Elizabeth Croushorn, Rhodes Batterman, Catherine Rhodes, Mary Gladys Burkholder, Jerolene Showalter, Reba Showalter, unidentified, Charlotte Rolston, and Fern Rolston; (middle row) ? Liskey, Charles Ritchie, Alice Ritchie, Lizzie Guy, Ruth Good, Mrs. J. Good, J.H.S. Good, Dr. O. Brunk, Will Swartz, Charles A. Heatwole, Swope Suter, Justis B. Heatwole, C.G. Senger, Eugene Suter, Cornelius Heatwole, Emanuel J. Suter, Dr. Timothy O. Heatwole, Jake Hartman, Perry Suter, Dr. W.J. Showalter, John Swartz, Frank Ritchie with his unidentified grandson, T.C. Suter, Frank Heatwole, Ellis Burkholder, John L. Rhodes, Aldine

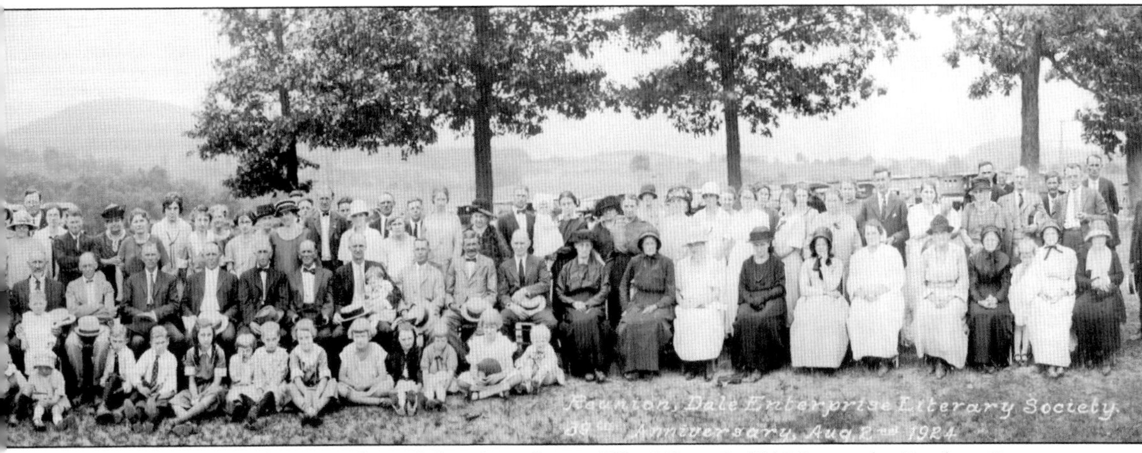

J. Heatwole, Millard Heatwole and daughter Janet, Ward Swank, Ed Heatwole, Reuben Suter, Sallie Heatwole, Sophia Heatwole, Ethel Rolston, Annie Showalter, Florence Showalter, Pearl Showalter, Fannie S. Deputy, Mrs. ? Nair, Mrs. Eugene Suter, and Lilly Weaver; (back row) Wilda Heatwole, Minnie Coakley, Walter D. Coakley, John Heatwole, Lizzie Miller, Mrs. F.L. Ritchie, unidentified, Preston Miller, Alice J. Heatwole, Edith Heatwole, Mrs. John G. Heatwole, Elva Miller, Lydia Heatwole, Margaret Whitmore, Vada Swartz, Lorene Showalter, Jake Kagey, Polly Lineweaver, John W. Wayland, John C. Myers, Malcolm Lilly, Elva Senger, Lilly Minnich, Lew Whitmore, Bessie Corbin, Alice Burkholder, Jennie Heatwole, unidentified, Justus Suter, Carl Heatwole, Lloyd Coakley, Galen Showalter, Graham Suter, Hiram Showalter, James Suter, Pete Shifflet, Herbert Senger, Marvin Suter, John G. Heatwole, Jacob Showalter, A.D. Heatwole, Carl Ritchie, William Swartz, Ina Ritchie, Lucille Ritchie, unidentified, Mrs. D. Harper, unidentified, Radie Ritchie, Arb C. Showalter, Laura Rhodes, Mrs. F. Heatwole, Reba Suter, Mrs. ? Suter, Mrs. ? Suter, Marie Suter, Mrs. ? Suter, Verdie Rhodes, unidentified, Raymond Corbin, Harry Heatwole, Floyd Corbin, Mrs. M. Heatwole, B.C. Senger, Ruth Suter, Olin Senger, Sadie Coakley, Mrs. Ed Heatwole, Earl Grove, Mrs. Elizabeth Grove holding Virginia, Mrs. Mike Whitmore, unidentified, Mary Deputy, unidentified, Florence Deputy, Vergie Senger, Annie Heatwole, Mabel Showalter, Grace Brunk, Charlotte Showalter, Mrs. Homer Swope, Mary E. Suter, Homer Swope, Mertie Kennedy, Mrs. ? Sublett, unidentified, Peter Hartman, Frank Sublett, Amos Shank, Hershey Weaver, Dan Heatwole, John Corbin, and Franklin Rhodes. (Eastern Mennonite University Collection.)

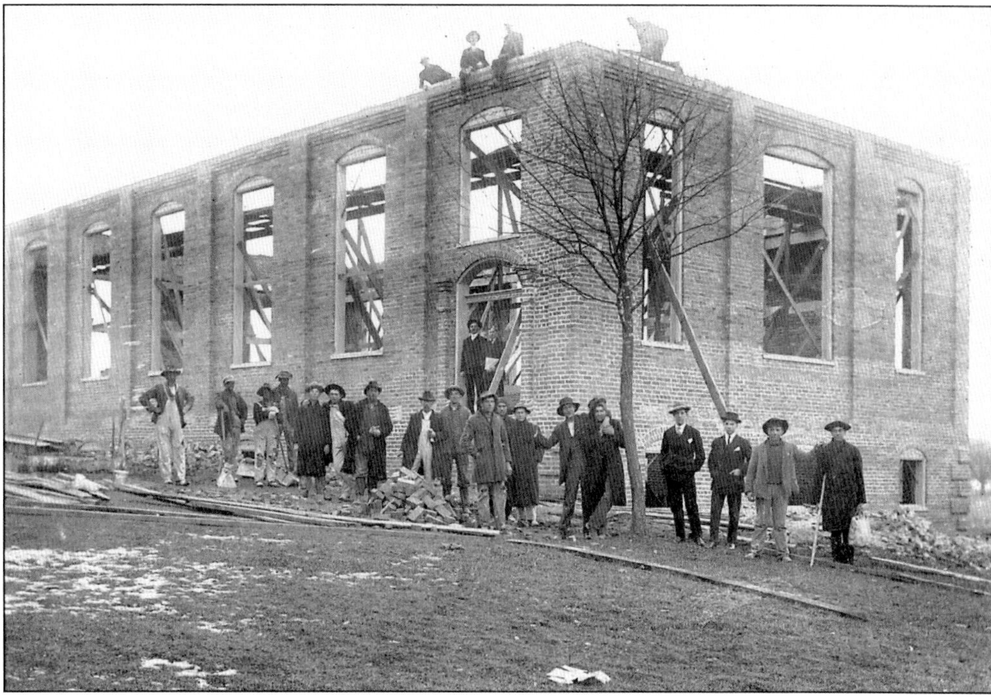

The weather is a factor in everyday life, and students and faculty at Bridgewater College were reminded of this fact in December 1907. In August of that year, the college's trustees agreed to partial funding of a gymnasium if the Bridgewater College Athletic Association could produce a substantial amount of the required funds. By the end of the year, the walls were completed, as shown in the photograph above; however, an unusually powerful windstorm blew them down on December 30 (below). (Jeffrey S. Evans Collection.)

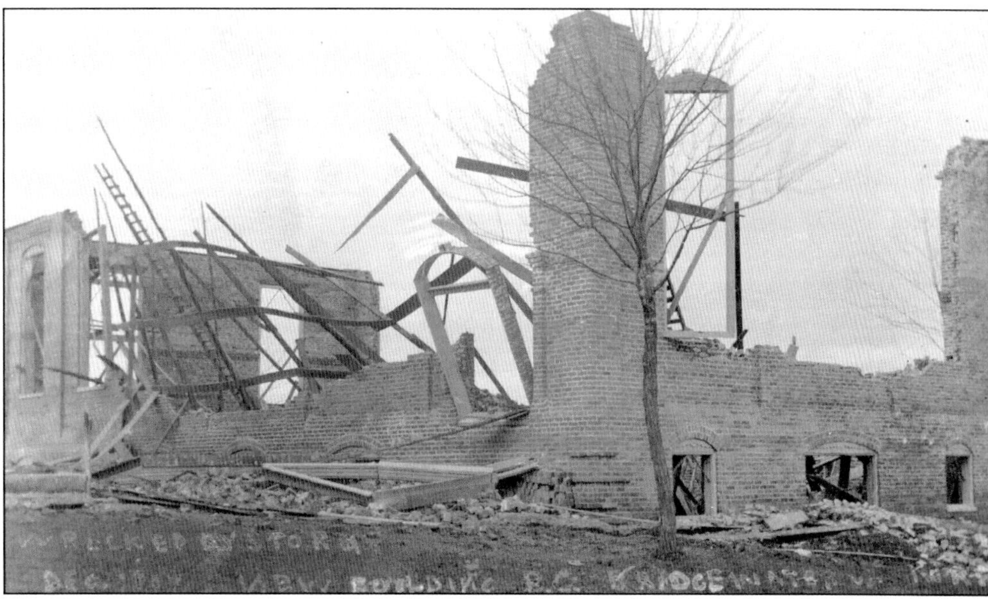

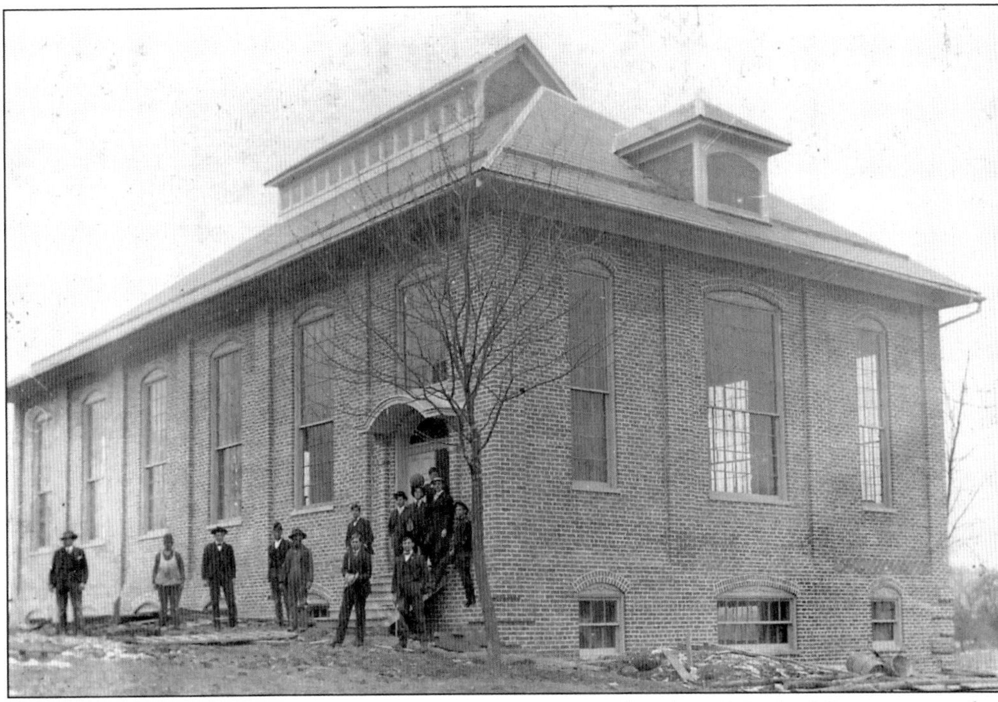

Undaunted, the construction crew set to work again immediately and the building was completed by June 1908 (above). At a final cost of nearly $8,000, the structure proved to be a bargain and soon filled multiple uses. Along with the basketball court, a stage at one end enabled the building to serve as an auditorium, and the chemistry department held classes in the basement from 1920 to 1926. Still, it was primarily a gymnasium, which the college felt would allow "the less strong to become stronger." Below, a class of students puts the gymnasium to use. (Jeffrey S. Evans Collection and Kermit Early Collection.)

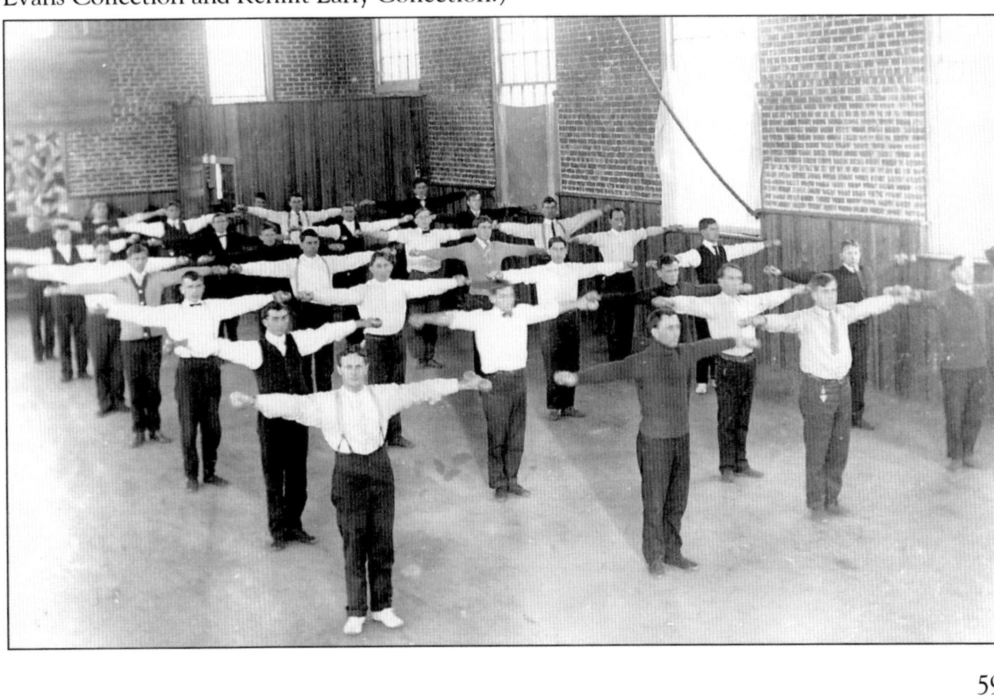

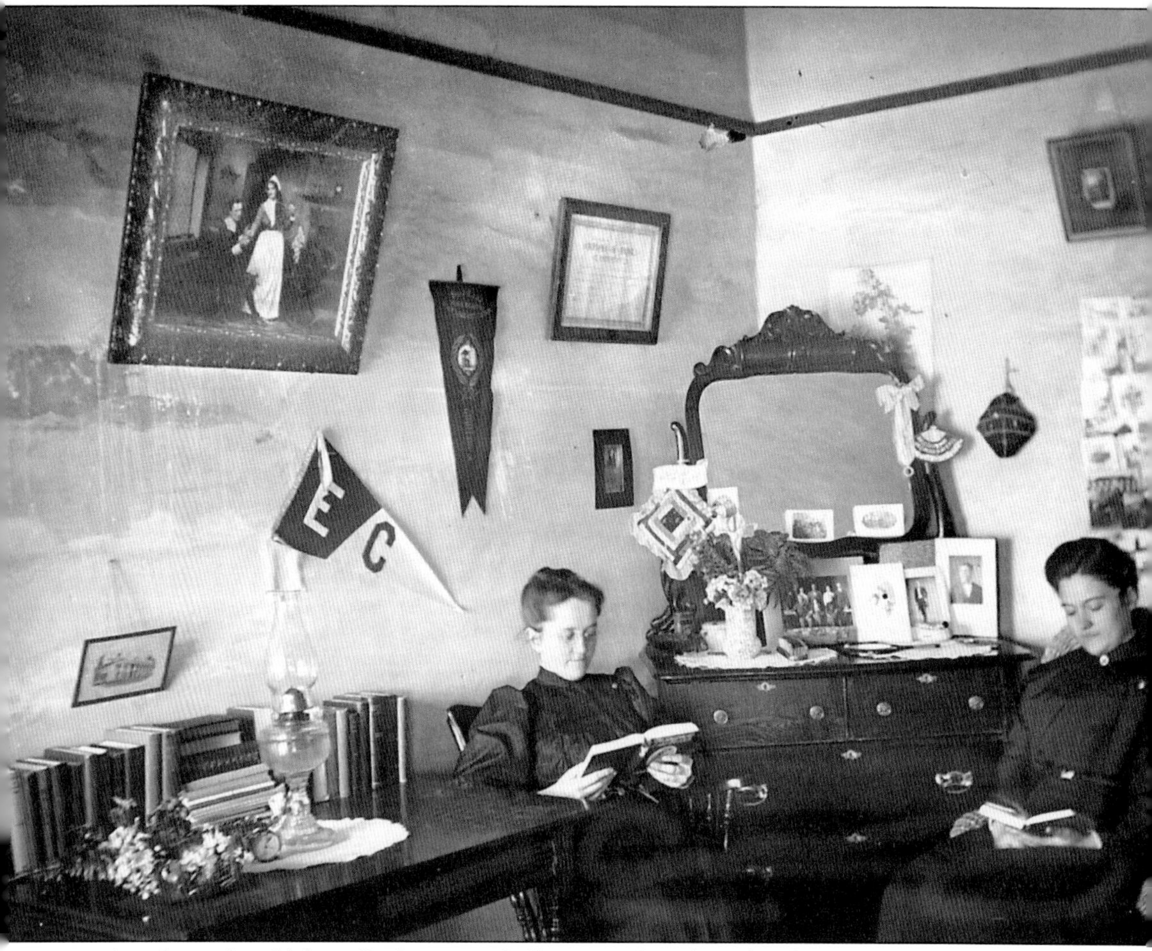

Another side of life at Bridgewater College was found in the dormitories. This photograph details the personal touches that Sally Zigler Myers (left) and Martha Garber (right) added to their room. They appear to be quite studious in this photograph from 1910–1911. (Eastern Mennonite University Collection.)

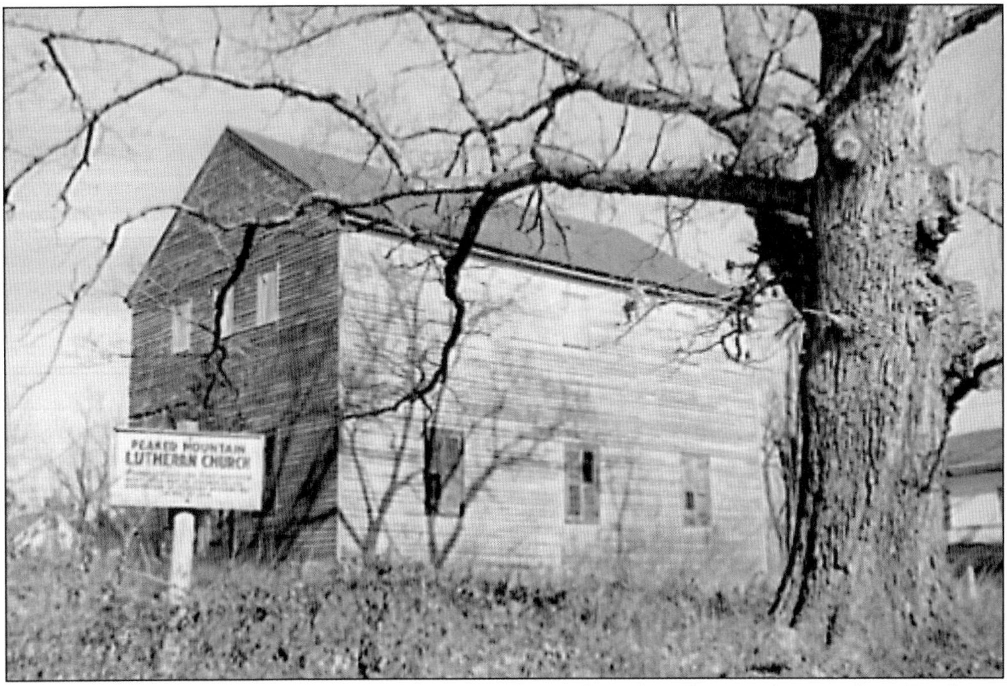

From the days of earliest European settlement, religion has played a significant role in Rockingham County's affairs. The Peaked Mountain Church, shown here in the 1940s, was in existence in the McGaheysville area as early as 1769. The church was originally a union church, serving both the Lutheran and the Reformed congregations of that area of the county. (Library of Congress Collection.)

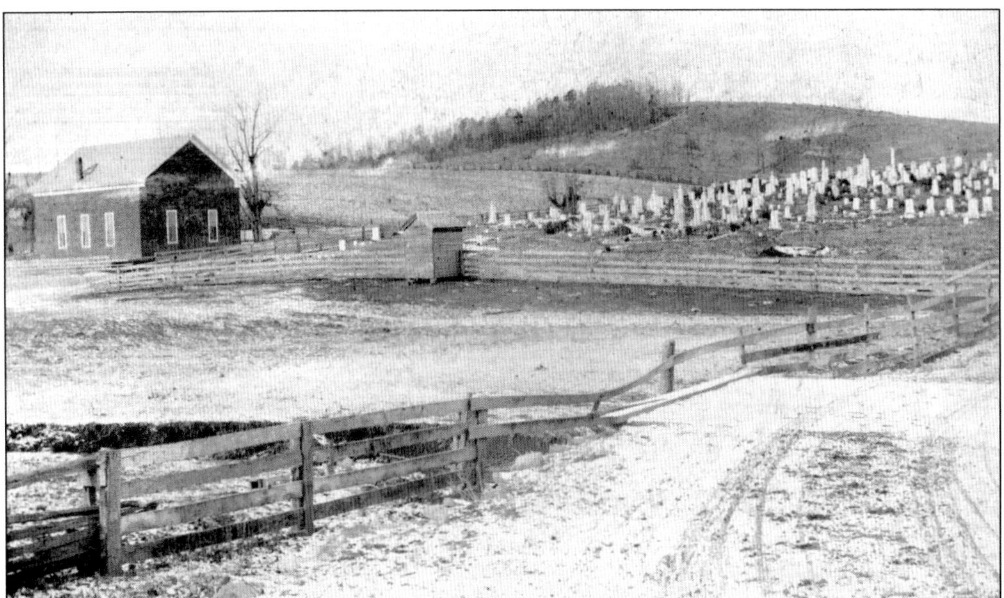

Friedens Church, several miles east of Mount Crawford, is home to one of the county's earliest congregations. Used by Lutheran and Reformed congregations as well, the church is recorded as being in existence in 1748. (Jeffrey S. Evans Collection.)

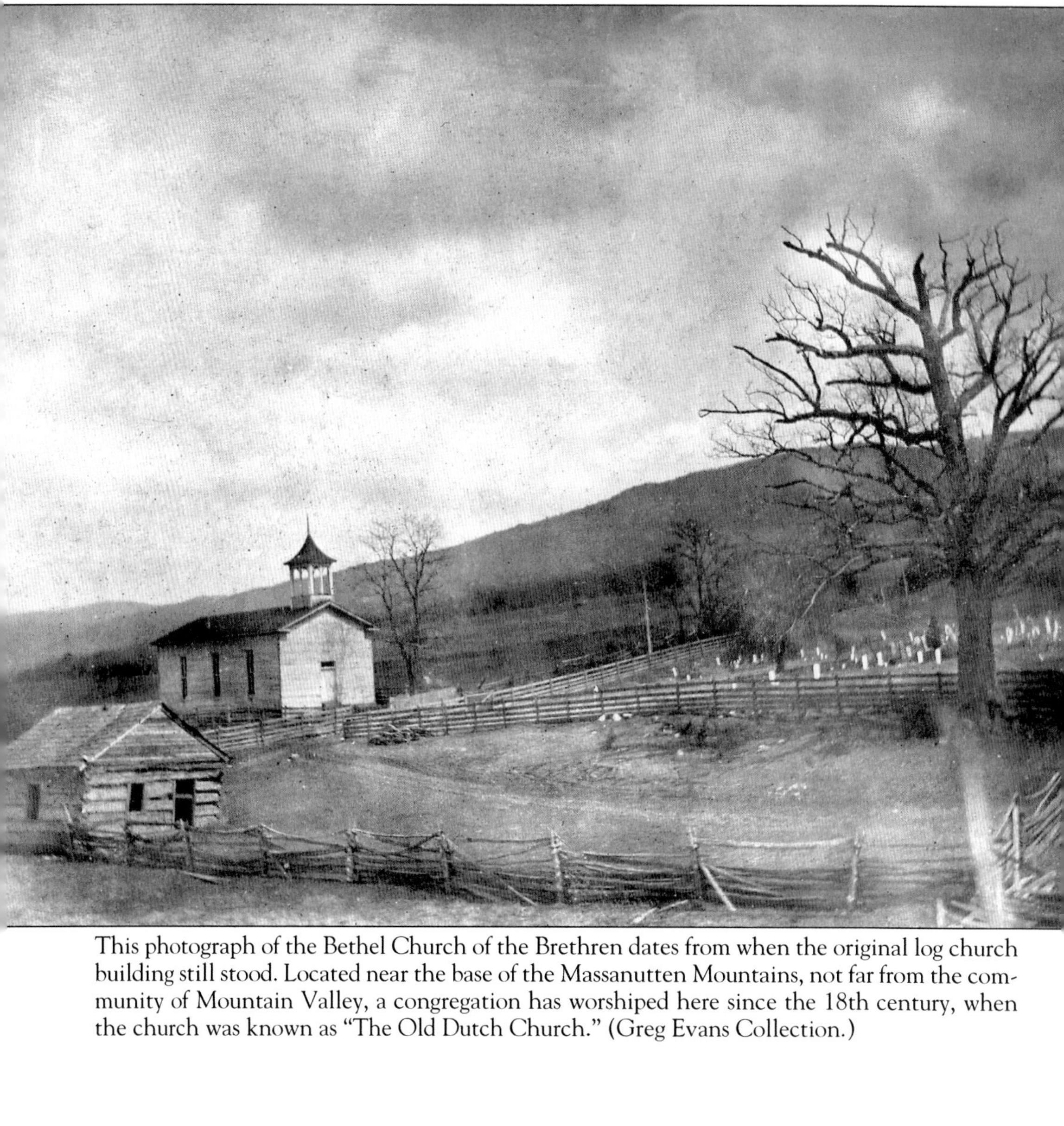

This photograph of the Bethel Church of the Brethren dates from when the original log church building still stood. Located near the base of the Massanutten Mountains, not far from the community of Mountain Valley, a congregation has worshiped here since the 18th century, when the church was known as "The Old Dutch Church." (Greg Evans Collection.)

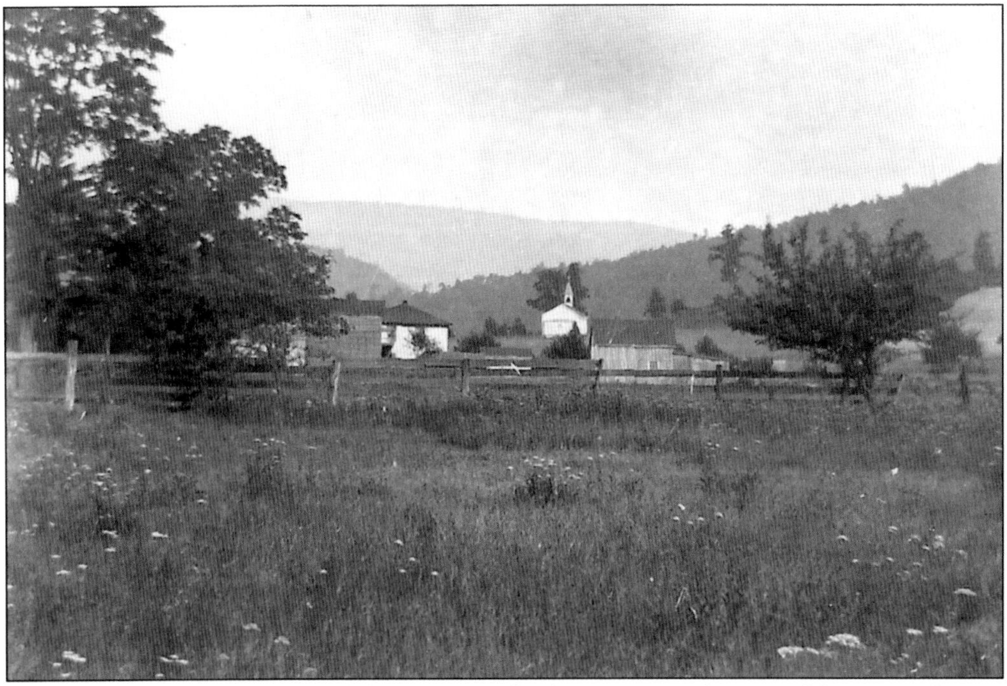

This photograph of a rural church at Dovesville demonstrates the peaceful setting of many Rockingham County churches. Now known as Bergton, the village is in the northwestern portion of the county. (Kent Botkin Collection.)

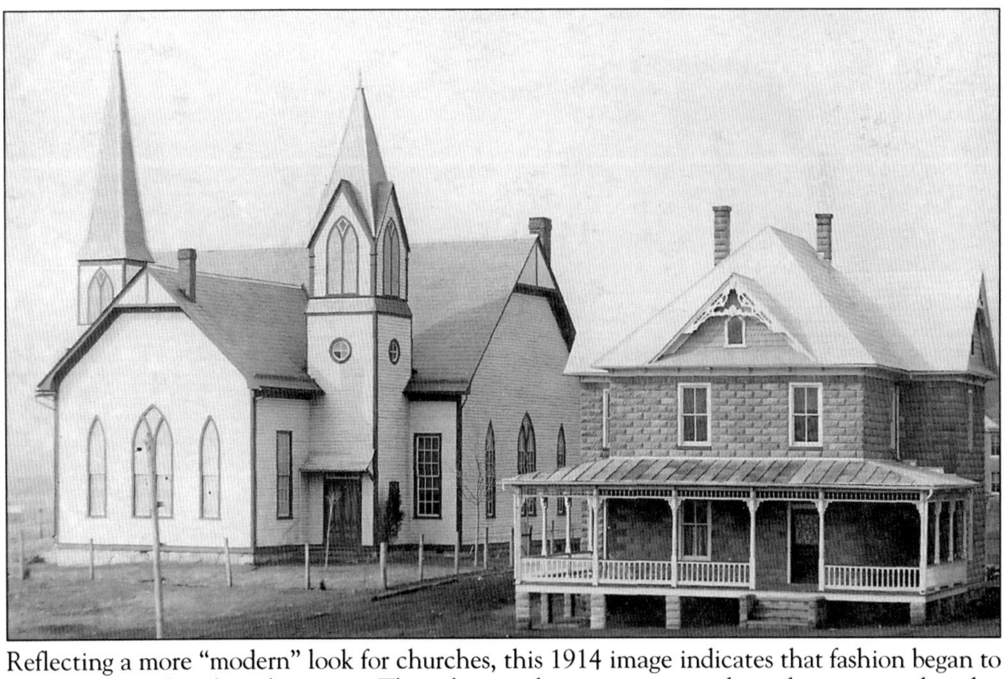

Reflecting a more "modern" look for churches, this 1914 image indicates that fashion began to play a role in church architecture. The substantial parsonage next door also suggests that this was a thriving congregation. The sender of this postcard reported that she was planning to attend a lawn party at Elkton that night. (Kent Botkin Collection.)

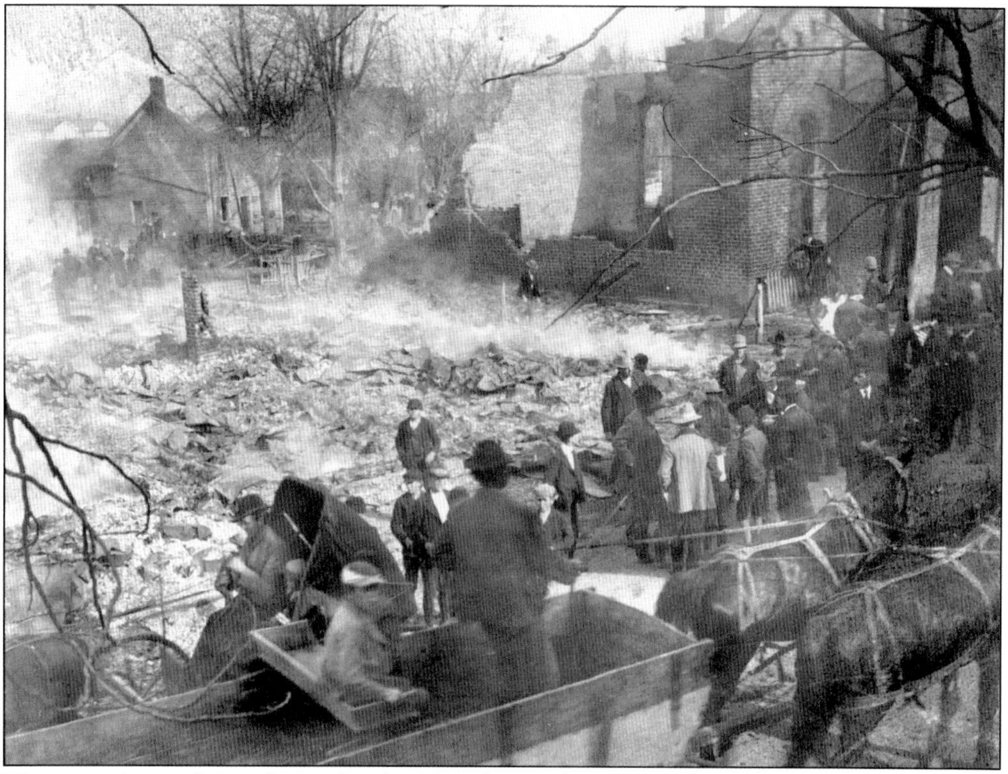

This rare photo of the aftermath of a 1903 fire at the intersection of Seminary Street (now College Street) and Main Street in Dayton shows the remains of the United Brethren Church, which had stood at the site since 1878. The fire also destroyed buildings on Seminary Street, including the Waverly Hotel. (Eastern Mennonite University Collection.)

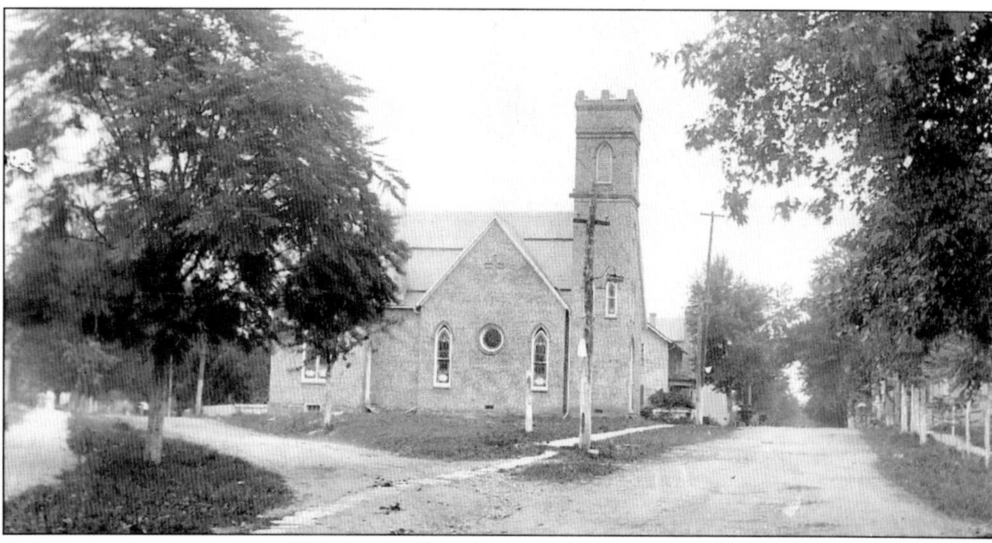

By March 1904, the United Brethren Church was rebuilt, as shown in this photograph. The cost of rebuilding was $6,100. In 1911, the triangular bank structure was built adjacent to the church; the post office operated in that building until 1940, when it moved to its present location on the east side of Main Street. (Eastern Mennonite University Collection.)

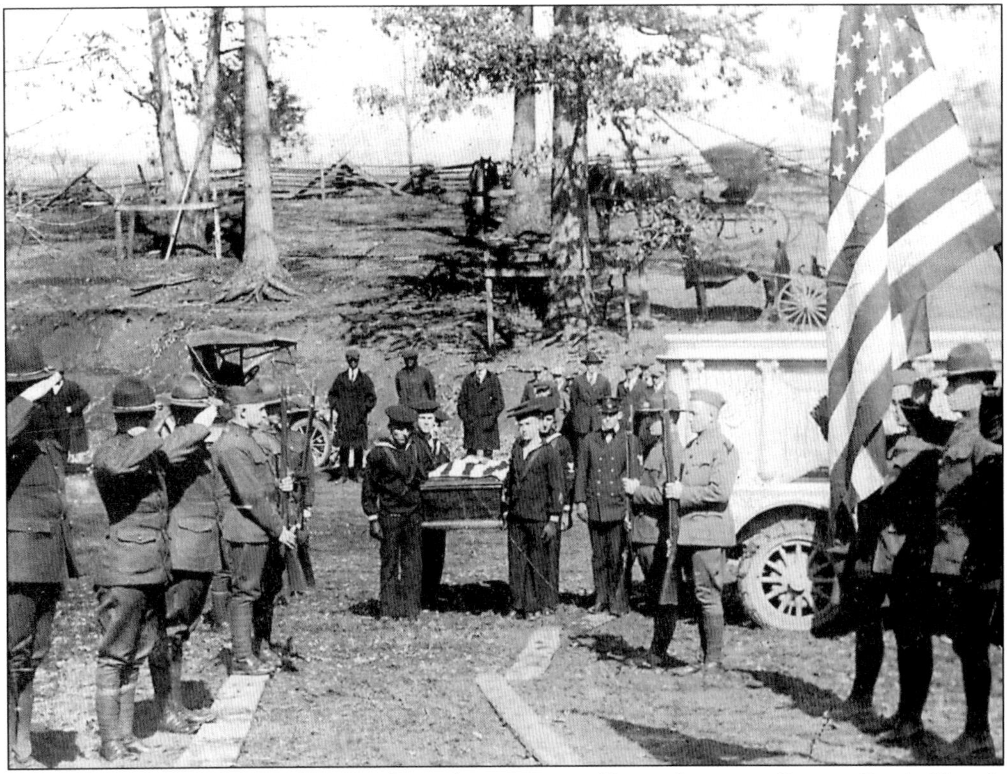

This photograph shows the military funeral procession of Leon Gentry at Beaver Creek Church of the Brethren in July 1919. Like many others, he was infected with the Spanish influenza that swept through the nation in 1918 and 1919. Gentry was a champion boxer for the navy. (Private collection.)

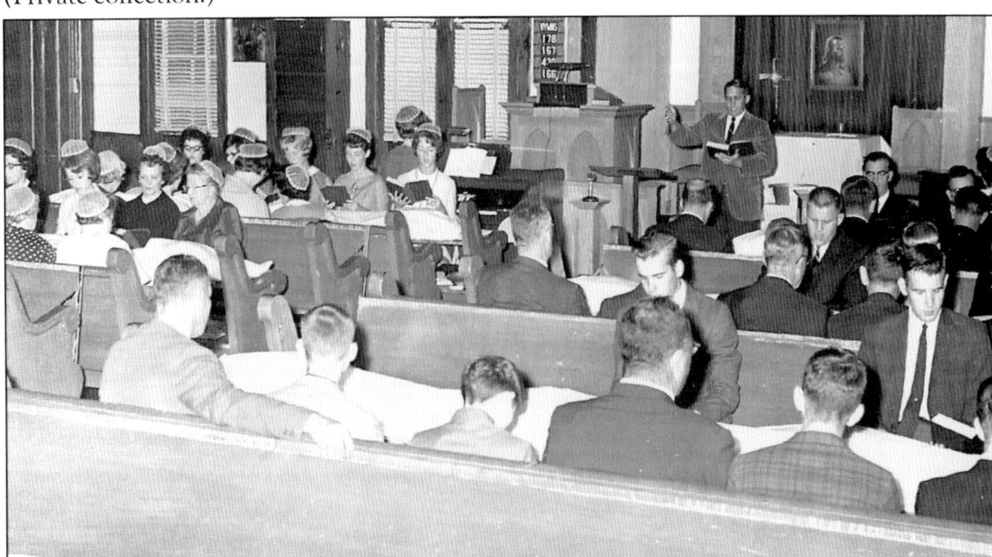

This photograph from the 1960s illustrates another ceremony that took place at Beaver Creek Church of the Brethren—Communion. This image also offers a unique look at the interior of the building, which was built in 1917. (Private collection.)

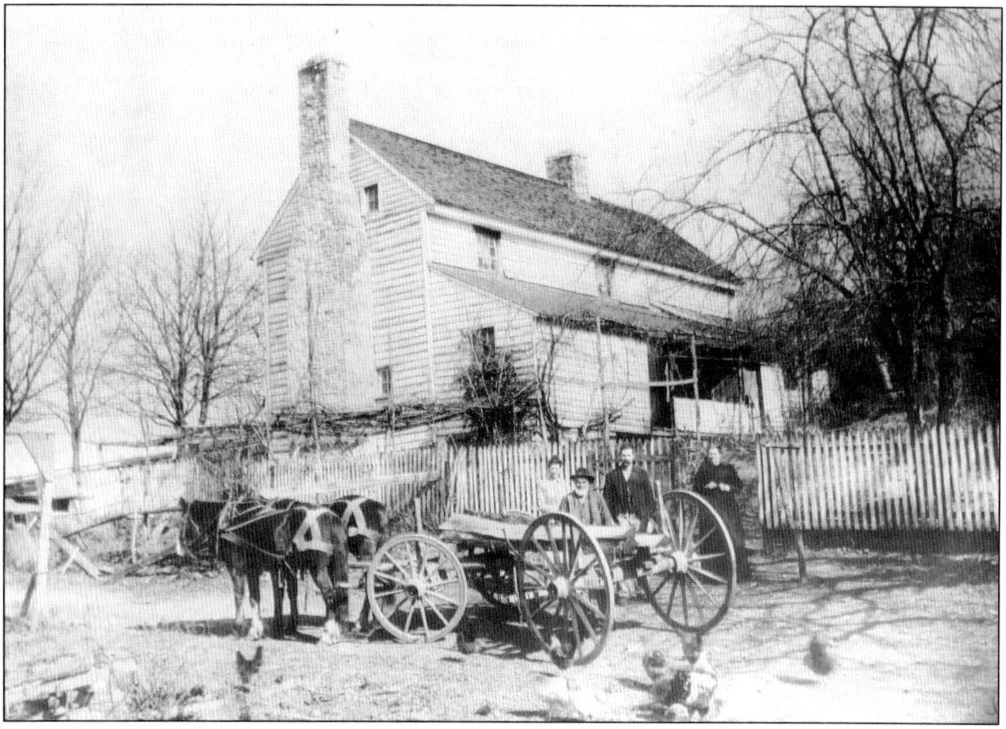

Shown at their Beldor home in the mountains of east Rockingham County, the Wyant family poses with their two-horse team and brood of chickens, essentials for the self-sufficient family of the late 19th century. Shown from left to right are Sally Wyant; her father-in-law, Jesse Wyant; Jesse's son, Charlie Wyant; and Martha Wyant, Jesse's wife. (Janet Downs Collection.)

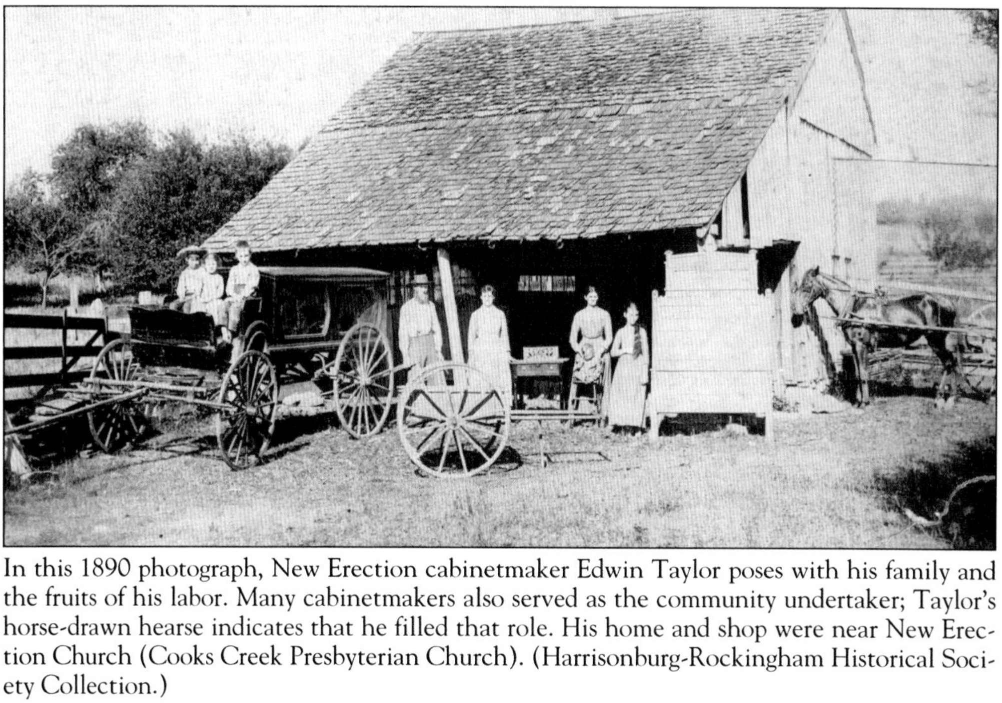

In this 1890 photograph, New Erection cabinetmaker Edwin Taylor poses with his family and the fruits of his labor. Many cabinetmakers also served as the community undertaker; Taylor's horse-drawn hearse indicates that he filled that role. His home and shop were near New Erection Church (Cooks Creek Presbyterian Church). (Harrisonburg-Rockingham Historical Society Collection.)

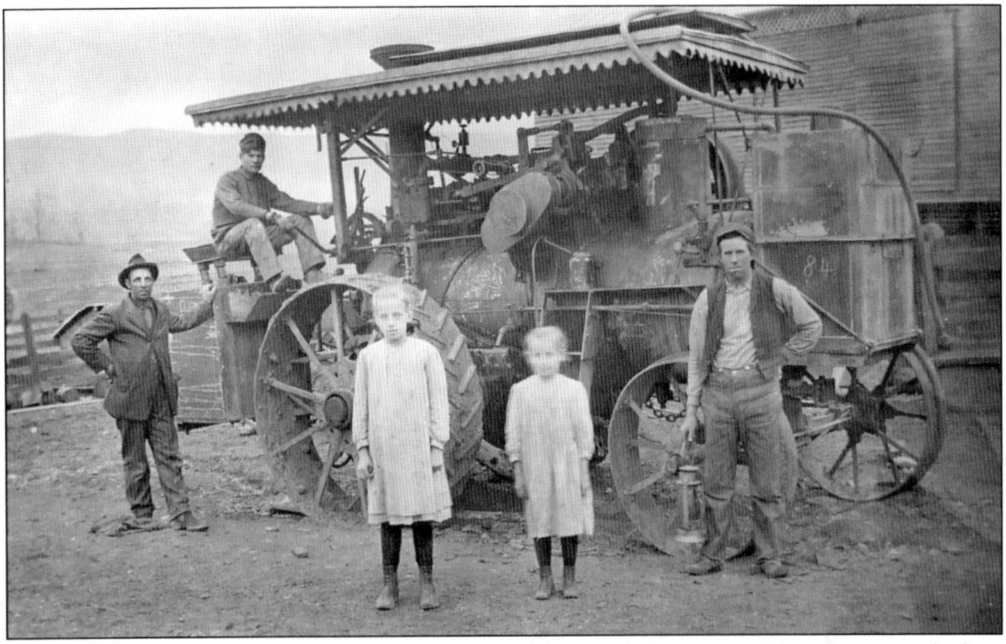

Since the time photographic images became possible, people have posed for pictures with their families, their possessions, and the achievements of which they are most proud. Here, an unidentified west Rockingham family poses with their steam engine, an important addition to many communities. (Jeffrey S. Evans Collection.)

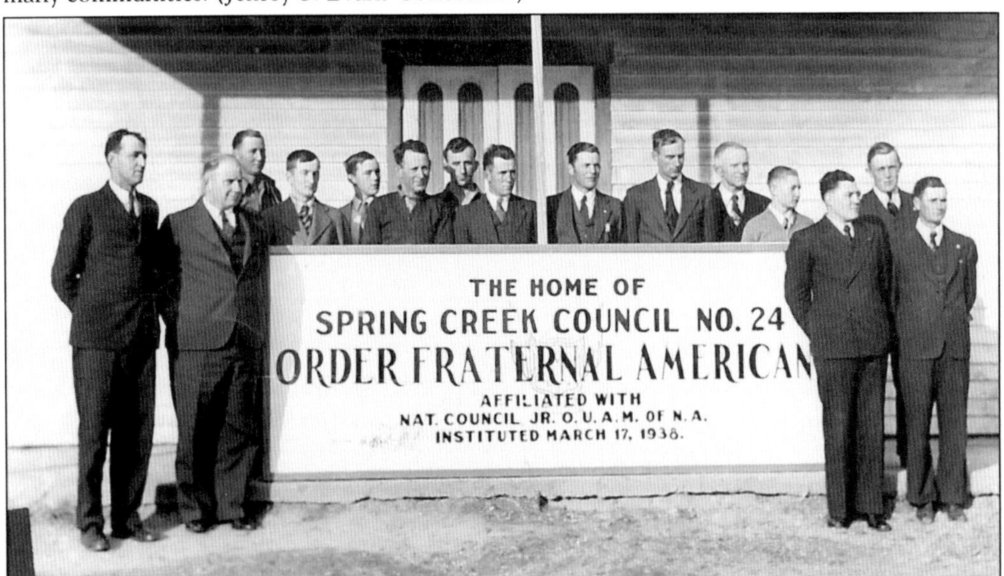

Organizations play a large role in many communities, and civic-minded individuals enjoy having a remembrance of their time together. In this photograph from the early 1940s, men from the Spring Creek area pose together as the local chapter of the Junior Order of the United American Mechanics of North America. Pictured from left to right are Everett Stearn, Roy Vanpelt, Hershel Miller, Hubert Wine, Garnet Simmons, Wilmer Simmons, Charles Taylor, Lenford Miller, Galen Miller Sr., Sam Taylor, ? Wheat, Morris Miller, Garnet Stover, Frank Hisey, and Elmer Miller. (Private collection.)

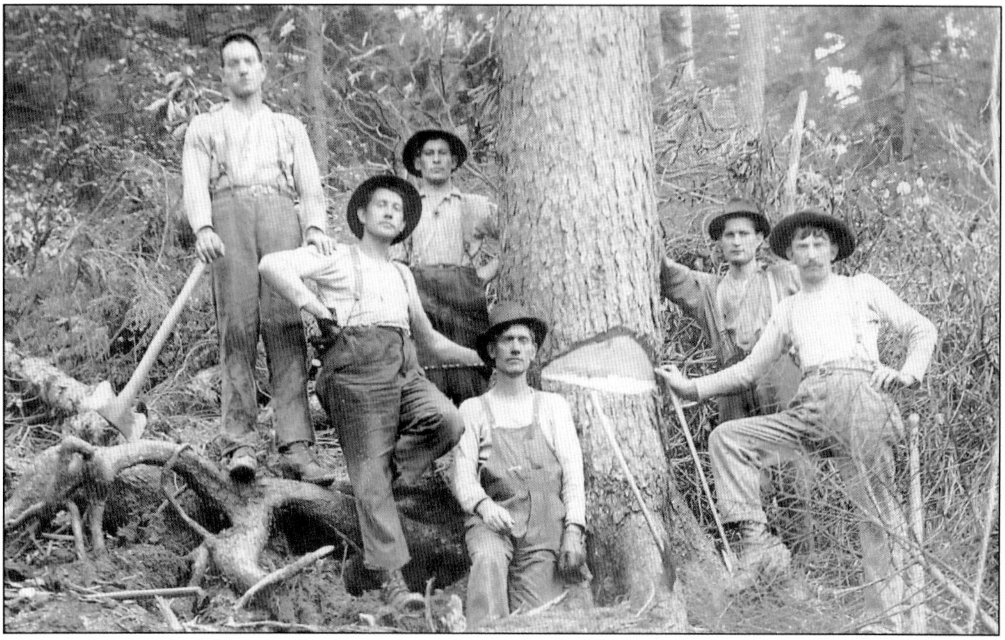

Obviously proud of their work, this group of unidentified lumbermen strikes a pose in the mountains of western Rockingham County. As other photos in this collection demonstrate, the timber industry was a major source of employment in the county, supplying the sawmills with logs and the tanneries with bark. (Jeffrey S. Evans Collection.)

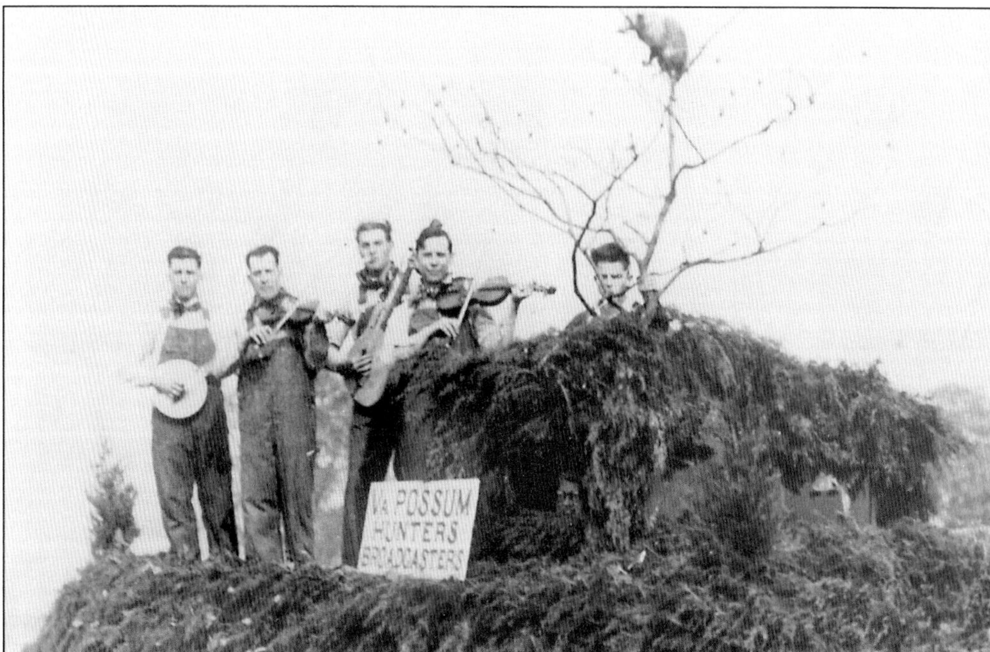

Posing on their float in the 1932 Winchester Apple Blossom Festival parade, Rockingham County musicians (left to right) Roy Todd, Emory Stroop, Myron Alshire, Ervin Jenkins, and Hop Muterspaugh serenade a live opossum in the tree. (Harrisonburg-Rockingham Historical Society Collection.)

Four

PASTIMES

Where images in the previous section were selected to demonstrate the variety of activities Rockingham County residents have been involved in, this chapter's photographs offer a sampling of how folks simply passed the time when they could shirk responsibility for a while. Whether picnicking, loafing, motoring, hobnobbing at a fashionable resort, or playing a game of baseball, the people in these photographs have all found a way to enjoy a respite from the cares of daily life. Perhaps the most extraordinary images of this section are those taken in Mount Crawford around 1900. Although the photographer and subjects in this series remain unidentified, the richness of each shot offers a window through which to view this brief period of time in one county's community. For this volume, the value of such images is not in knowing who these people are; instead it lies in witnessing how they lived the carefree moments of their lives.

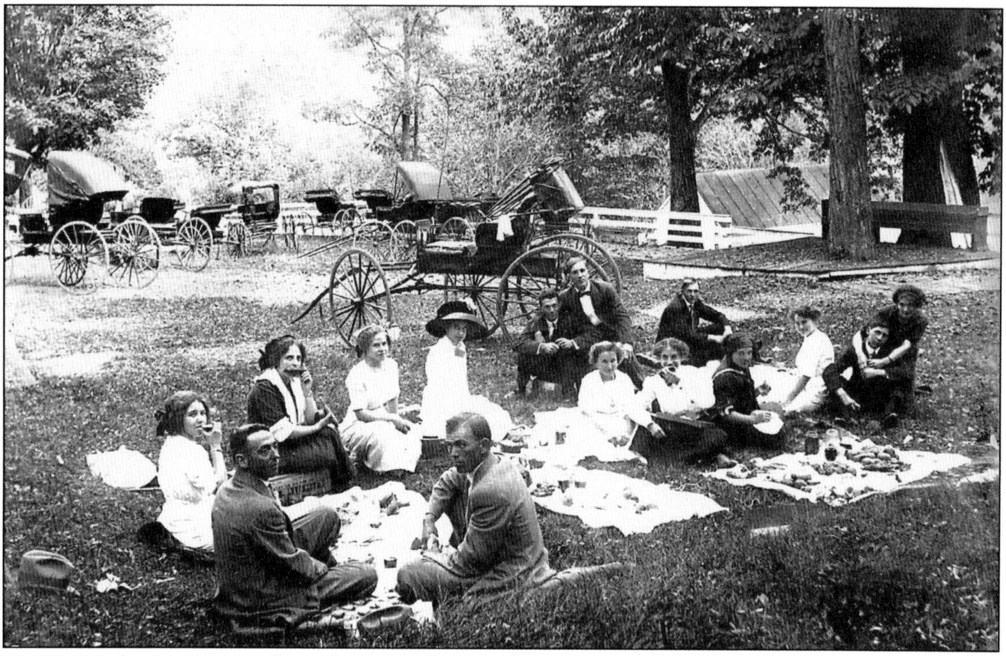

Picnics in the mountains have long been a favorite pastime on a leisurely weekend afternoon. Here a group of friends enjoy "dinner on the ground" at one of Rockingham County's picturesque mountain retreats. (Kermit Early Collection.)

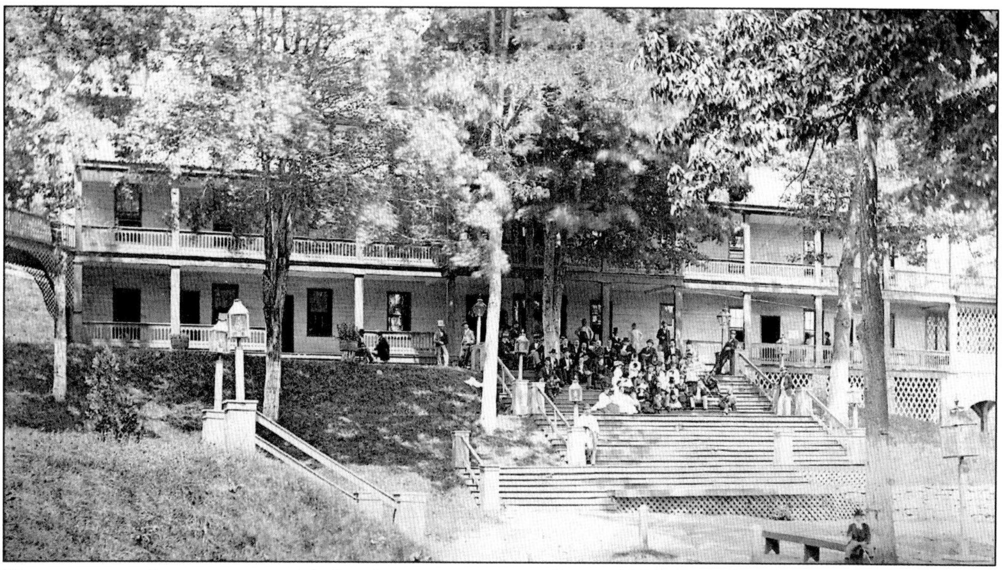

First promoted as a resort with healing waters as early as 1825, Rawley Springs hit its heyday around 1885, several years before fire destroyed a number of the buildings. This photograph of the Virginia Hotel came with an interesting note listing the "Fat Men of Rawley." Included on the roll, with a combined weight of 1,540 pounds, are R.D. Morrison of Baltimore, Maryland; E.A. Soullard of Savannah, Georgia; J.M. Graves of Rawley, Virginia; Rev. S.S. Roszell of Harrisonburg, Virginia; Hon. William Milnes Jr. of Shenandoah Iron Works; S.B. Luck, the manager at Rawley Springs; and J.P. Houck, of Shenandoah Iron Works. (Massanutten Regional Library Collection.)

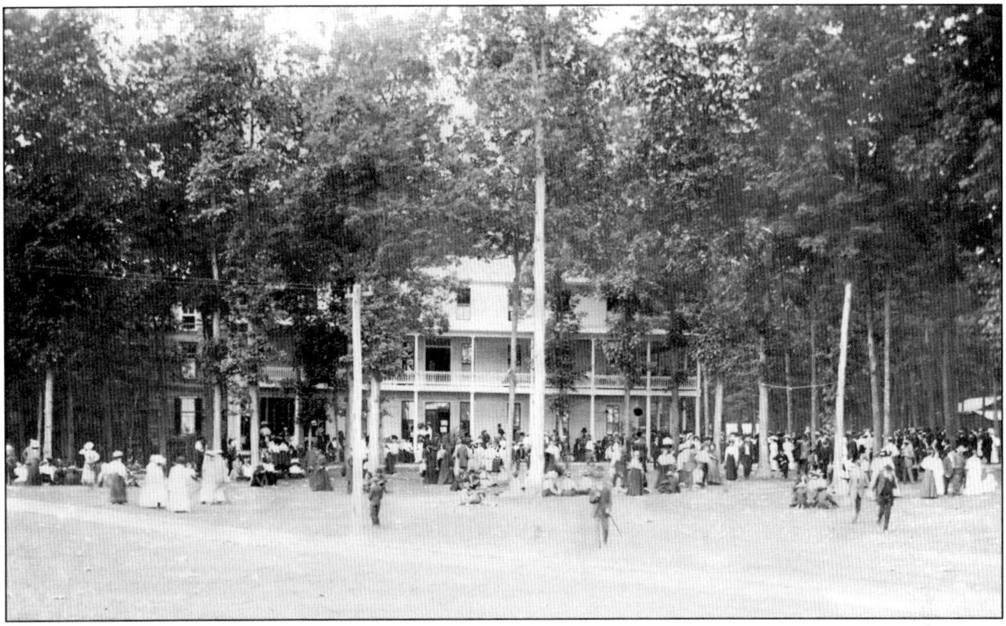

Opening in the 1860s, Assembly Park in the Park View community north of Harrisonburg lived up to its name. It was the place where residents assembled for revival meetings, lectures, agricultural fairs, "match games of baseball," and later even school, as members of the Mennonite community purchased the building in 1916 to establish Eastern Mennonite University. (Eastern Mennonite University, Menno Simons Archives Collection.)

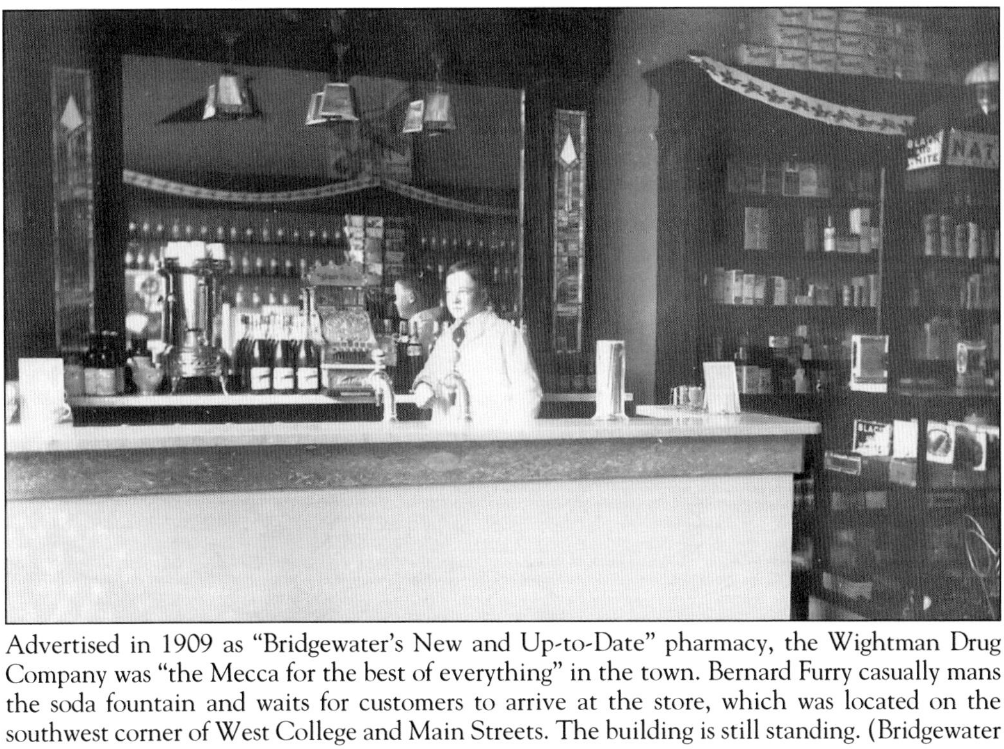

Advertised in 1909 as "Bridgewater's New and Up-to-Date" pharmacy, the Wightman Drug Company was "the Mecca for the best of everything" in the town. Bernard Furry casually mans the soda fountain and waits for customers to arrive at the store, which was located on the southwest corner of West College and Main Streets. The building is still standing. (Bridgewater College Collection.)

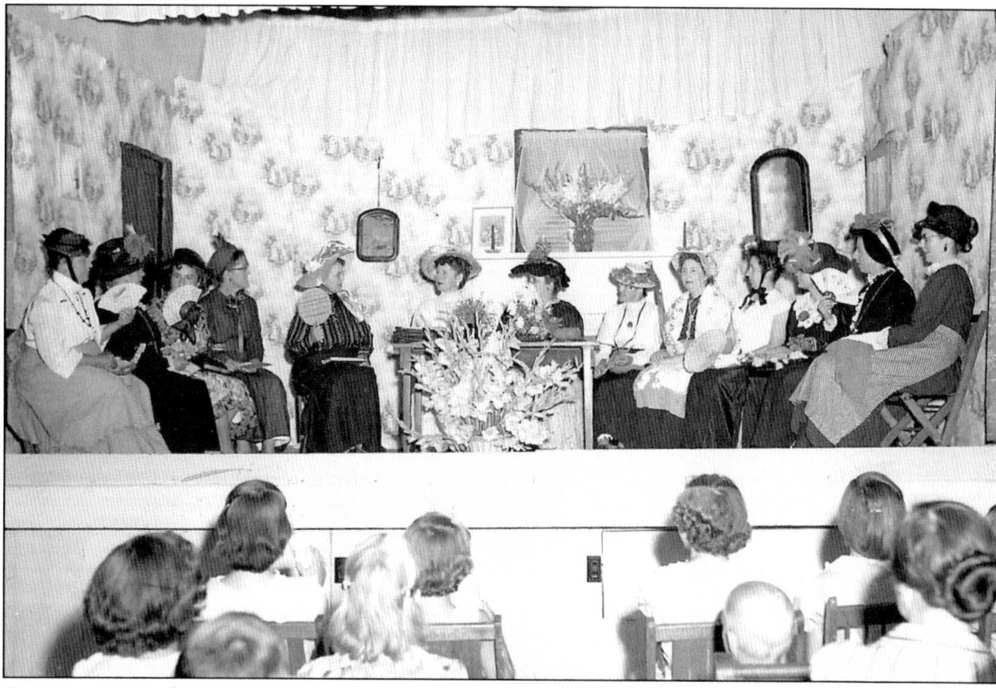

Communities often sponsor events to raise money or simply to get together for a good time. Women from the nearby Sangerville area performed this 1950s play in the Spring Creek Town Hall, and although the title has been lost, the memories of many such events linger in this historic building that continues to serve as gathering place. (Private collection.)

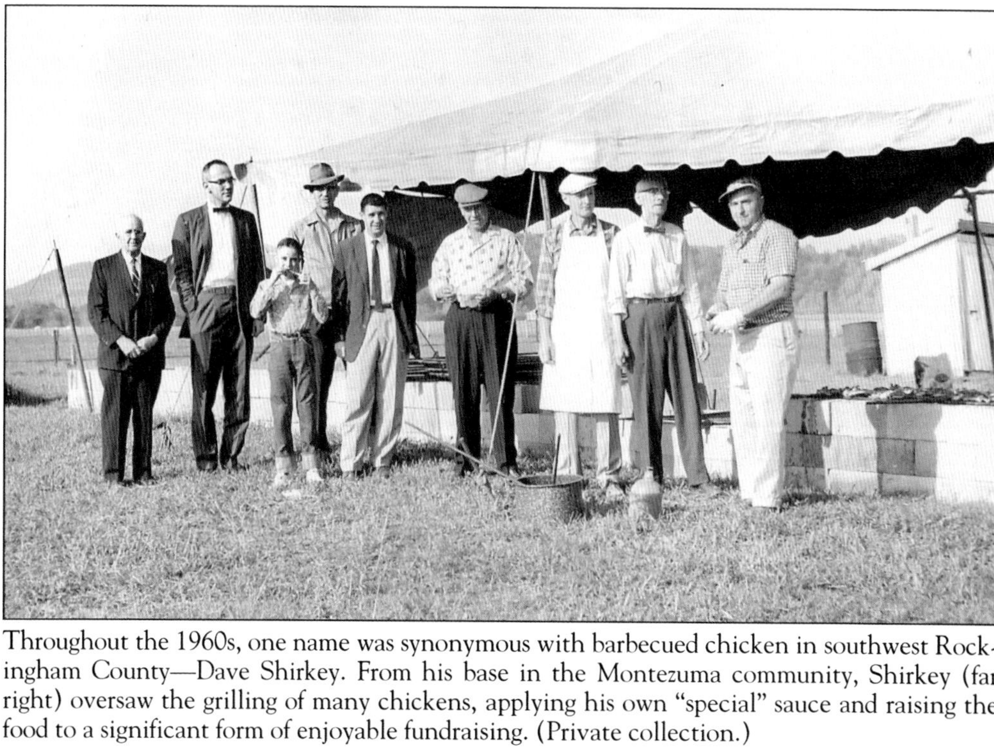

Throughout the 1960s, one name was synonymous with barbecued chicken in southwest Rockingham County—Dave Shirkey. From his base in the Montezuma community, Shirkey (far right) oversaw the grilling of many chickens, applying his own "special" sauce and raising the food to a significant form of enjoyable fundraising. (Private collection.)

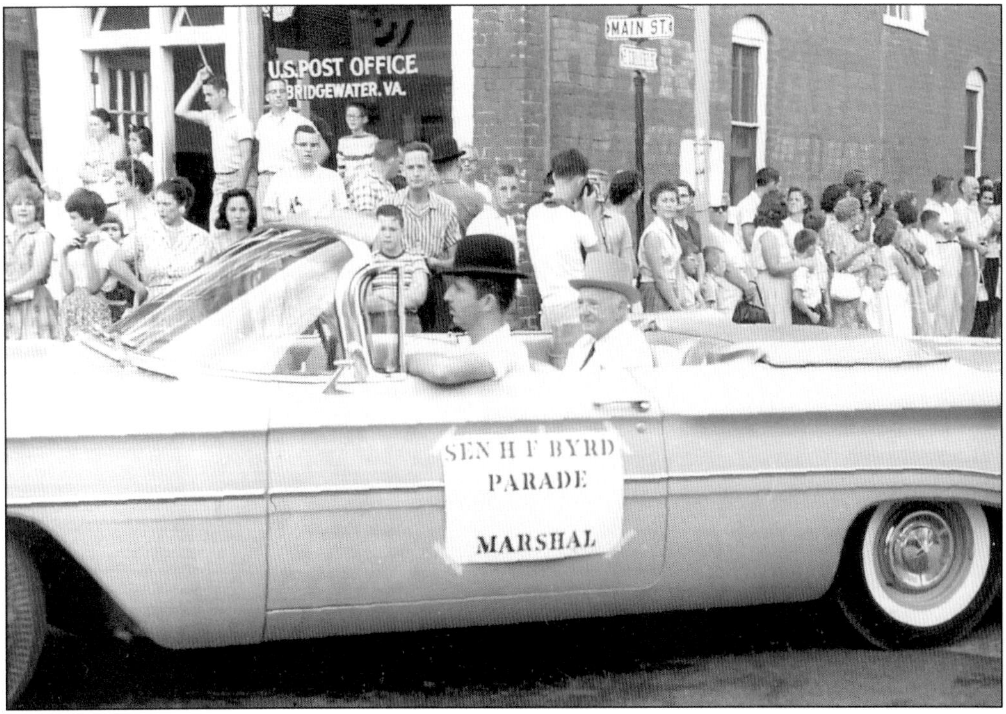

Parades have long been a favorite pastime for participants and observers alike. This Bridgewater parade featured Sen. Harry F. Byrd Sr. as grand marshal and roller skating majorettes. These photographs also offer another glimpse of the Sipe building at corner of Main and College Streets. (Private collection.)

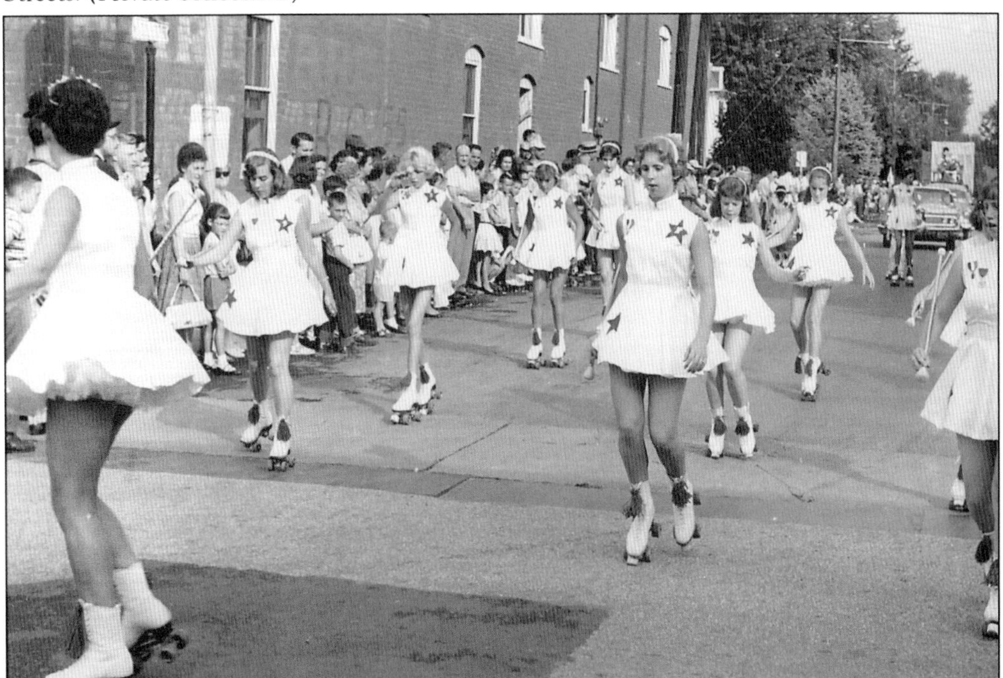

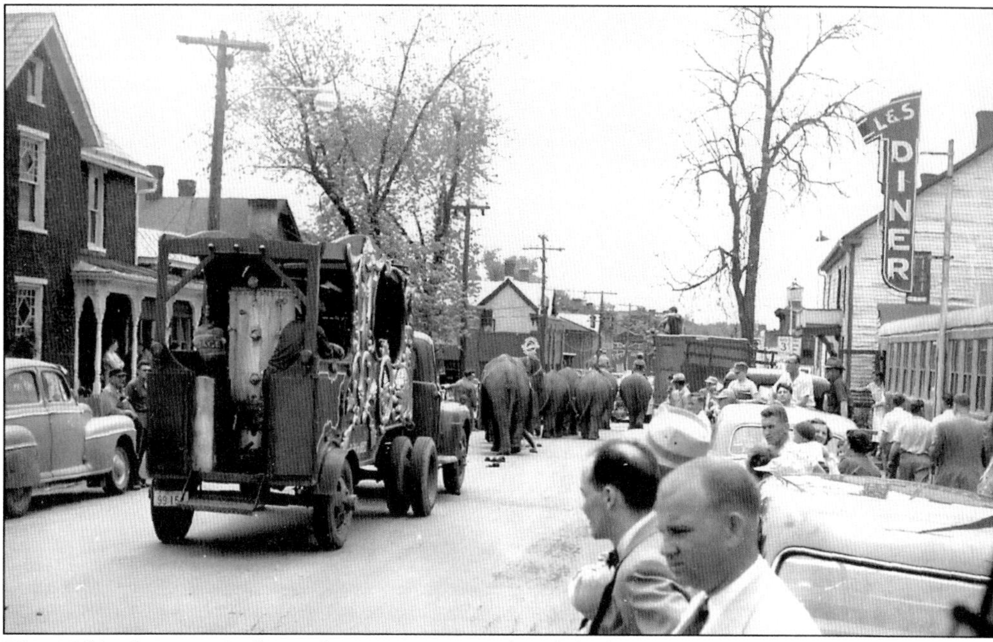

This 1950s photograph shows the uncommon sight of elephants marching past the popular L&S Diner on Liberty Street in Harrisonburg. The circus and the elephants are long gone, but the L&S continues to treat patrons from the area. (Private collection.)

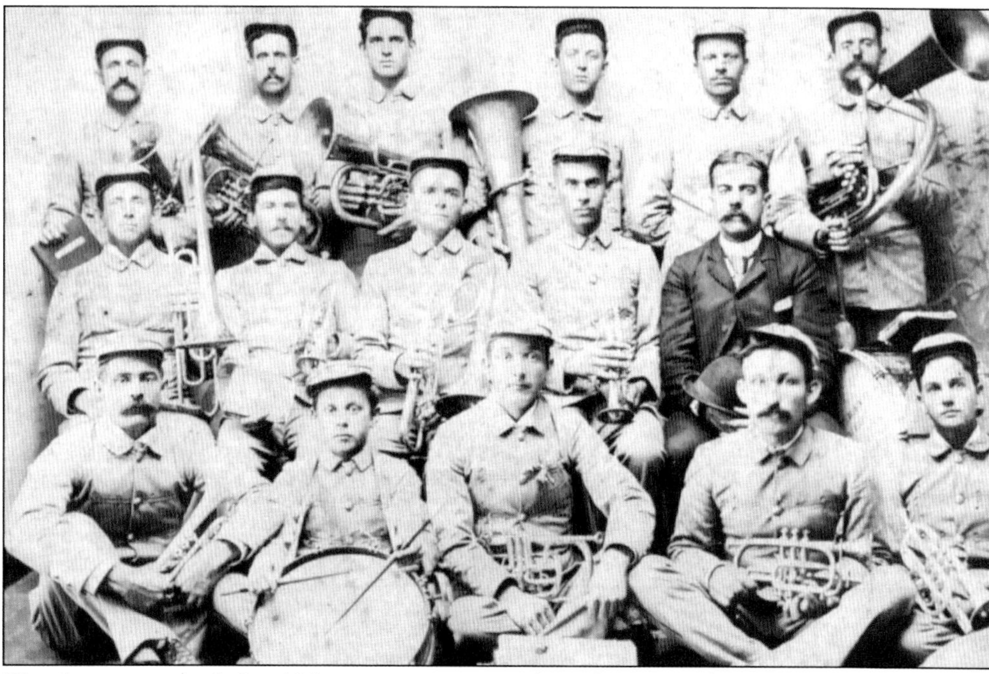

The last quarter of the 19th century witnessed a phenomenal increase in the number of community bands. Even smaller hamlets such as Cross Keys, with help from neighbors in Mill Creek, mustered a band, although the community claimed only about 50 residents in 1912. This photograph was taken October 9, 1894. (Harrisonburg-Rockingham Historical Society Collection.)

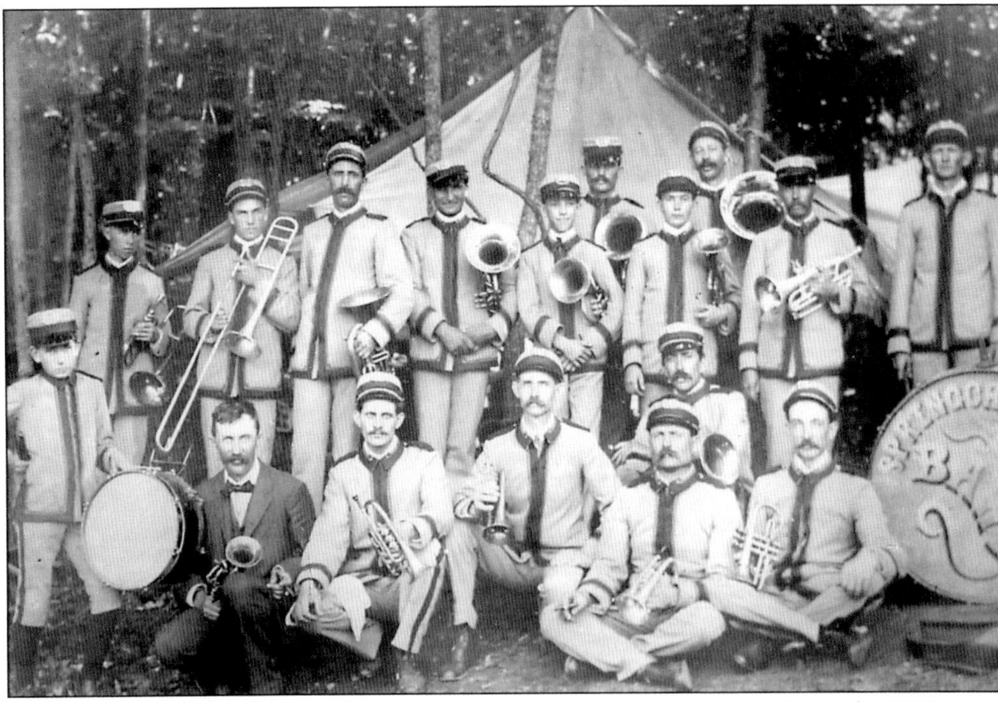

The Spring Creek band, shown here, entertained their thriving community in the 1890s until after the century turned. Formed in 1896, the Bridgewater Concert Band (below) livened up many occasions in that town and was a featured group when President William McKinley visited Harrisonburg in 1898. As automobiles made travel from home easier, entertainment could be enjoyed outside of one's town or village, and the abundance of bands eventually dissipated. (Harrisonburg-Rockingham Historical Society Collection; Greg Evans Collection.)

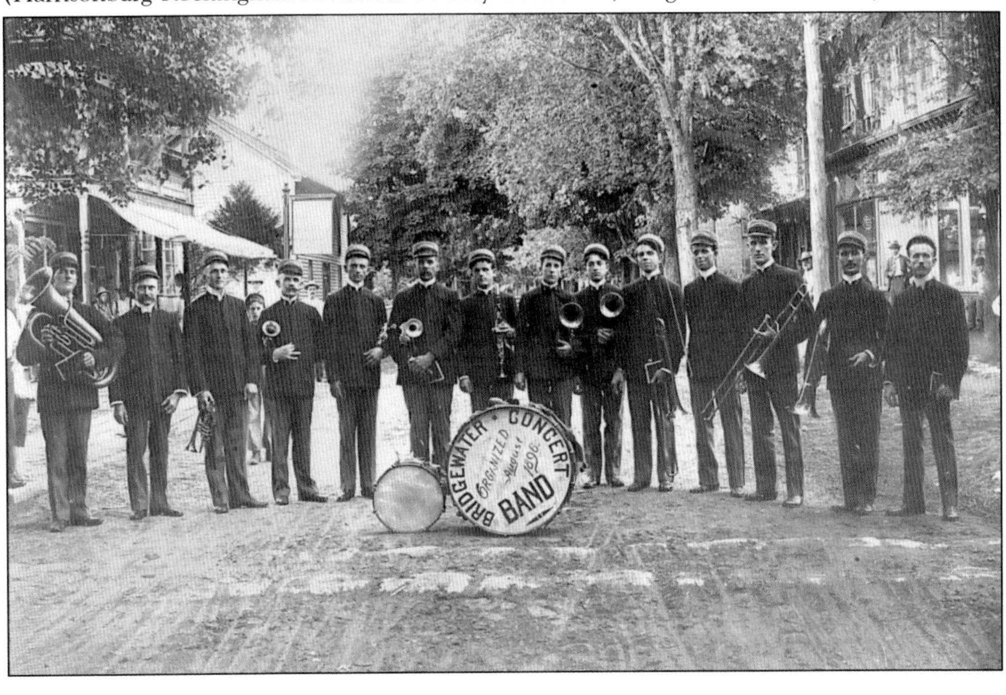

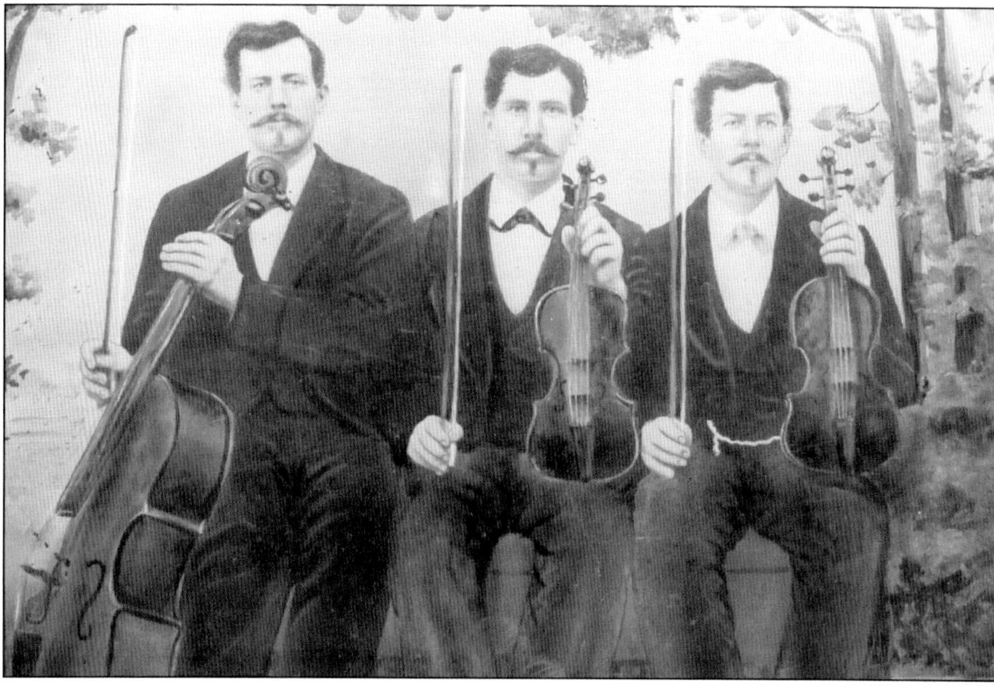

Dances have always been a pleasant source of diversion in Rockingham County, and string bands were booked on many weekends throughout the year. This group from the eastern portion of the county includes, from left to right, Ben Long, Ike Hudlow, and Will Long. Their turn-of-the-century play list featured "Soldier's Joy," "Jenny Lind Polka," "Military Schottische," and "Over the Waves." (Harrisonburg-Rockingham Historical Society Collection.)

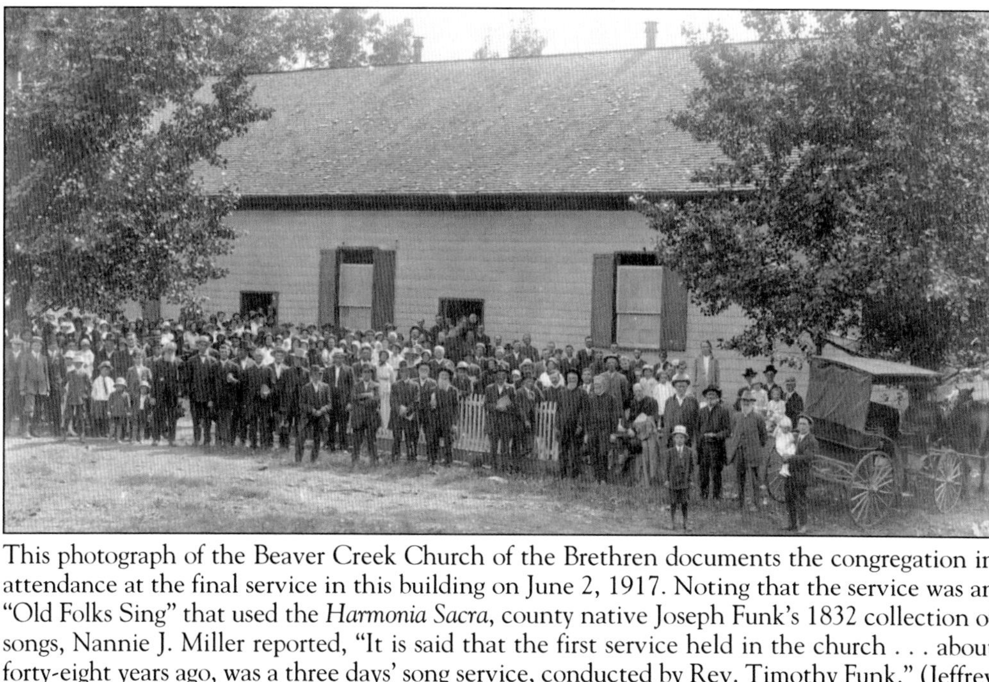

This photograph of the Beaver Creek Church of the Brethren documents the congregation in attendance at the final service in this building on June 2, 1917. Noting that the service was an "Old Folks Sing" that used the *Harmonia Sacra*, county native Joseph Funk's 1832 collection of songs, Nannie J. Miller reported, "It is said that the first service held in the church . . . about forty-eight years ago, was a three days' song service, conducted by Rev. Timothy Funk." (Jeffrey S. Evans Collection.)

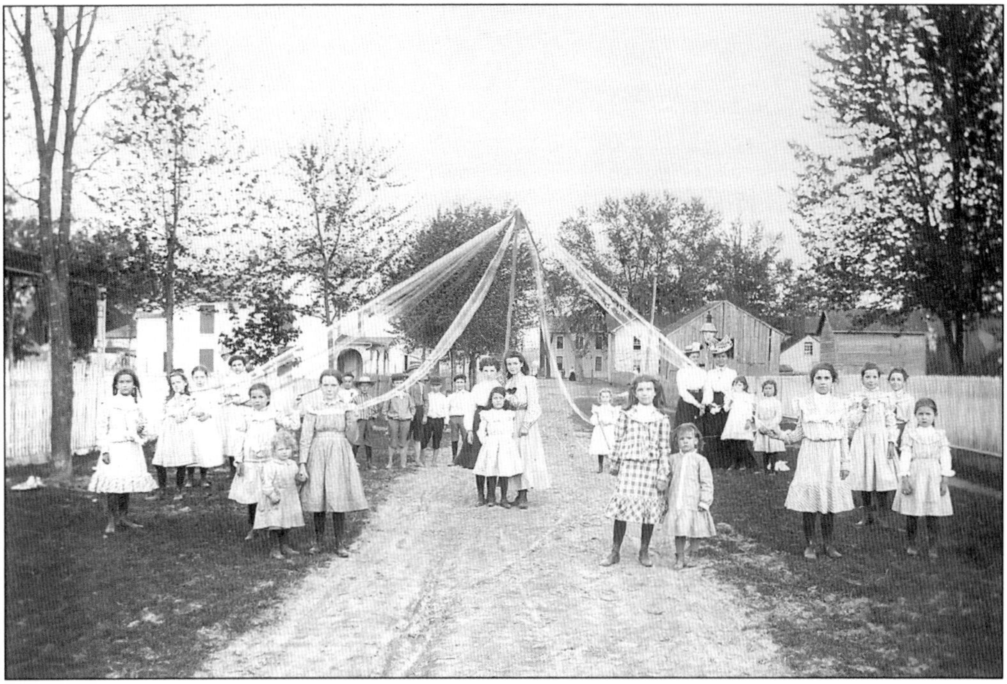

Holidays are a time for celebration and the renewal of traditions. These photographs illustrate two customs that are seldom observed in the 21st century; above, a group of young folks in Bridgewater pose around a may pole; below, a group of belsnickels in Singers Glen demonstrate a less universal tradition around 1910. Continuing the Christmas custom of dressing outlandishly and visiting neighbors are, from left to right, Joe Lee, John Lee, Fred Ritchie, Claude Ritchie, Ben Lee, Claud Lee, Buck Swank, and Scott Brewer. (Kent Botkin Collection; Private Collection.)

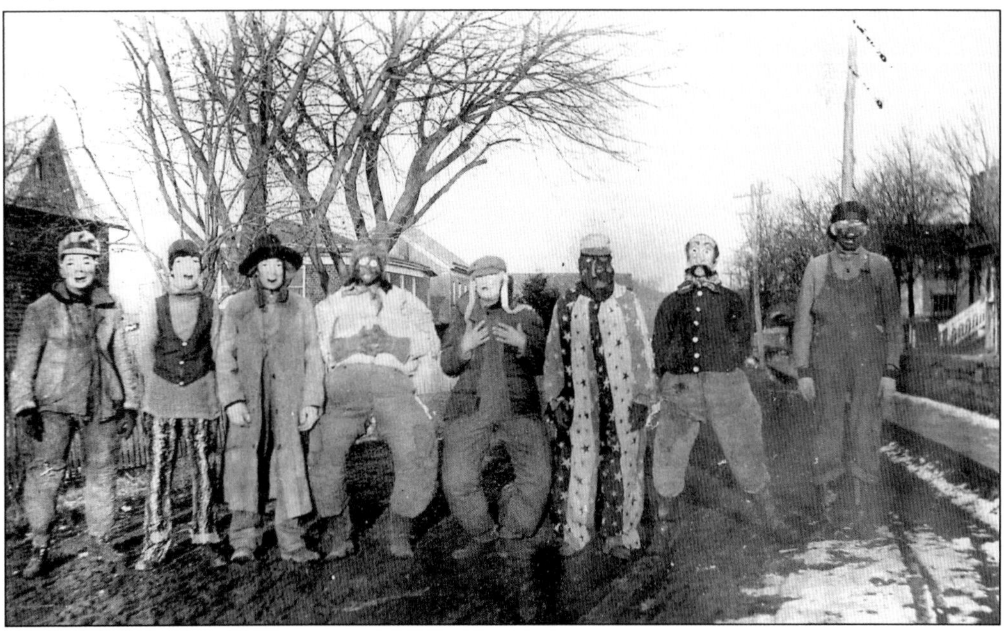

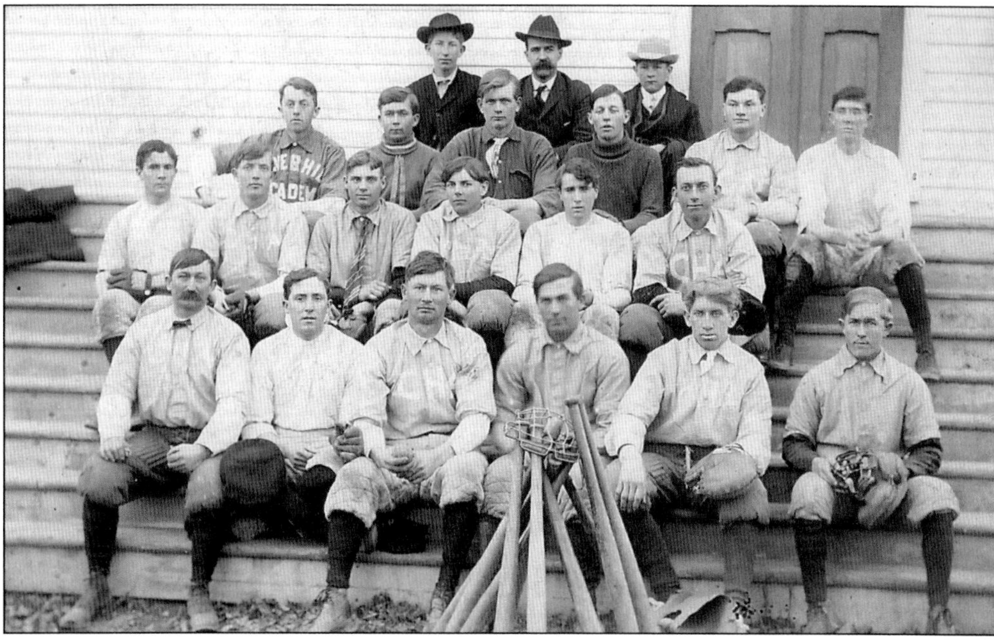

The importance of baseball to Rockingham County cannot be disputed. Members of the Clover Hill Academy club, photographed around 1900 on the steps of the Spring Creek Methodist Church, may have been preparing to face their neighbors from the Spring Creek School. (Private collection.)

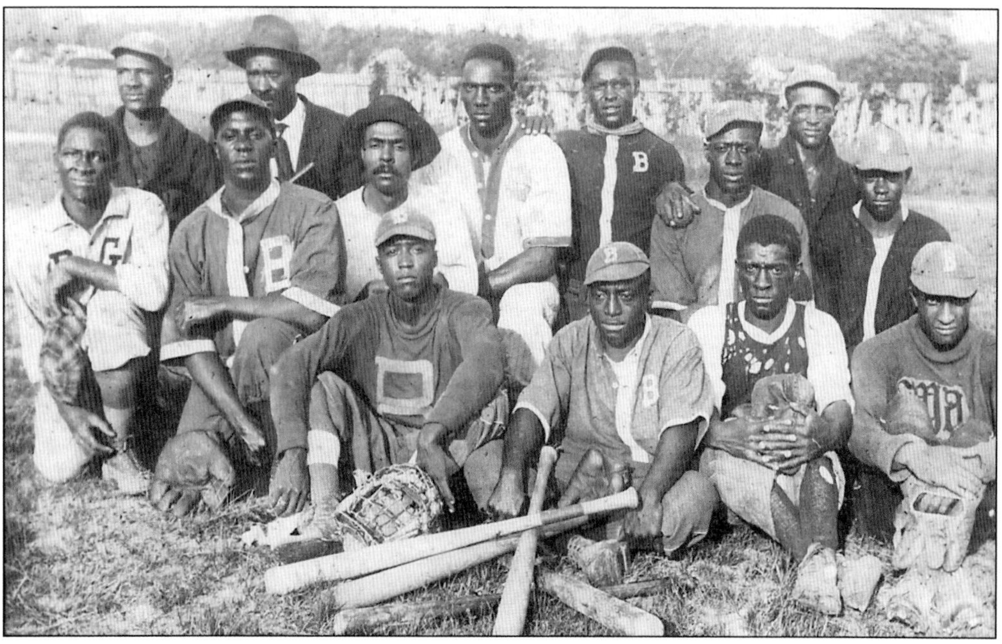

As in much of the nation before integration, Rockingham County had a rich tradition of African-American baseball. In the 1940s, the county supported two black clubs: one in Harrisonburg managed by Junious Whitelow and the other in Bridgwater led by Roscoe Burgess. The Bridgewater team is pictured here before the two teams merged to form the Harrisonburg AC's. (Greg Evans Collection.)

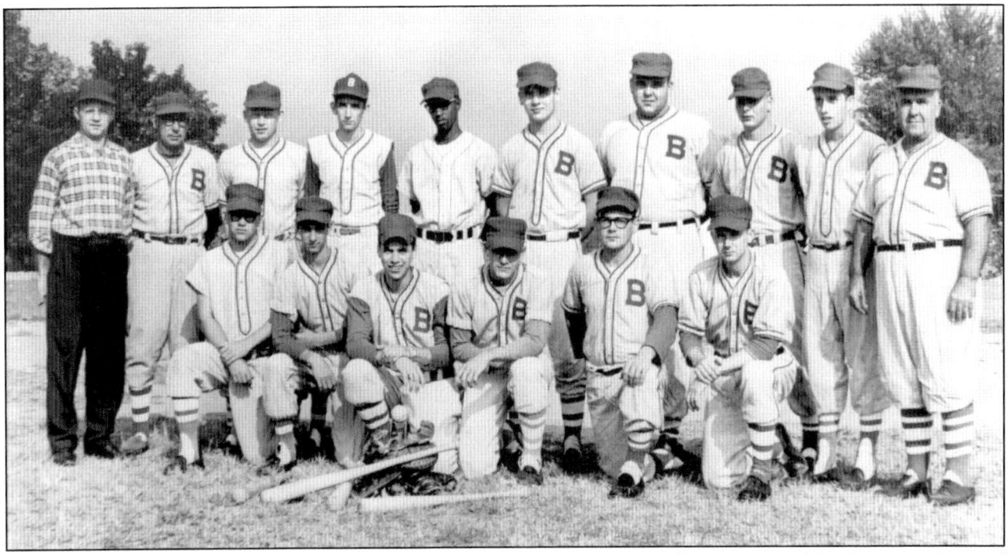

The Rockingham County Baseball League, formed in 1924 at the urging of *Daily News Record* editor J.R. "Polly" Lineweaver, continues as a league in 2004, making it the oldest continuous amateur baseball league in the nation. The 1962 Bridgewater league champions are pictured from left to right: (front row) Ray Lynn Heatwole, Donny Fulk, Kenny Newman, Tommy Huffman, Keith Spitzer, and Johnny Hensley; (back row) Harry L. Simmons (coach), Harry Whitmore (coach), Shirley Ringgold, Tommy Fulk, Ted Temple, Dewayne Rhodes, Griff Gilkerson, Wayne Whitmore, Wayne Hypes, and Carl "Pidge" Rhodes Sr. (manager). (Private collection.)

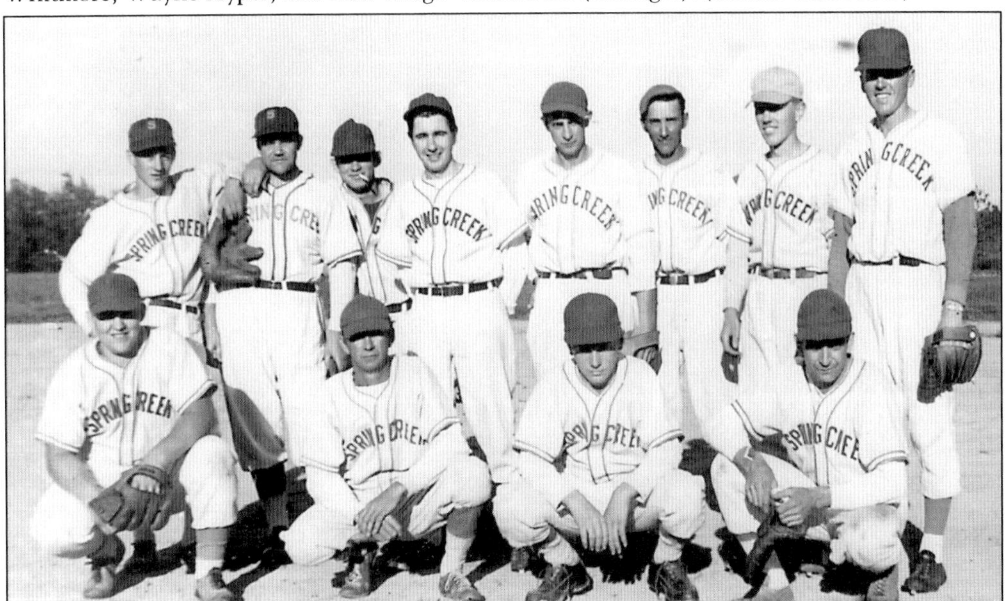

Spring Creek, along with Briery Branch, Broadway, Bridgewater, Dayton, Keezeltown, and Linville-Edom, fielded a team in the first season of the Rockingham County Baseball League. The following members of the 1950 Spring Creek club are pictured from left to right: (front row) Dennis Wright, Jack Tumer, Carl McNett, and DeRay Miller; (back row) Norman Mongold, Bobby Spitler, Tom Cromer, Ralph Heatwole, Stanley Cassidy, Carney Tumer, Harold McNett, and Roland McNett. (Private collection.)

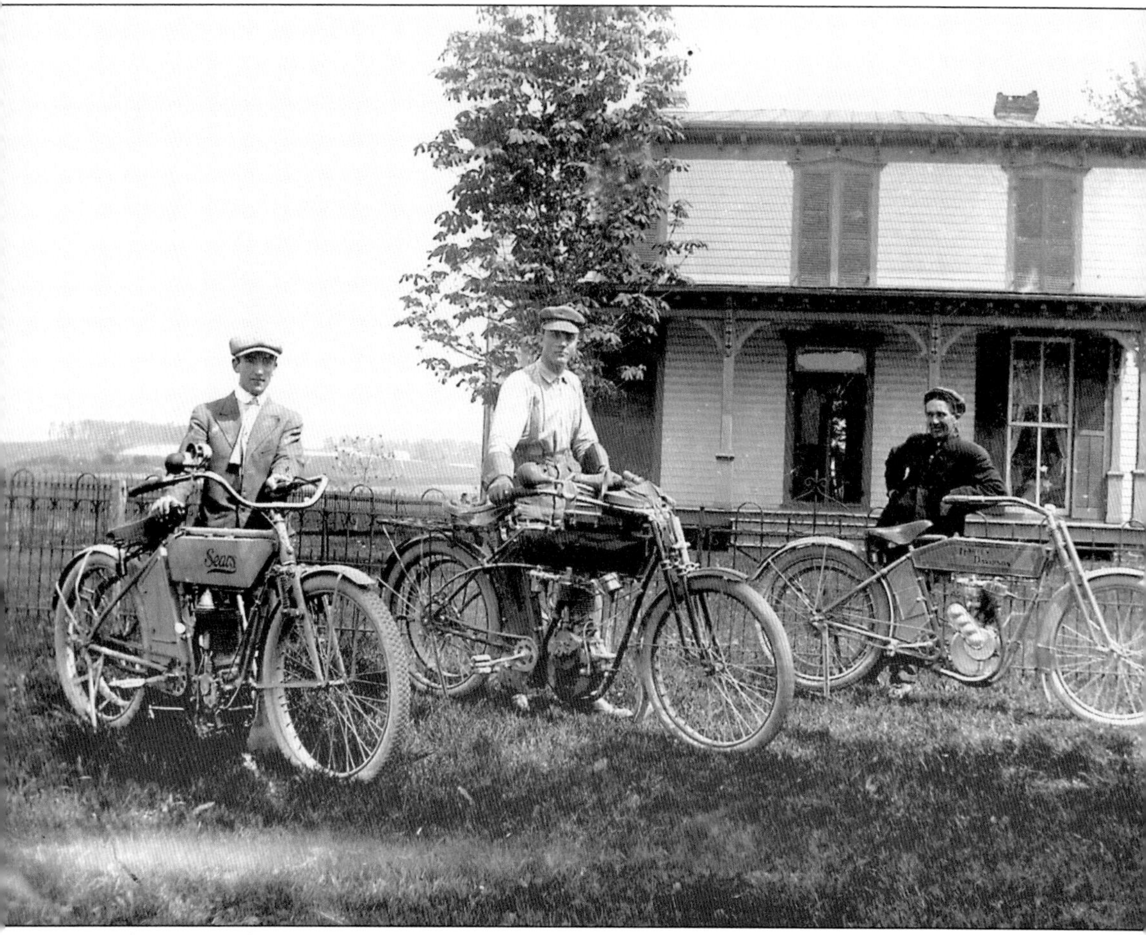

Advances in the transportation world not only increased mobility but also encouraged traveling by car or motorcycle for pleasure. O.K. Early (middle) poses with his unidentified friends, who are riding a Sears model (left) and a Harley-Davidson (right). (Kermit Early Collection.)

While serving in the National Guard in the early 1930s, Hubert Wine of Spring Creek motored around the county on a Harley-Davidson motorcycle. (Private collection.)

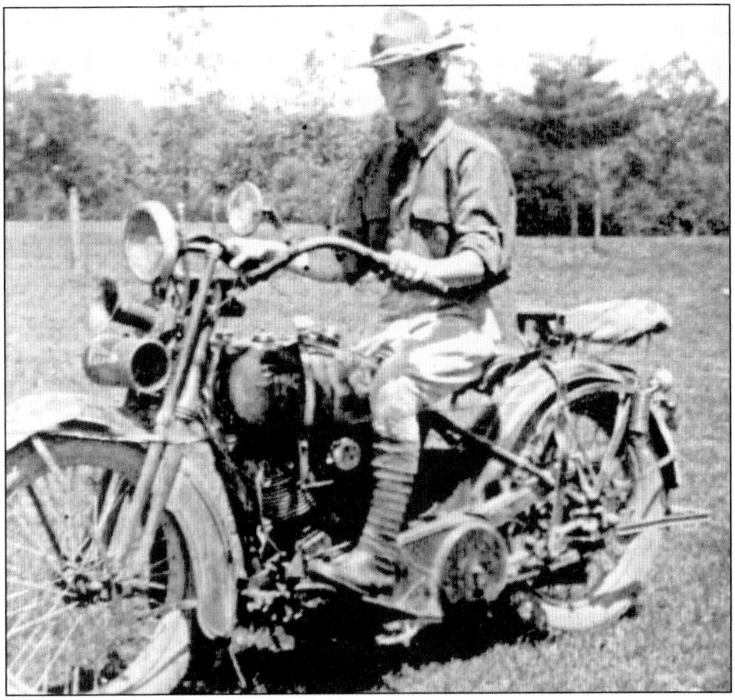

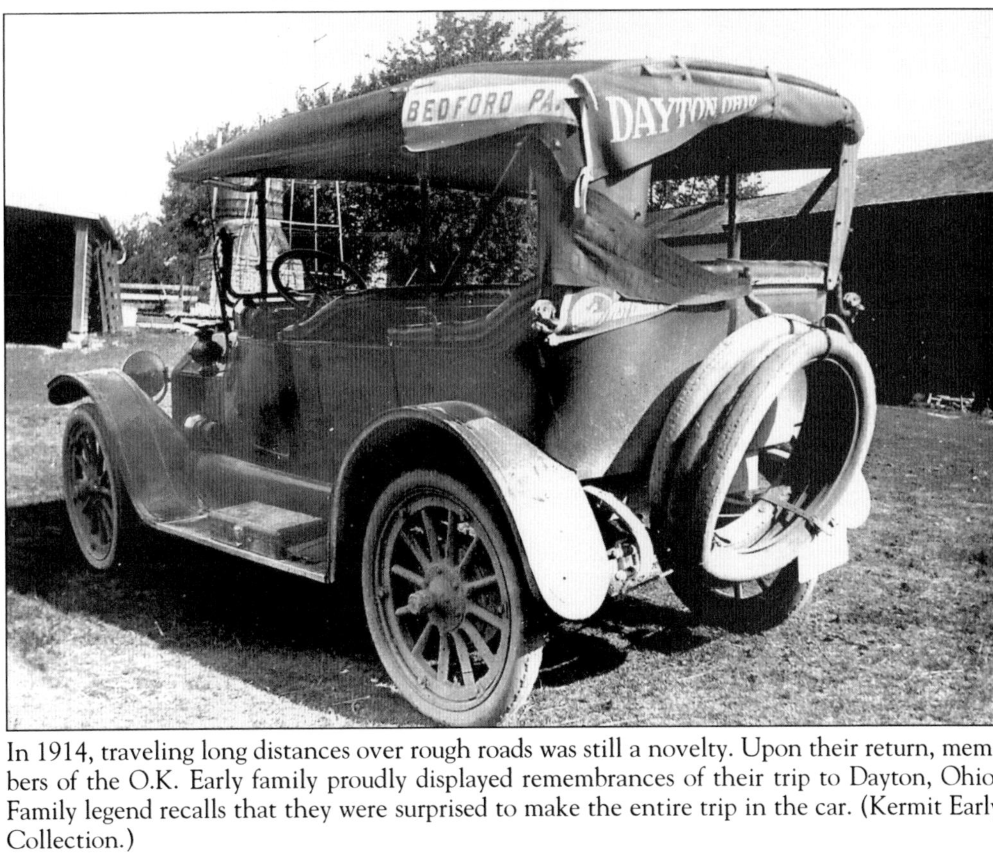

In 1914, traveling long distances over rough roads was still a novelty. Upon their return, members of the O.K. Early family proudly displayed remembrances of their trip to Dayton, Ohio. Family legend recalls that they were surprised to make the entire trip in the car. (Kermit Early Collection.)

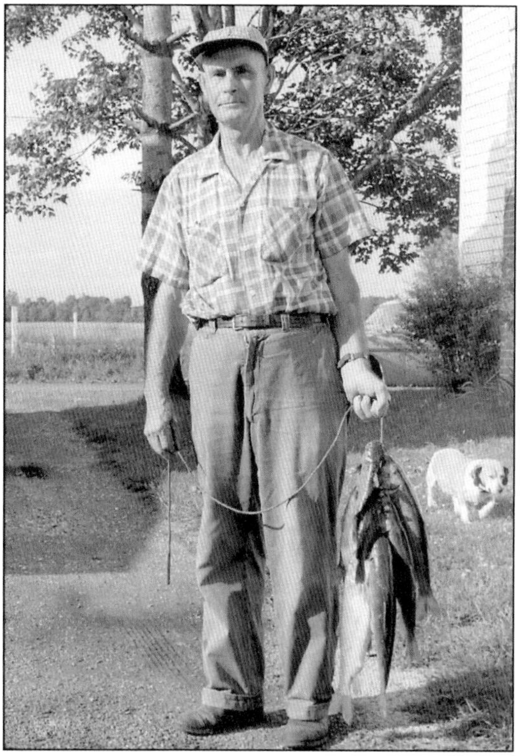

Many people believe that any day spent fishing is a good day. Elmer Miller suggests that it is an even better day when you are successful. This 1950s photograph attests to the bounty of Rockingham County's waters, in this case Spring Creek in the southwestern portion of the county. (Private collection.)

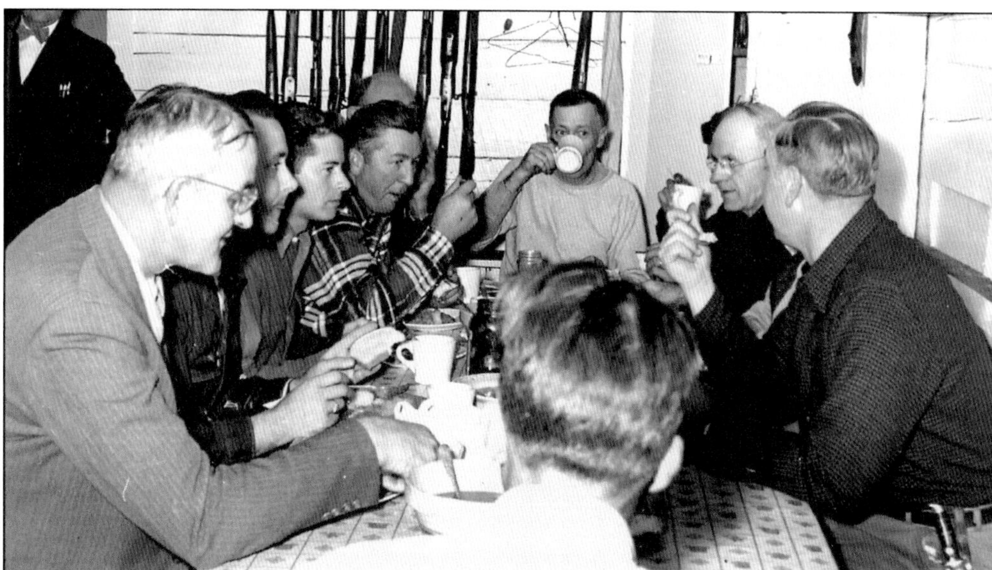

This is an image of supper at the Spring Creek Hunt Club, located near Flag Pole Knob in the Allegheny Mountains. Local men often hosted hunters from outside of the area, and in this 1940s image, Weldon Click (seated third from left), Hershel Miller (fourth from left), Walter Click (second from right), and Raymond Carr (right) converse with their visitors. While fellowship is often a part of the hunting experience, Harrisonburg's *Daily News Record* reported in January of 1951 that 56 bears had been killed in Rockingham County during the past hunting season, proving that hunting was also a serious business. (Private collection.)

A trip to the mountains does not always mean one must carry a firearm. The trails through the Blue Ridge, Massanutten, and Allegheny Mountains have enticed hikers for generations. Four friends pause for a portrait before embarking on their ramble around 1920. Pictured are, from left to right, Marion Suter, Earl Heatwole, Frank Swope, and Raymond Burkholder. (Private collection.)

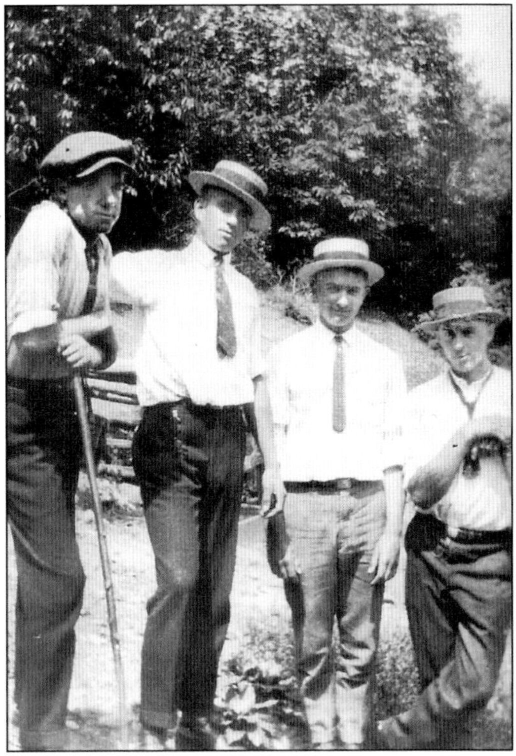

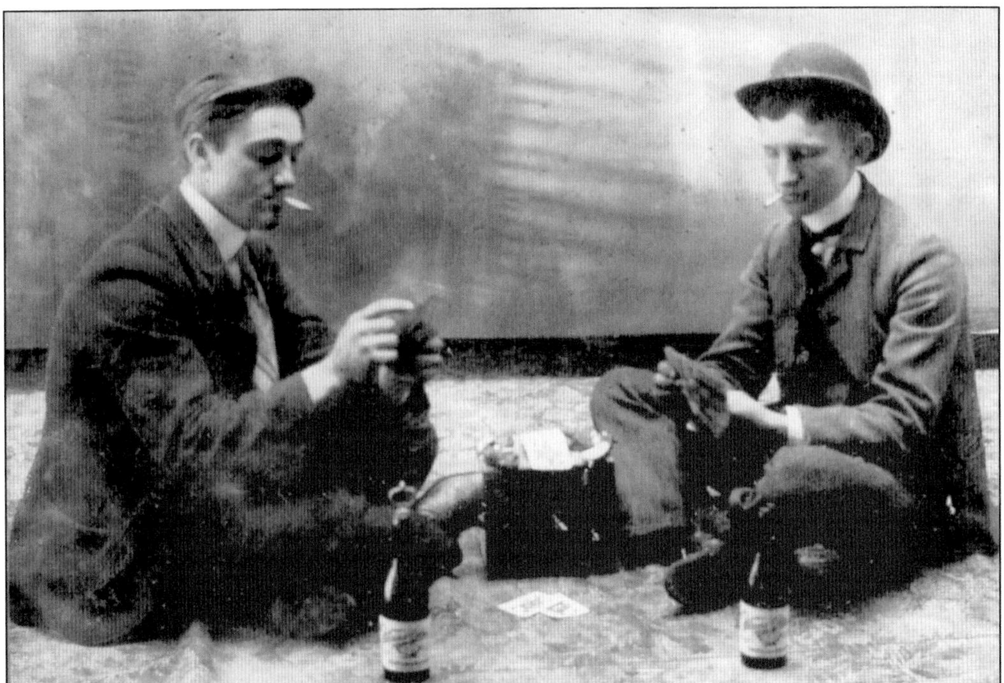

This pair of unidentified Dayton lads demonstrates a number of different ways to pass one's time in the early 20th century—obviously before prohibition. (Harrisonburg-Rockingham Historical Society Collection.)

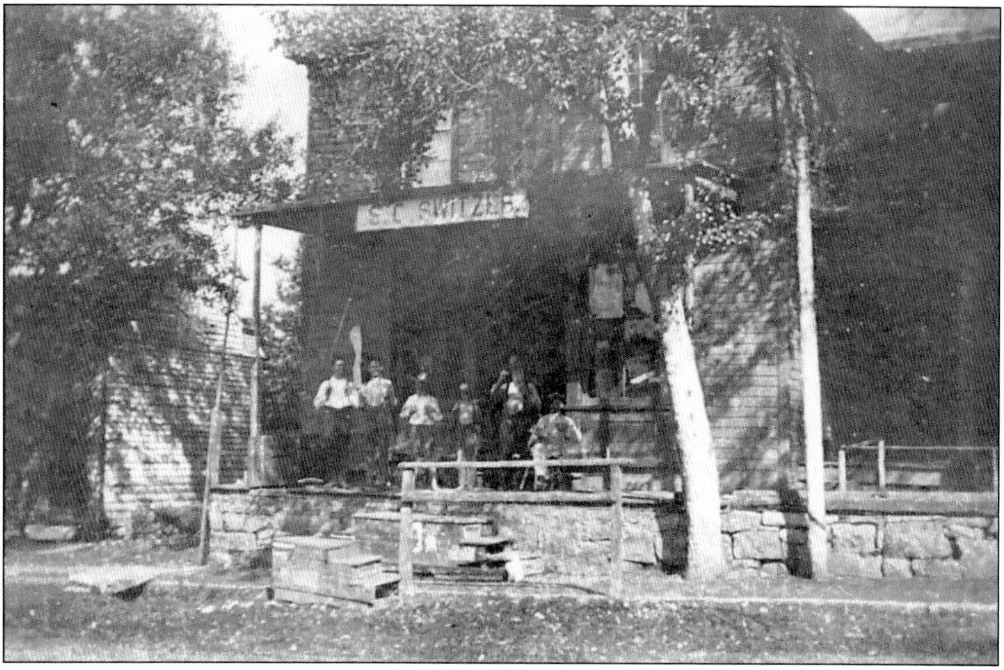

The following photographs, all from a single photo album from around 1900, feature people passing the time in Mount Crawford. Although the photographer and those pictured are unknown, many of the shots were taken either inside Switzer's store or in the surrounding neighborhood. The store building and adjoining house still stand on the east side of Main Street. (Jeffrey S. Evans Collection.)

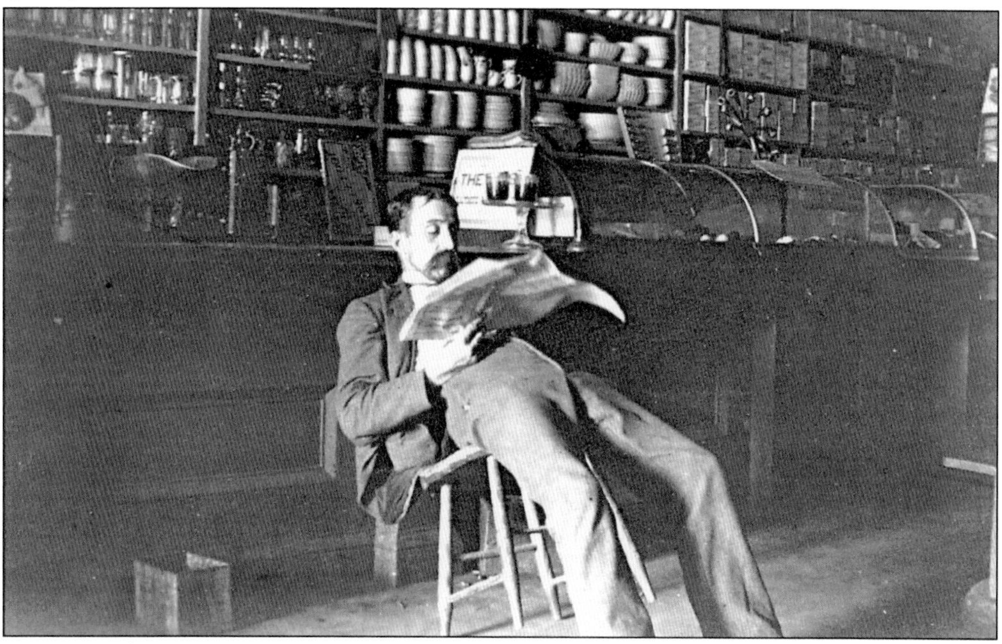

A patron of S.C. Switzer's store relaxes with a paper. Note the merchandise on the store's shelves; items include ceramic tableware, lanterns, and lampshades. The volume of items indicates that Switzer had a steady clientele. (Jeffrey S. Evans Collection.)

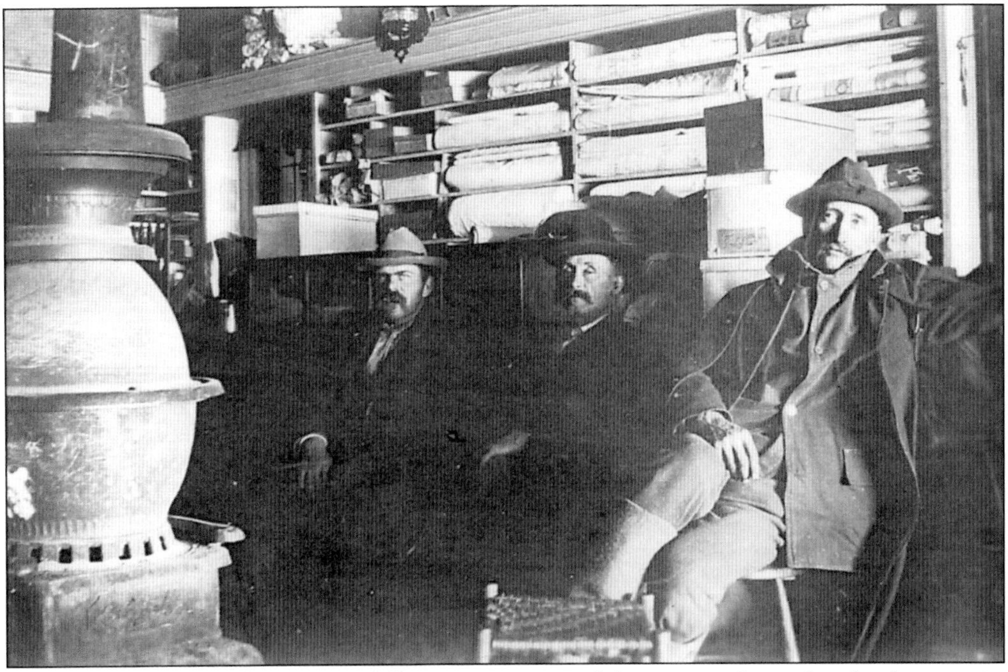

Across the store from the previous lollygagger, a group of three warm themselves by the stove in front of the cloth material display. The footstool in the foreground suggests that such an activity was encouraged. (Jeffrey S. Evans Collection.)

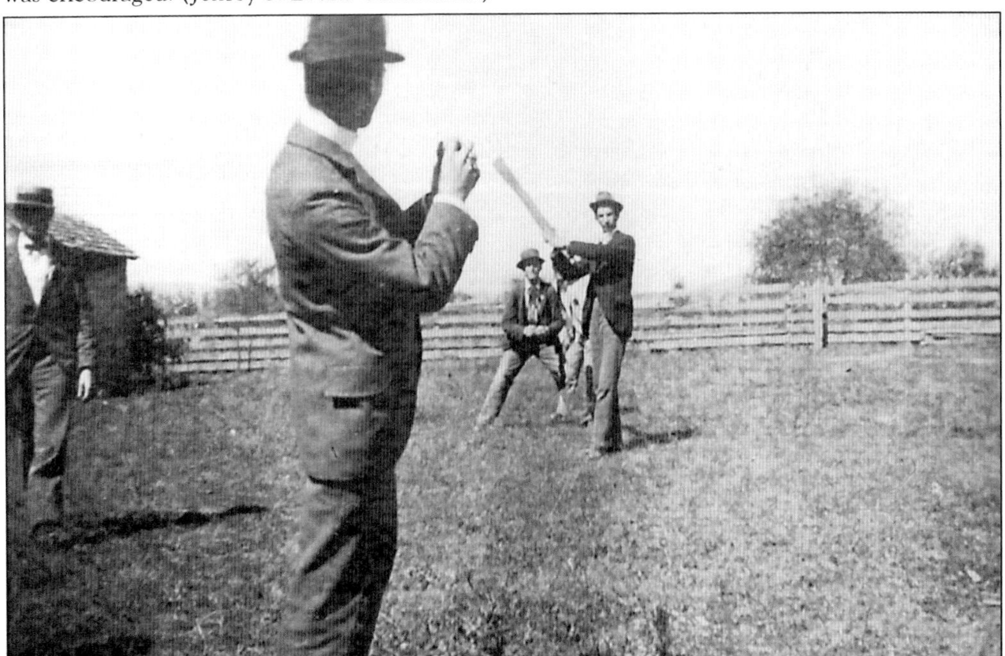

As noted previously, baseball has a long history in Rockingham County. Here, several men demonstrate the common backyard variety of the sport. Mentions of the sport appear in memoirs placing the game's appearance in the county in the mid-19th century. (Jeffrey S. Evans Collection.)

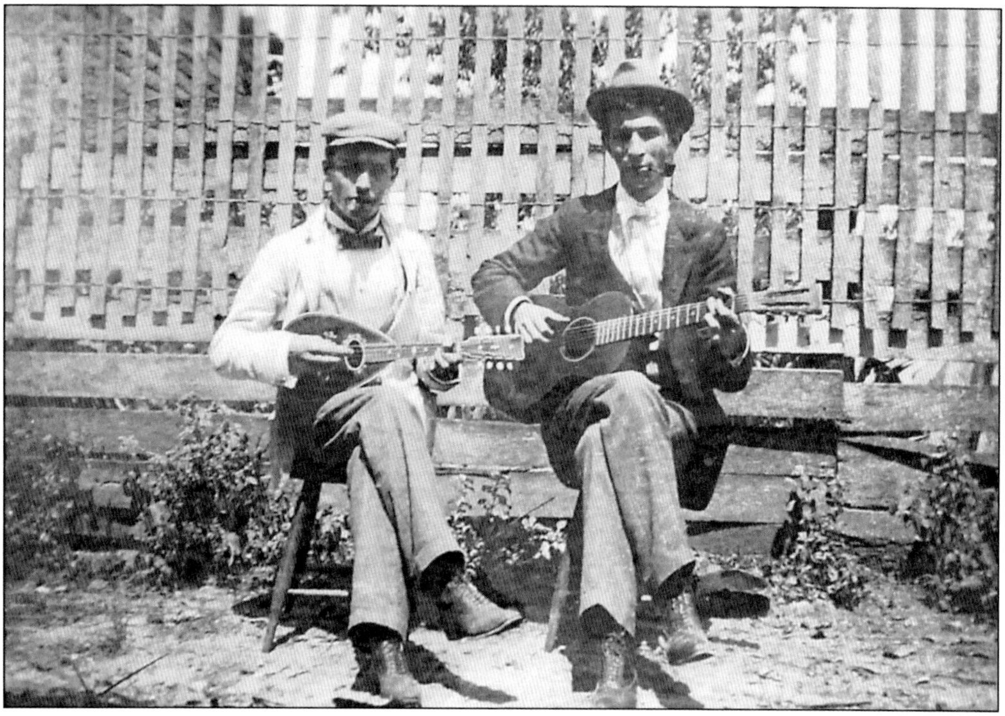

Music has been a part of county life since the area was settled. Above, the common parlor instruments, a mandolin and guitar, are held ready for a performance. Below, two Mount Crawford residents demonstrate their dancing skills; it appears that the men are executing the style known as flat footing or clogging. (Jeffrey S. Evans Collection.)

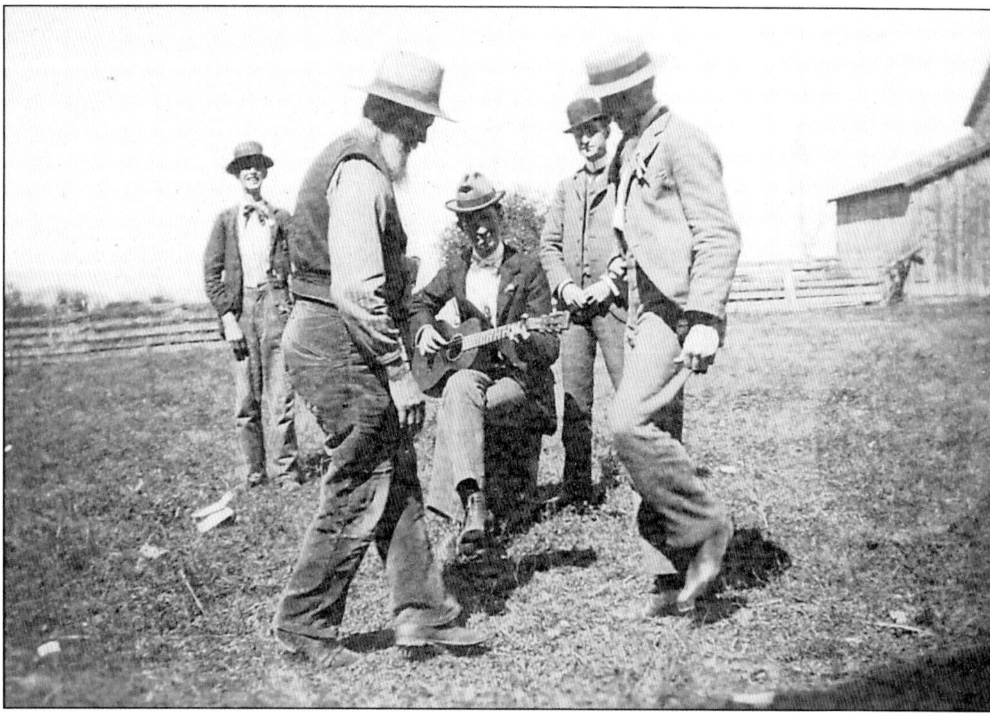

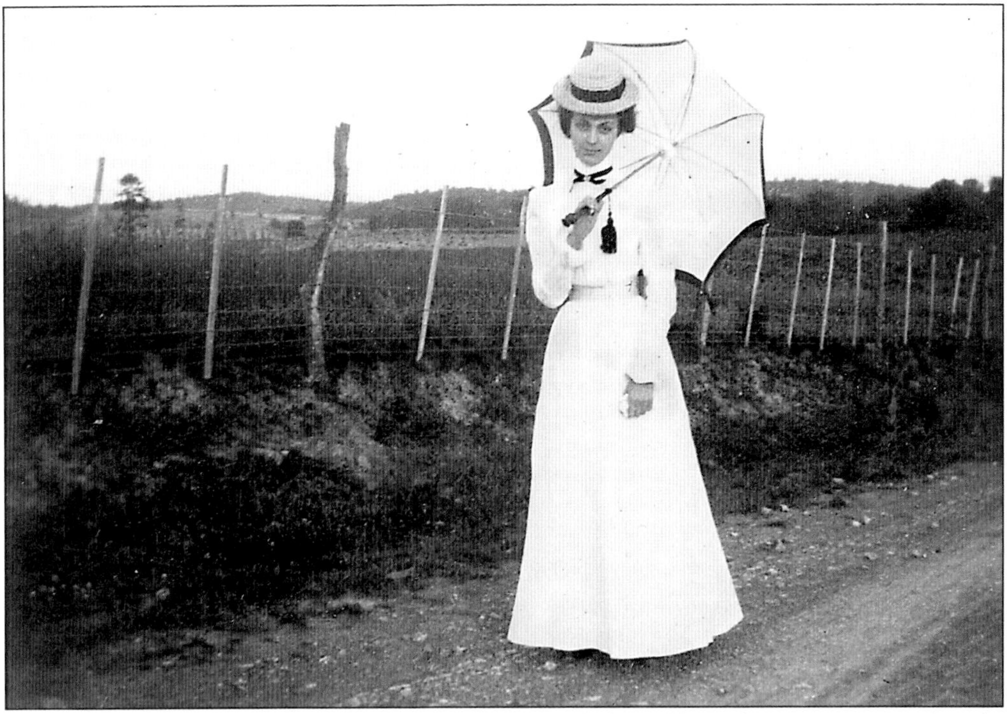

The ladies of Mount Crawford appear to have been as fashionable as those in any part of Rockingham County. Whether strolling with a parasol (above) or ice-skating on the river with a beau (below), the proper hat and attire seems to have been readily available to the women of the town. (Jeffrey S. Evans Collection.)

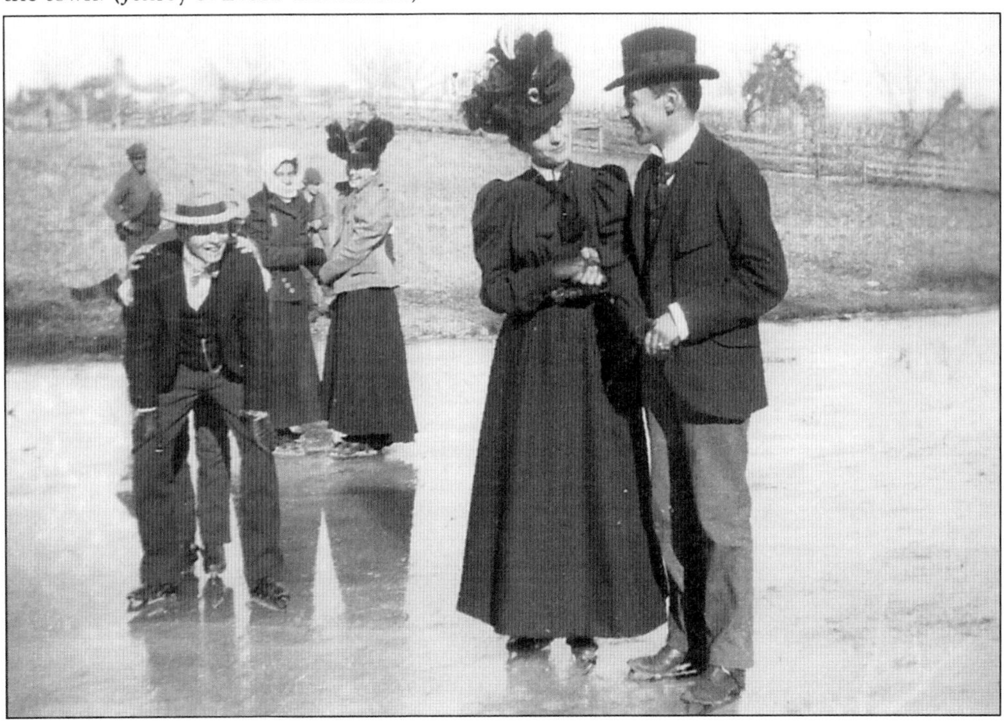

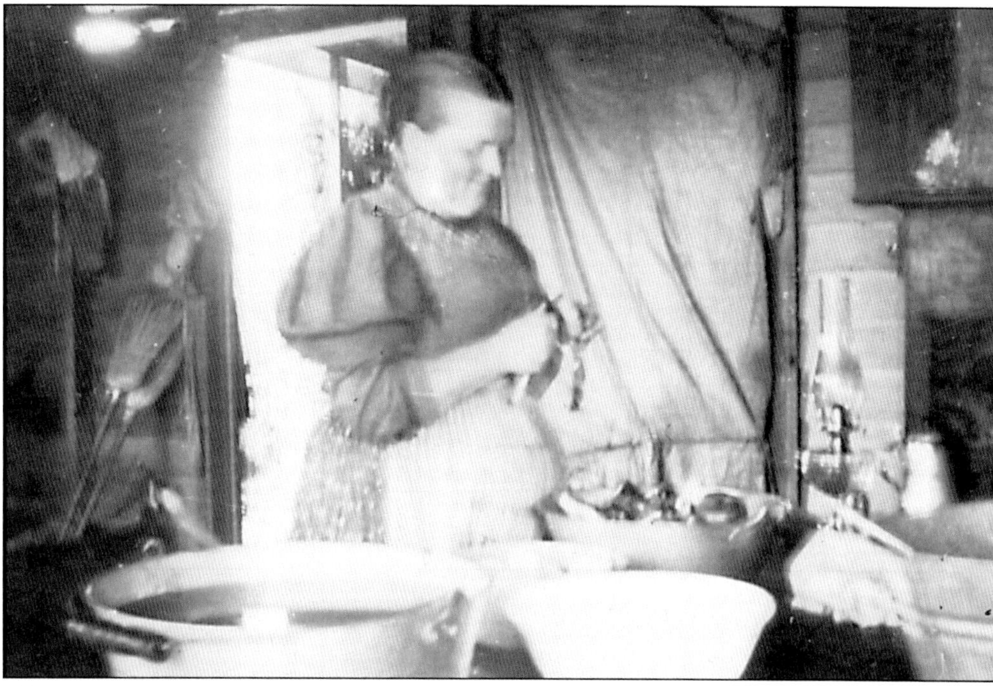

Of course life was not always spent whiling away the time; women continued to prepare meals and complete the other tasks of daily life. This rare photograph of a woman in the kitchen shows a side of life not often photographed during this time period. (Jeffrey S. Evans Collection.)

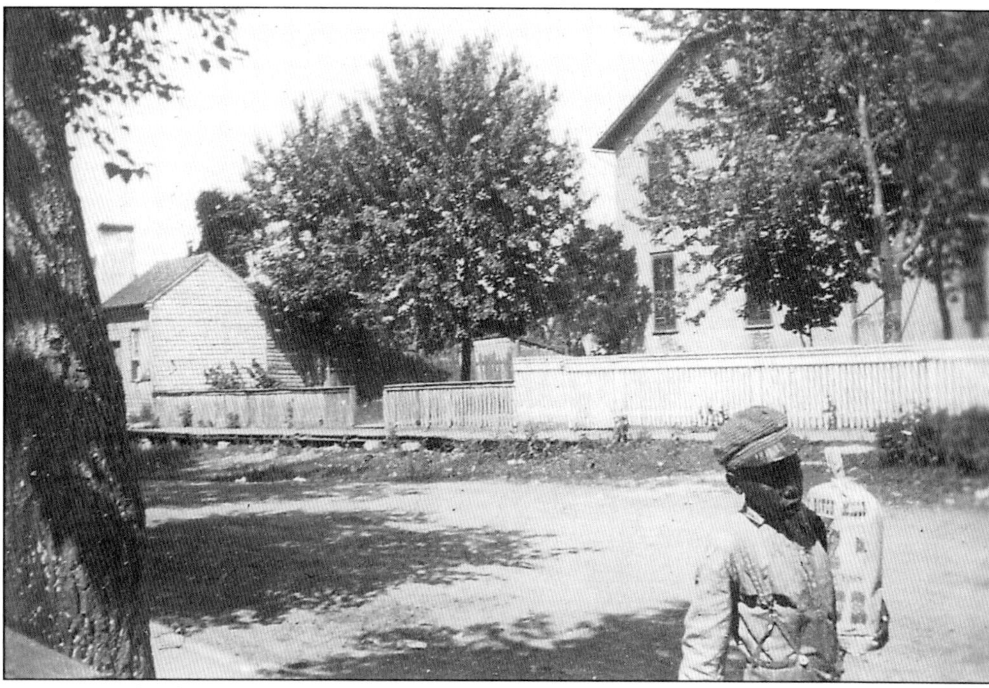

Toting a sack of flour from one of Mount Crawford's two mills was probably a regular task. Brothers J.F. and J.S. Crawn opened North River Mills, which is printed on the bag in this photograph, in 1886. (Jeffrey S. Evans Collection.)

Five

Highways and Byways

Rockingham County's location in the heart of the Shenandoah Valley has made it a center of travel and commerce since the 18th century. The Great Wagon Road leading southwest from Philadelphia carried many migrants to the west, and gaps in the mountains encouraged the development of roads to the east and west. This selection of photographs aims at providing a glimpse of the highways themselves as well as the activities and commerce that sprung up around them. Tourists to the valley found numerous spots to rest along the Valley Pike and U.S. Route 33, and excursions off of these main roads onto the "byways" revealed the delights of county towns and villages and offered further views of the county's rural landscape. In 1935, John W. Wayland reported sightings in the county of cars from Oklahoma, California, Texas, Illinois, New Mexico, New York, Pennsylvania, New Jersey, and various other states, indicating that traffic was indeed moving through Rockingham County. On Labor Day of that year, he noted that 3,453 out-of-state automobiles passed through Harrisonburg. Still, the highways and byways of the county are not all about tourism, and the images reproduced here reflect the sights that residents experienced as they lived, worked, and traveled in Rockingham County.

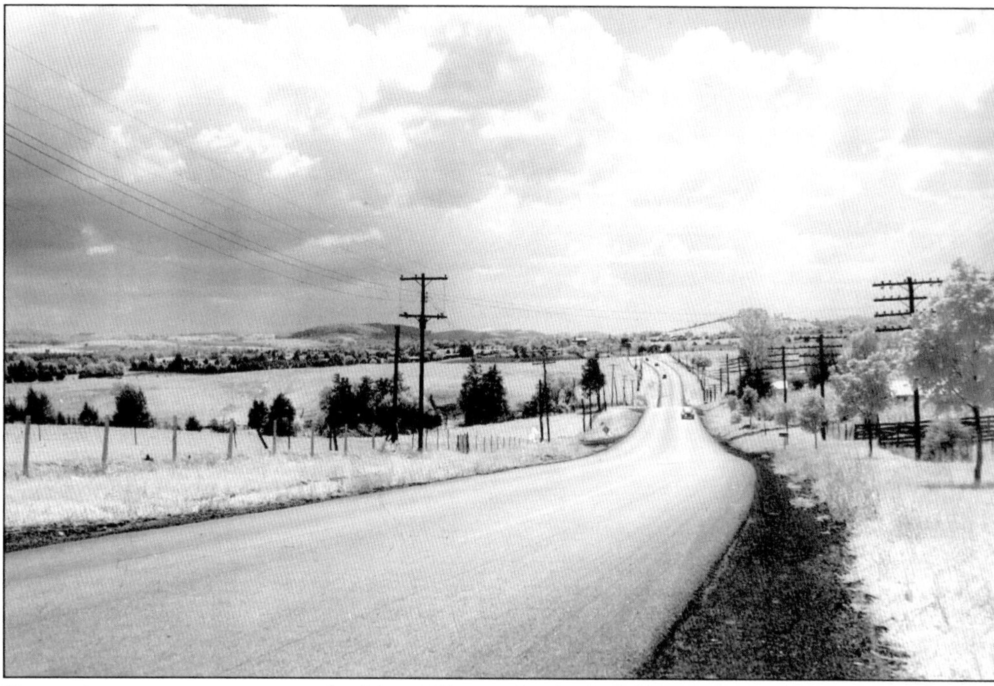

Known by names as various as the Great Wagon Road, the Valley Pike, and U.S. Route 11, this road has been the main north and south route through the county for centuries. This photograph by William Flick around 1940 reveals a northern portion of the highway's scenic beauty as it rolls through farmlands. (Massanutten Regional Library.)

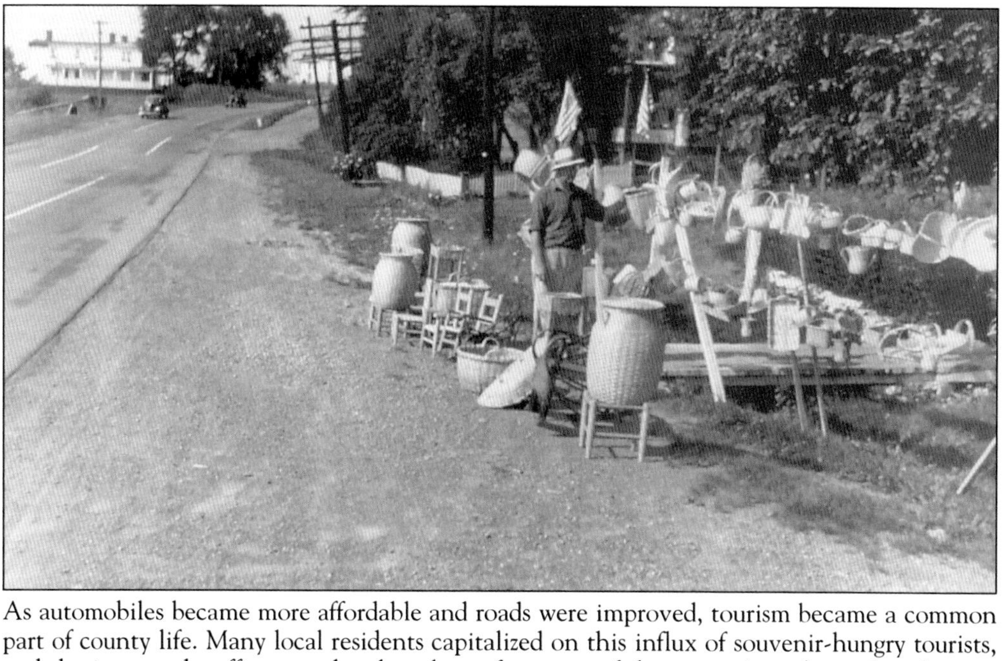

As automobiles became more affordable and roads were improved, tourism became a common part of county life. Many local residents capitalized on this influx of souvenir-hungry tourists, and the increased traffic proved to be a boon for many of the county's traditional craftsmen. In this photograph from the 1940s, white oak–basket maker George Shifflett peddles his finely crafted works along the Valley Pike at Lacey Spring. (Private collection.)

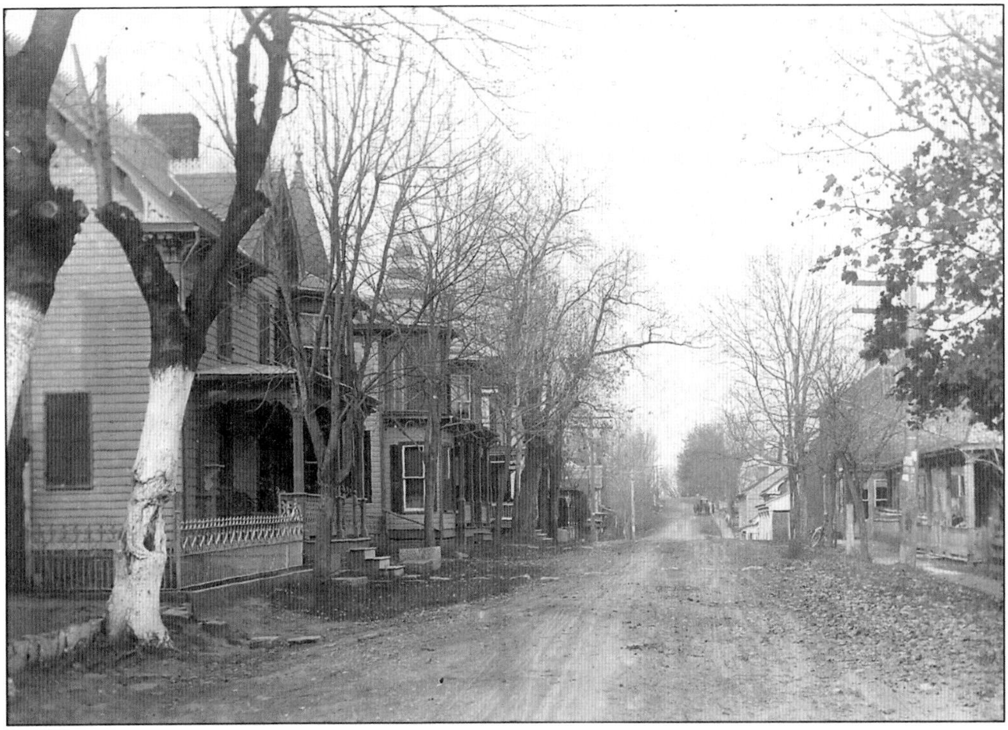

On the southern end of Rockingham County, the Valley Pike serves as Main Street for Mount Crawford. Known as "turnpike towns," villages like this one grew up along the main road through the Shenandoah Valley and tended to stretch out along the highway rather than expanding in gridded blocks. (Jeffrey S. Evans Collection.)

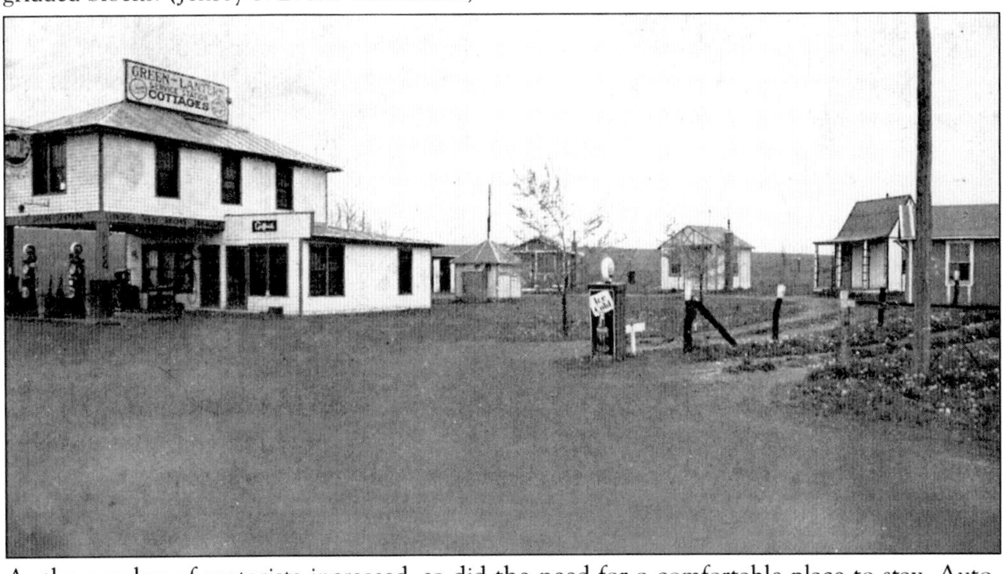

As the number of motorists increased, so did the need for a comfortable place to stay. Auto-camps appeared along highways, but these required travelers to pack camping gear for their journey; motels and cottage camps quickly became present on the landscape. The Green Lantern Cottage Camp was built in the 1920s, along the Valley Pike just south of Harrisonburg. (Kermit Early Collection.)

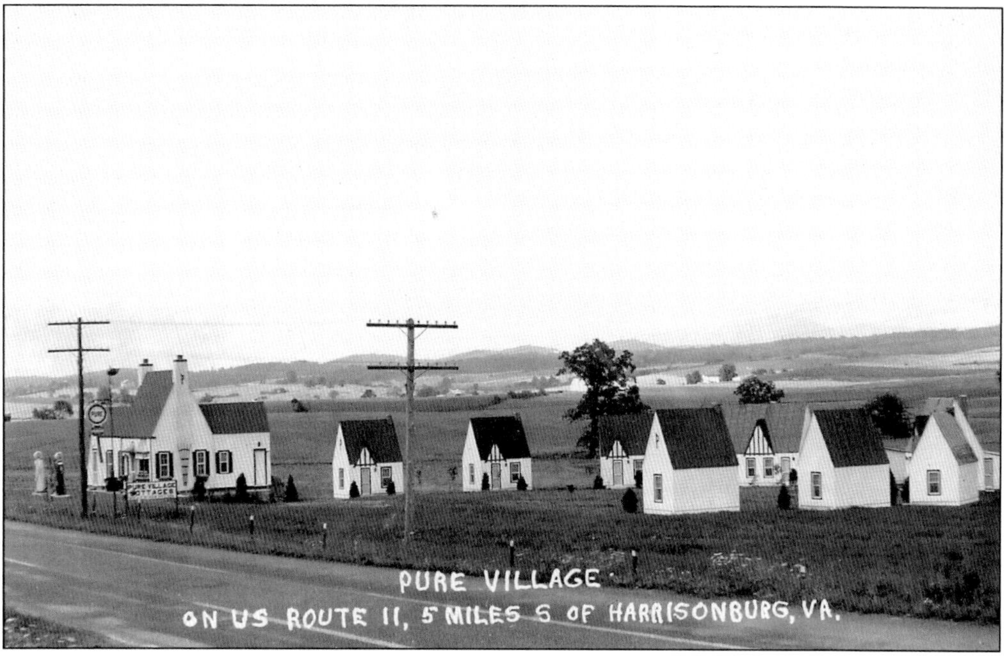

By the mid-1930s, gasoline companies realized that a natural extension of their services would be to offer comfortable overnight accommodations. The Pure Oil Company approached O.K. Early and asked him to build one of their recognizable cottage style stations with the addition of tourist cottages—the result was Pure Village, pictured here in 1936. (Kermit Early Collection.)

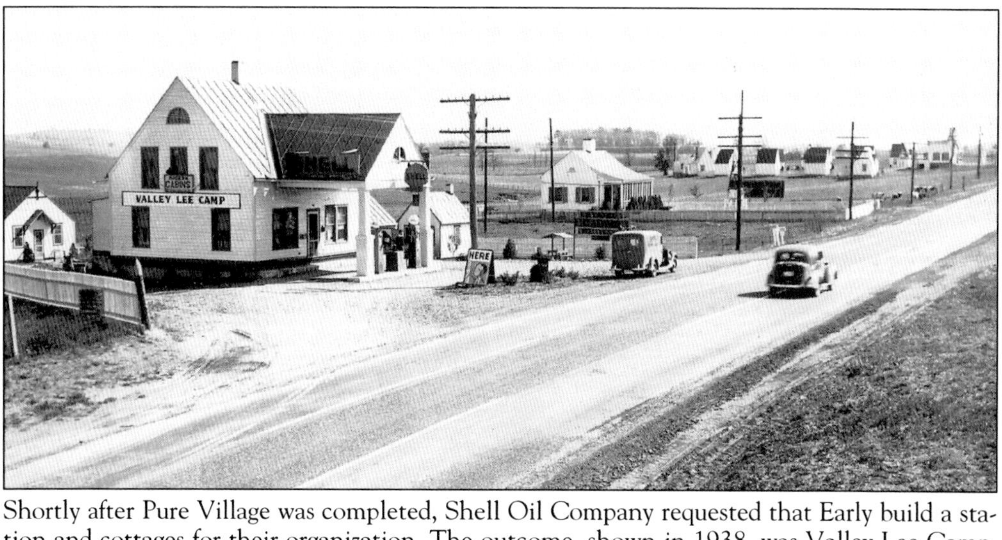

Shortly after Pure Village was completed, Shell Oil Company requested that Early build a station and cottages for their organization. The outcome, shown in 1938, was Valley Lee Camp, taking its name presumably from the Shenandoah Valley's connection to the Civil War. Both Valley Lee and Pure Village were just a few miles south of Harrisonburg; Pure Village can be seen in the distance. (Kermit Early Collection.)

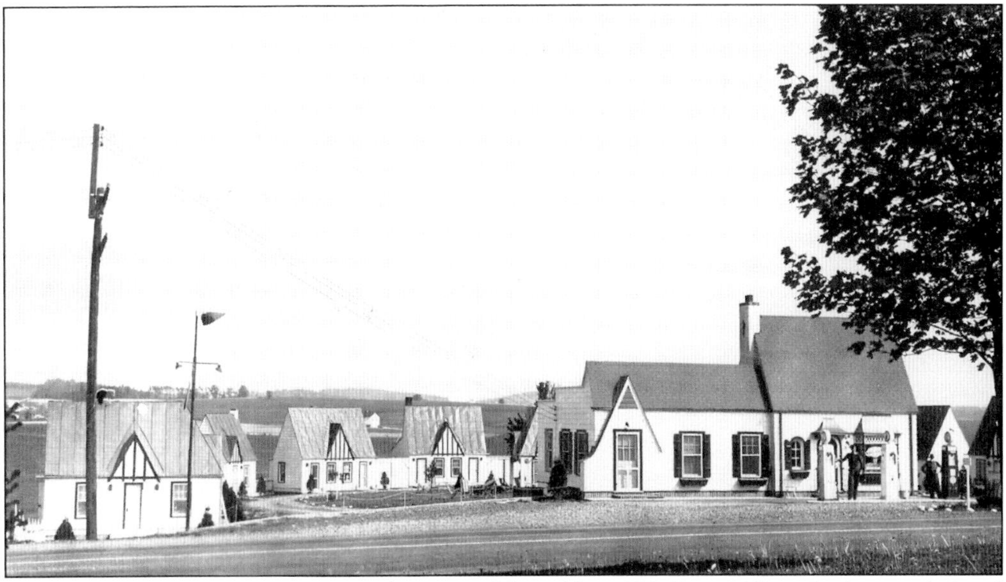

These cottage clusters were extremely successful, and by 1938, Pure Village had expanded and offered garages for travelers' automobiles (above). By the 1950s, the motel advertised that the rooms came complete with Simmons furnishings and offered a restaurant for hungry visitors. The photograph below, taken in 1958, illustrates the growth of Pure Village over the years and also reveals its rural setting. The stream flowing behind the village is Blacks Run. (Kermit Early Collection.)

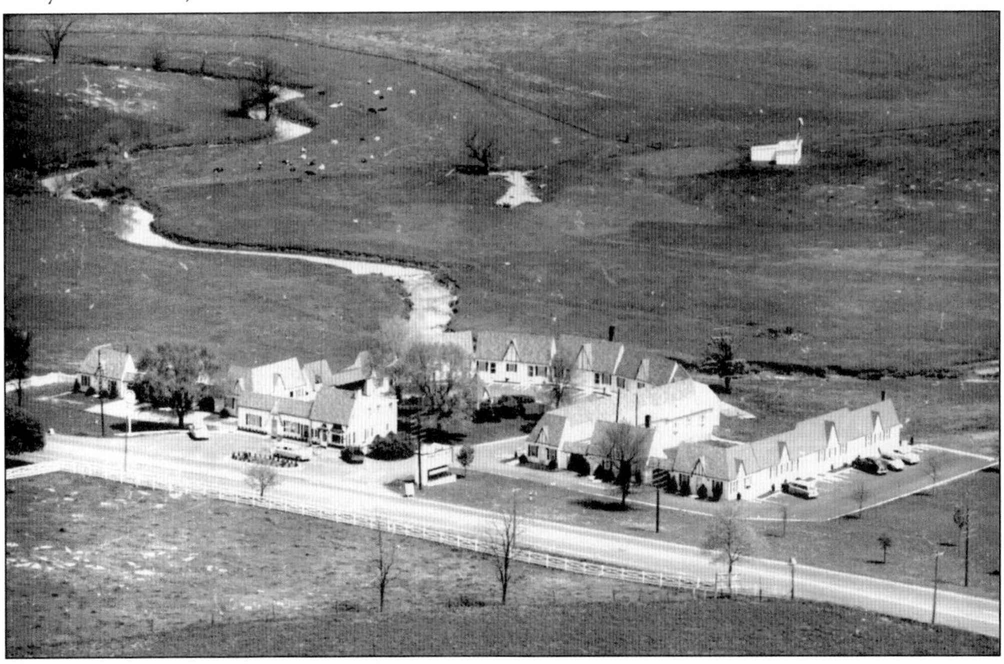

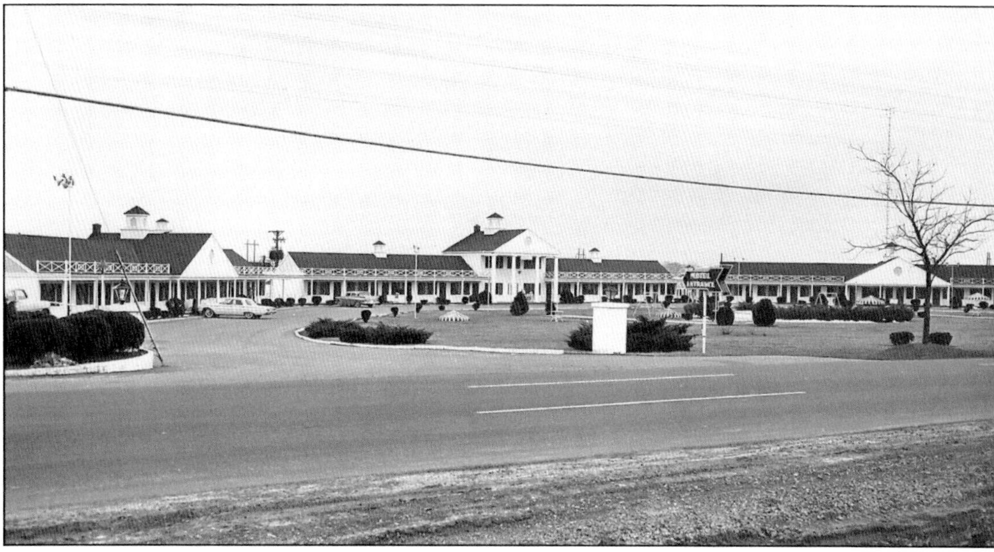

Another well-known stopover on the Valley Pike south of Harrisonburg is the Belle Meade Motel. In continuous operation since the 1950s, the complex became part of the Red Carpet Inn chain in the 1970s and continues to offer weary travelers a place to stay and a hot meal. (Harrisonburg-Rockingham Historical Society Collection.)

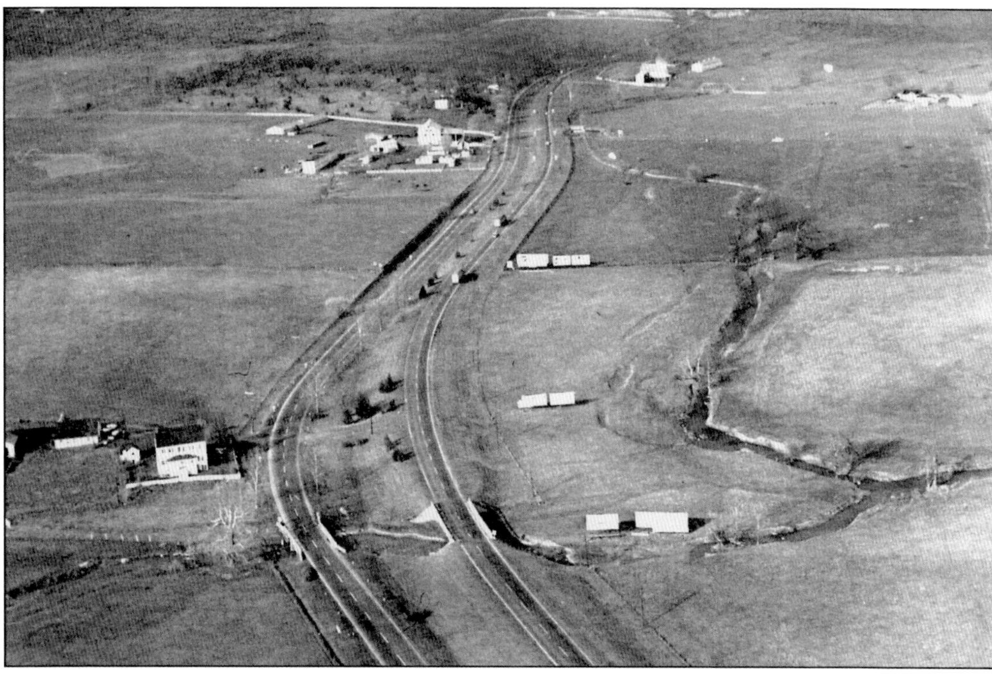

Changes continue to take place along the section of the Valley Pike that runs through Rockingham County. This late 1950s image of an area just north of Mount Crawford illustrates the completion of the modern four-lane section of Route 11. Located near an exit off Interstate 81, the abundant countryside pictured here is rapidly giving way to industry and to businesses hoping to lure travelers. (Private collection.)

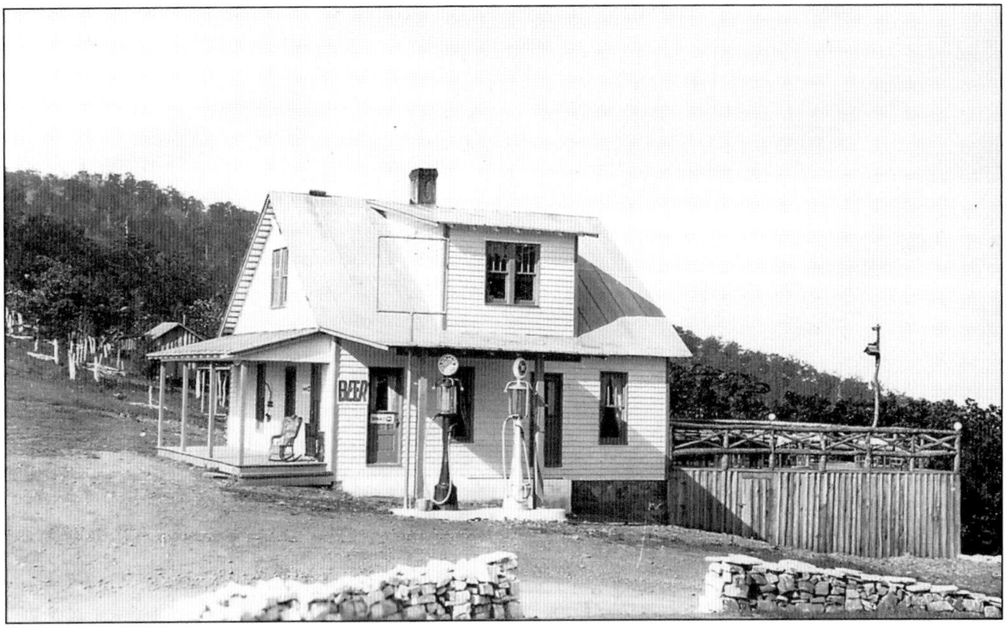

The Valley Pike is not the only major highway to pass through Rockingham County; U.S. Route 33 bisects the county from east to west. Ed Friddle's gas station, located on the pinnacle of Shenandoah Mountain, marked both the beginning of the county's western boundary as well as the state line between Virginia and West Virginia. (Harrisonburg-Rockingham Historical Society Collection.)

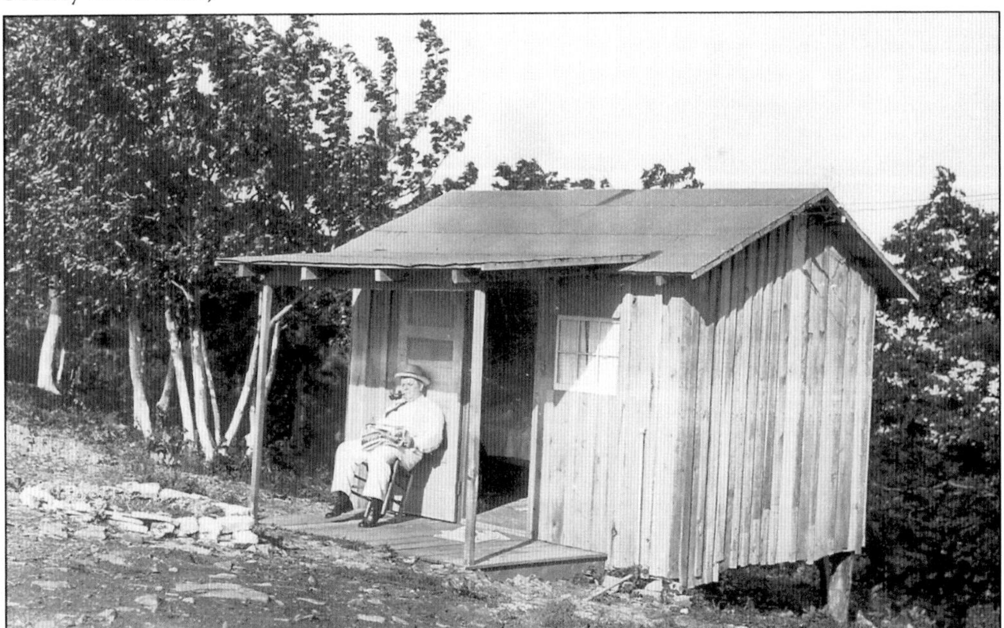

Like the motor courts along the Valley Pike, Friddle's also offered a place to rest. Though not as elegant as those in the valley, these cottages may have provided a welcome respite for the weary traveler heading through the mountains. (Harrisonburg-Rockingham Historical Society Collection.)

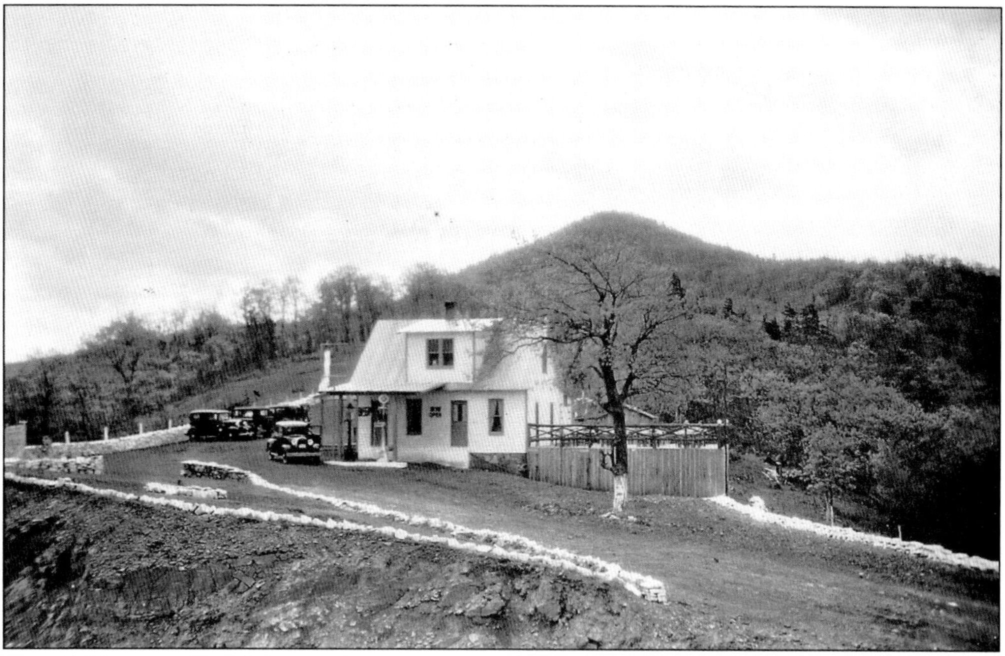

This 1933 view of Friddle's reveals two interesting aspects of the landscape: the road was not yet paved to this point, and the mountaintop in the background remained bare. Shortly after this photograph was taken, the High Knob tower, below, was constructed to help watch for forest fires in the George Washington National Forest, much of which lies in Rockingham County. Other knobs in the mountain chain were home to towers, including Reddish Knob, which offered parking for those seeking a vista. (Private collection.)

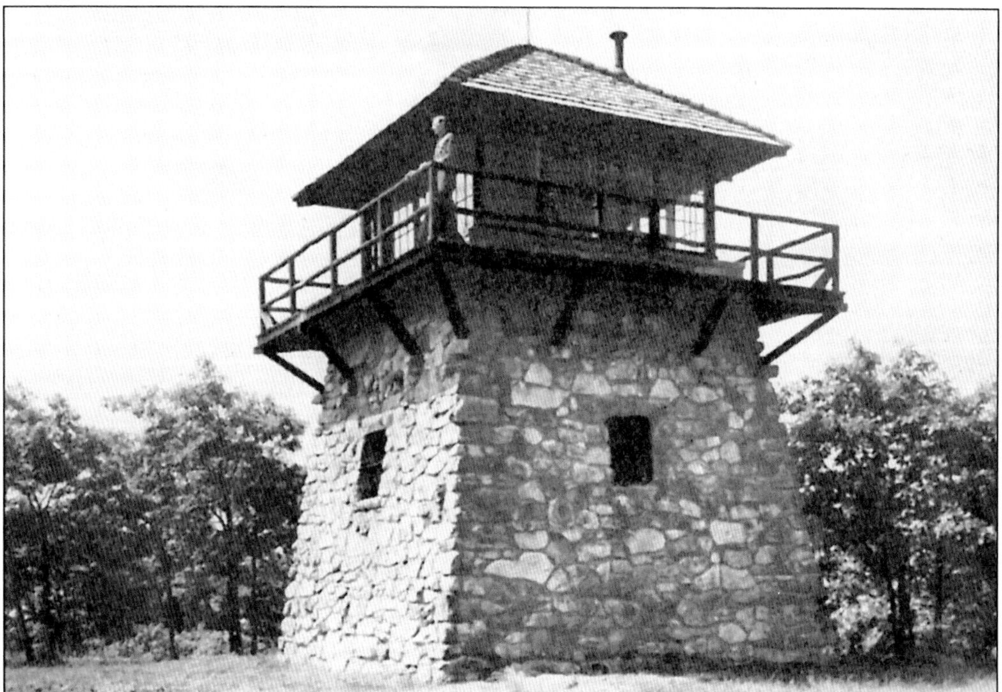

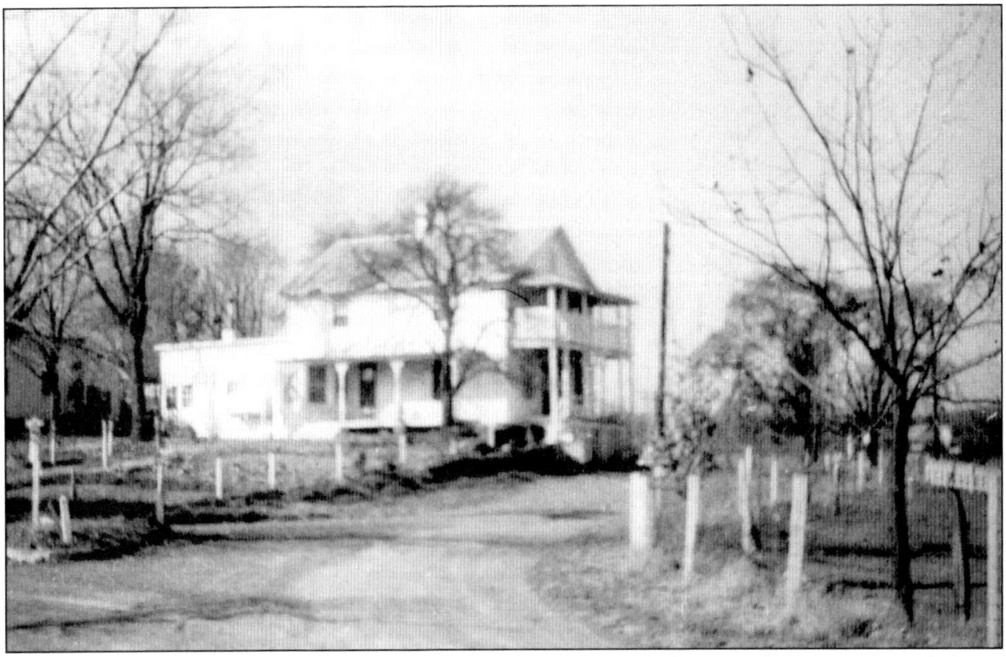

If motorists heading east made it past Friddle's and continued along Highway 33 toward Harrisonburg, they would encounter the community known as Dale Enterprise. Owned and operated by various families through the years, the store stands directly on the road near old Route 33's intersection with Silver Lake Road from the south. Stores such as this were found in all communities, providing convenient necessities. (Kermit Early Collection.)

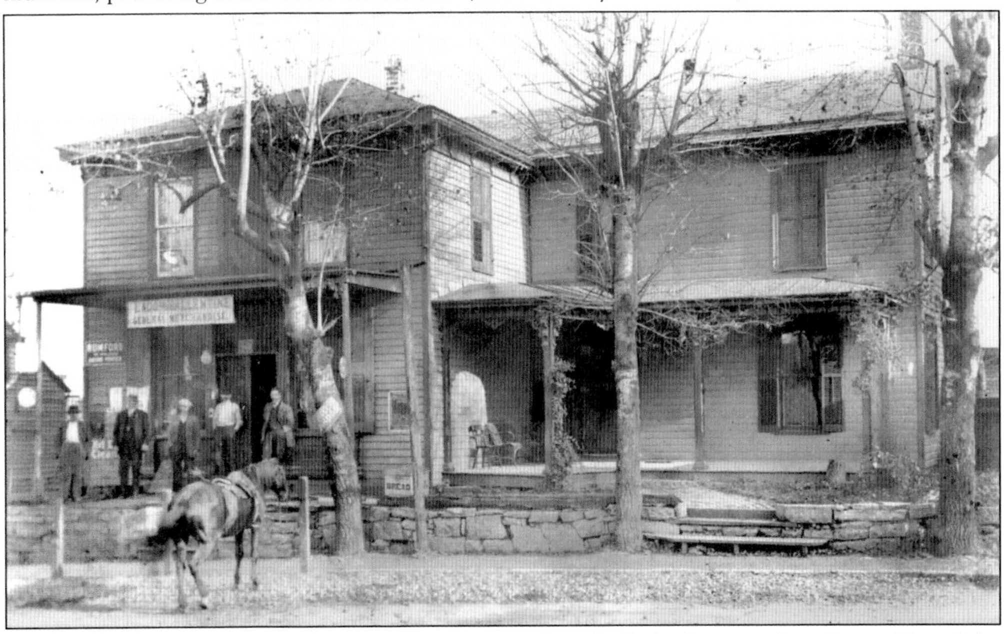

Previously known as S.C. Switzer's store in Mount Crawford, the business has changed hands by the time of this photograph from about 1910. Signs advertising Coca-Cola, Old Dutch Cleanser, Bull Durham Cigars, and Rumford Baking Powder indicate the "department" store role that such stores played in a community. (Jeffrey S. Evans Collection.)

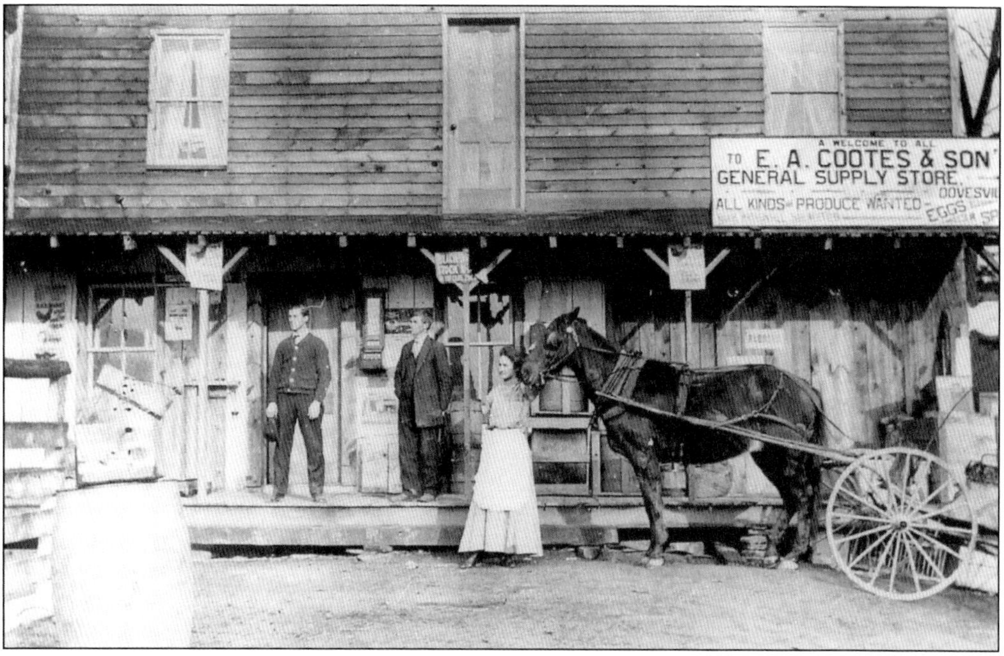

E.A. Cootes, a businessman from northwest Rockingham County, operated two stores in that region in the late 19th century. One was in the community that bears his name, Cootes Store, and the other was in Dovesville (now Bergton). In isolated villages, a general supply store was essential. (Harrisonburg-Rockingham Historical Society Collection.)

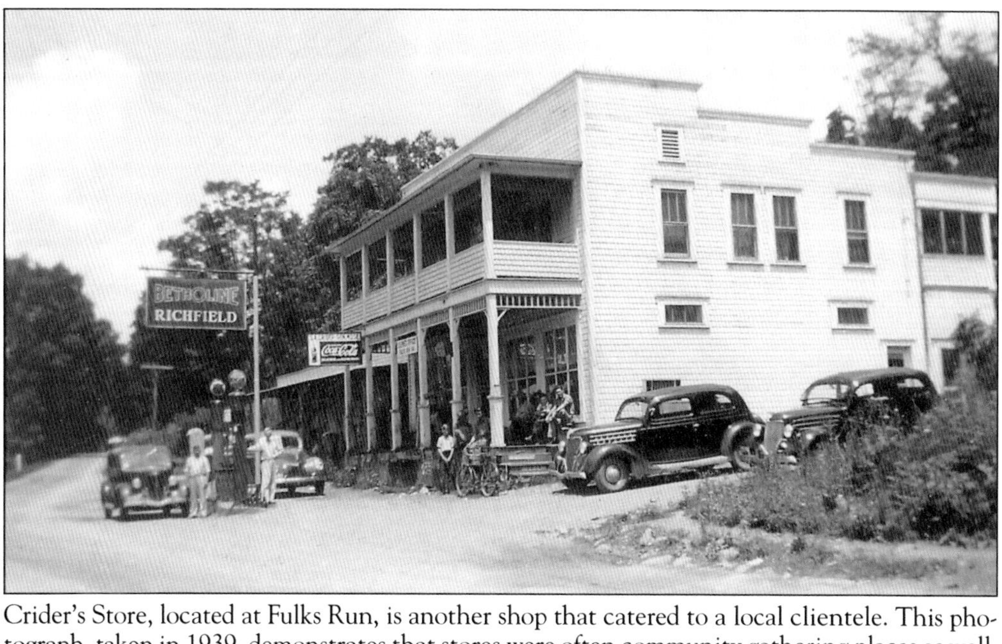

Crider's Store, located at Fulks Run, is another shop that catered to a local clientele. This photograph, taken in 1939, demonstrates that stores were often community gathering places as well. Crider's Store, although no longer open, is still standing. (Harrisonburg-Rockingham Historical Society Collection.)

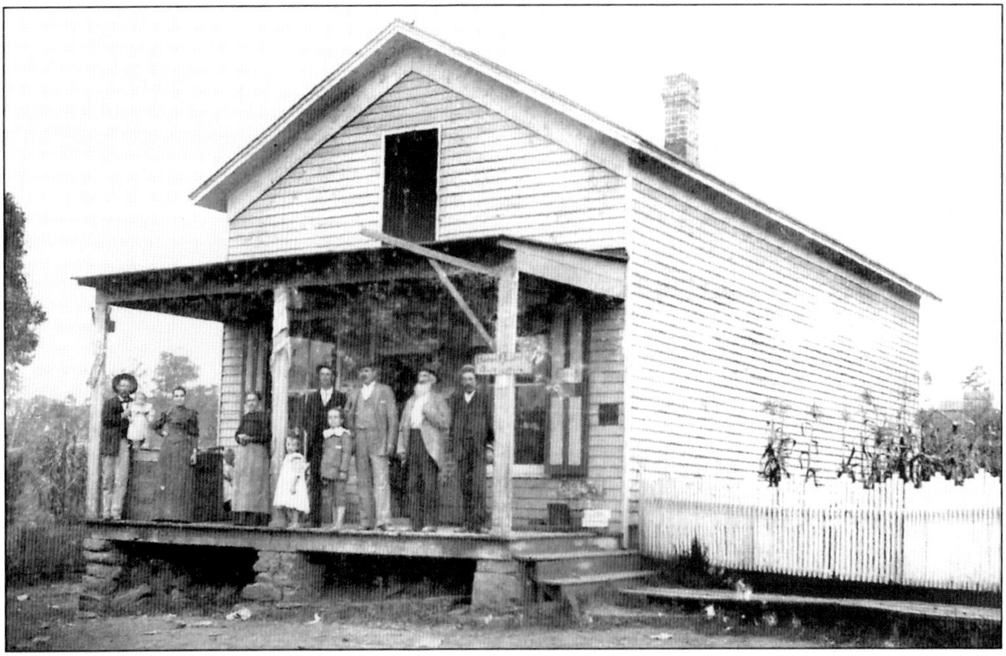

Built in 1890 by Edwin Funk, S.H. Swank's store in Singers Glen has also served as the village's post office since 1914, when Swank's daughter, Maud Swank Lee, became postmistress. Upon her retirement in 1961, Mrs. Lee's daughter, Nancy Lee (Mitzi) MacAllister, took over the position, which she filled until 1995. The building continues to house the Singers Glen Post Office. (Eastern Mennonite University Collection.)

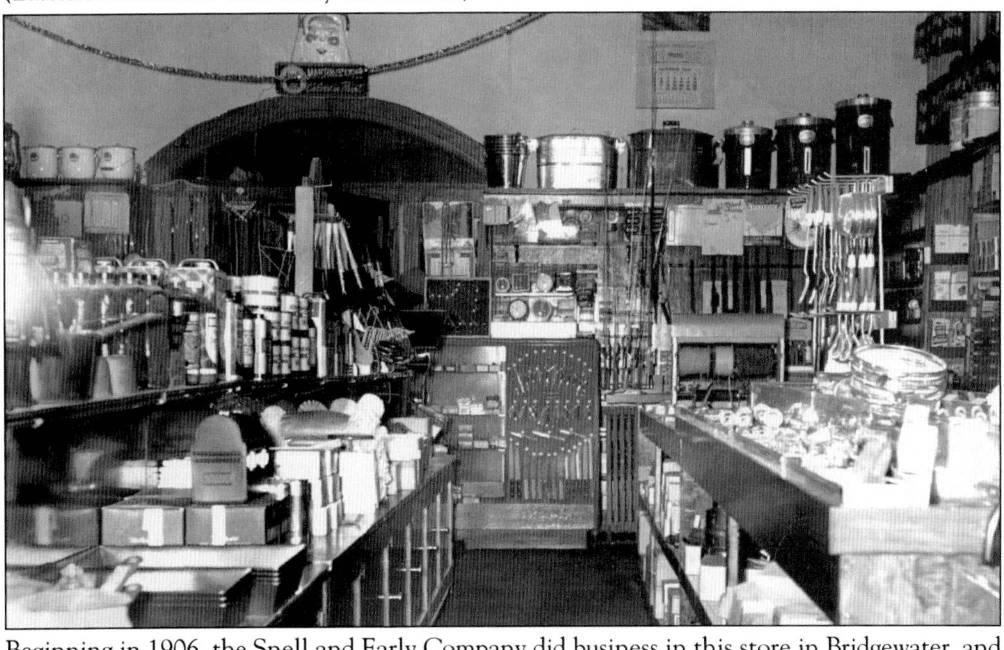

Beginning in 1906, the Snell and Early Company did business in this store in Bridgewater, and in 1937, the Rockingham Milling Company opened a hardware and feed store there. The building is located on the west side of South Main Street. This Christmas photograph illustrates the numerous items that one may have purchased as a present. (Private collection.)

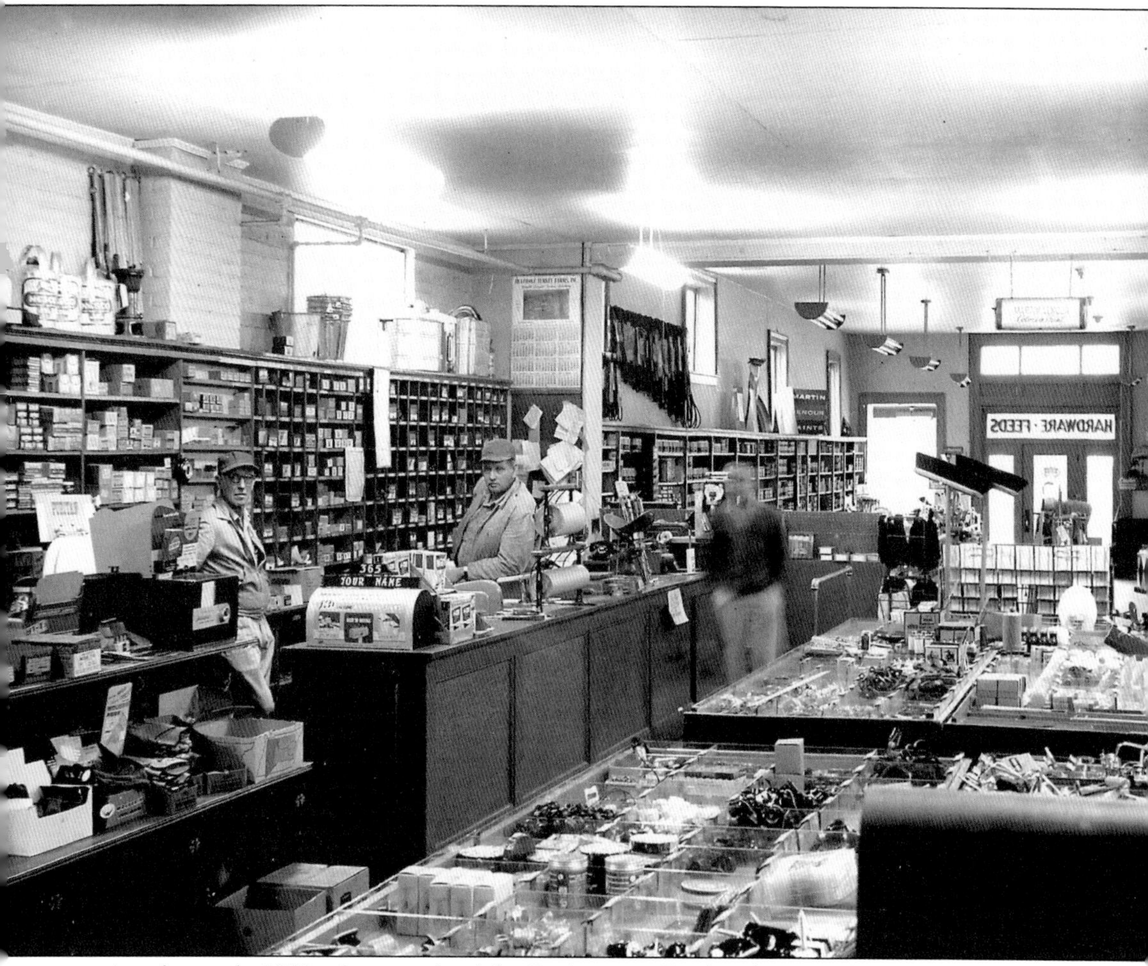

Another early 1950s photograph of the Bridgewater Rockingham Milling Company's interior shows two employees, Gilbert Long (left) and Otho Miller (center), along with the well-supplied shelves that offered Martin Senour paints, Wolverine work gloves, and d-Con rat poison. The blurry fellow on the right is Norman Thacker. The company closed this branch in 1975. (Private collection.)

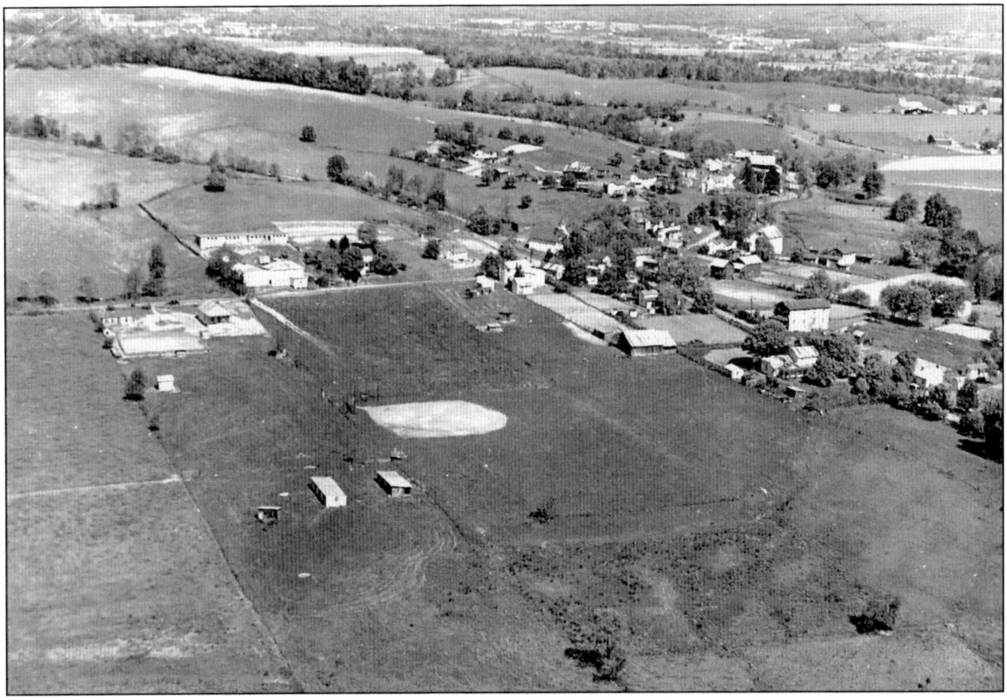

Looking to the northwest, this aerial view of Spring Creek emphasizes the rural setting of many of the villages in Rockingham County. Taken in the late 1940s, the photograph shows the Spring Creek baseball field in the center and the town hall on the right. (Private collection.)

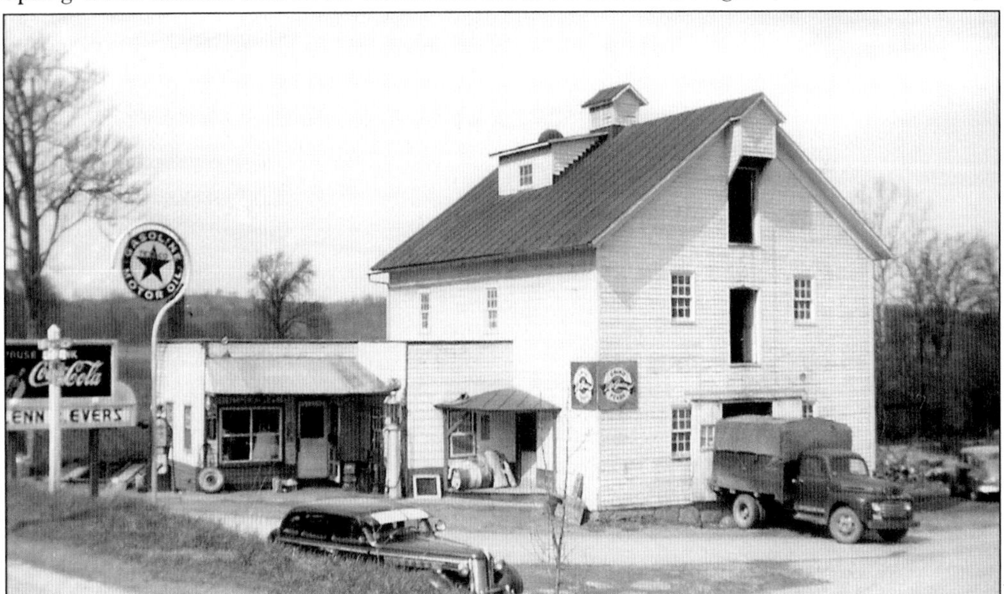

In many of the county's rural communities, a mill served as a center of news and gossip as well as commerce. Glenn Evers owned the Spring Creek mill when this photograph was taken in April 1951. The small store, or "superette," on the left was added to the mill in 1936. The structure was built in the late 1860s to replace one burned during the Civil War. (Eastern Mennonite University Collection.)

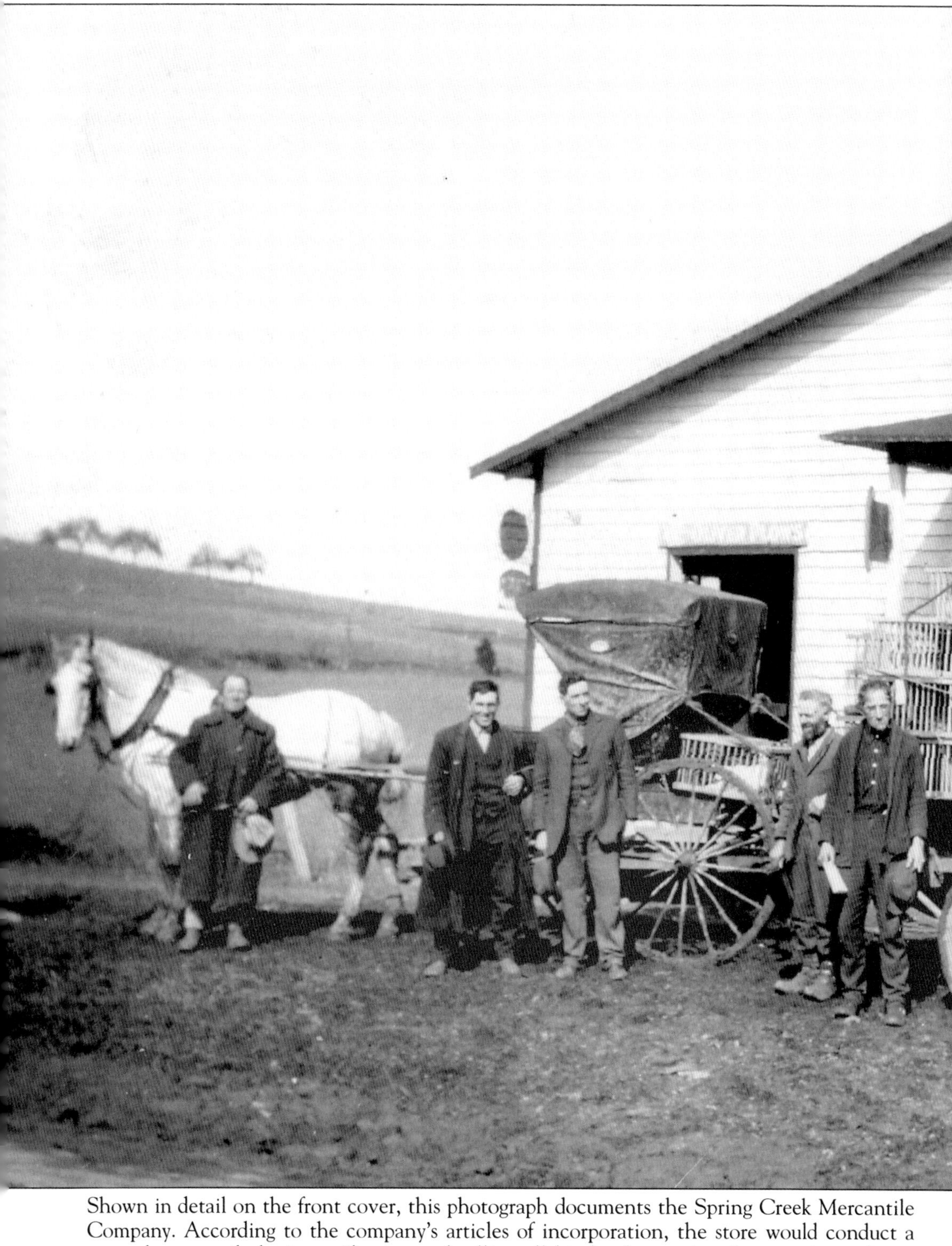

Shown in detail on the front cover, this photograph documents the Spring Creek Mercantile Company. According to the company's articles of incorporation, the store would conduct a general mercantile business, "buying and selling all kinds of groceries, farm products, fruits, confectionaries, stationary, drugs, paints, hardware, farming implements, dry goods, boots and

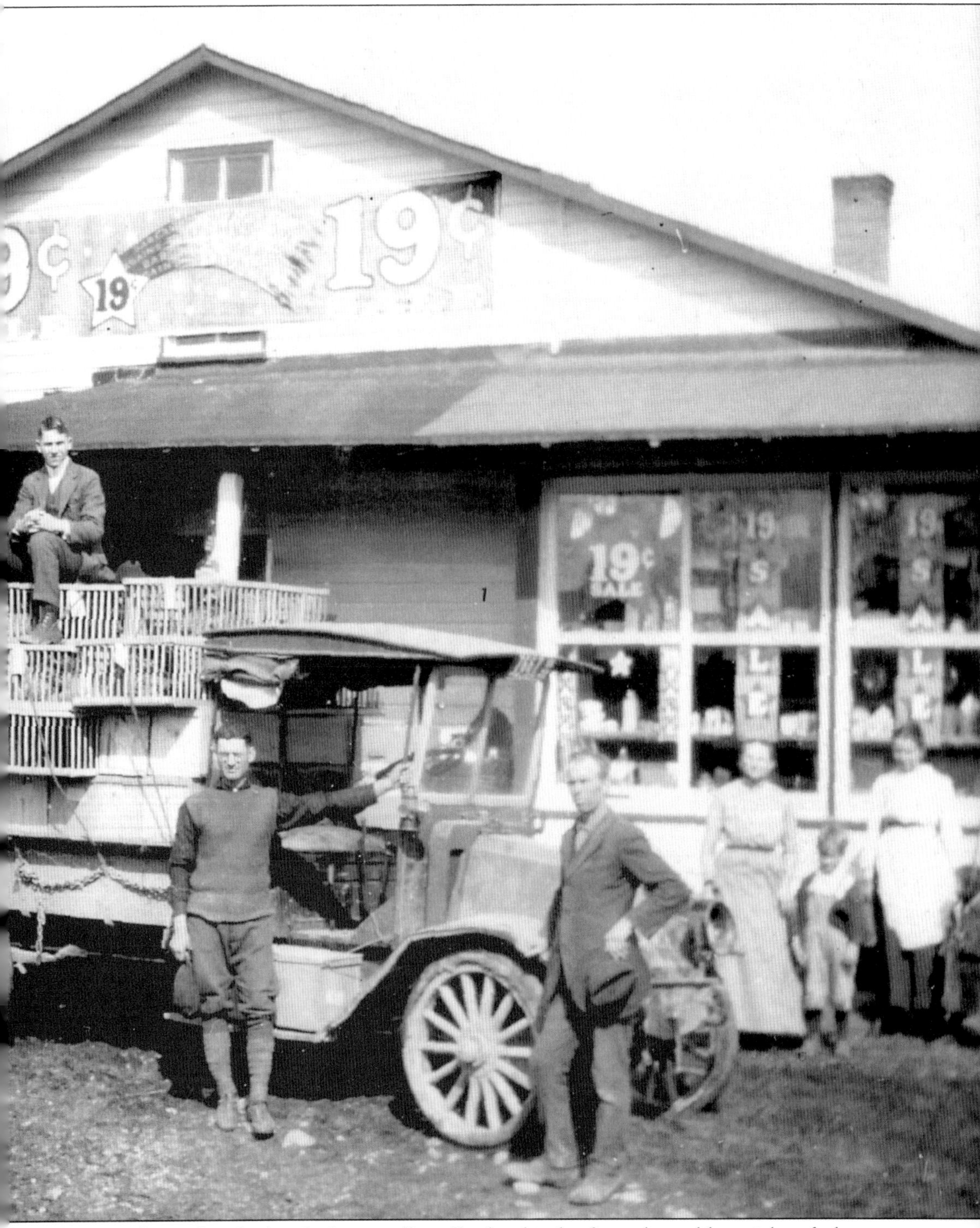

shoes, coal, wood and other fuels, as well as all other kinds of merchantable articles of whatever description." Incorporated on July 30, 1918, the Board of Directors consisted of J.W. Hess, F.E. Wine, S.C. Heltzel, I.C. Zimmerman, S.L. Hess, H.G. Patterson, R.E. Myers, W.W. Wine, and C.D. Sanger. (Private collection.)

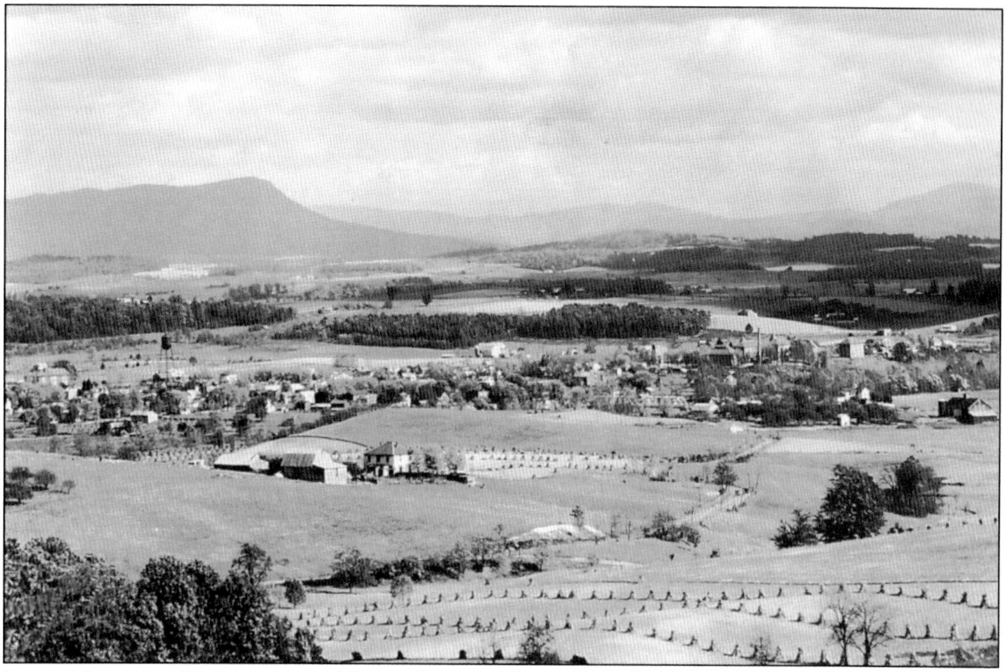

Located on the Harrisonburg-Warm Springs Turnpike, the town of Bridgewater stretches northward from the banks of North River. Originally known as Magill's Ford and later Bridgeport, the town of Bridgewater was chartered in February 1835. This panoramic view by Harry Staley looks eastward over the town toward the Massanutten Peak. (Bridgewater College Collection.)

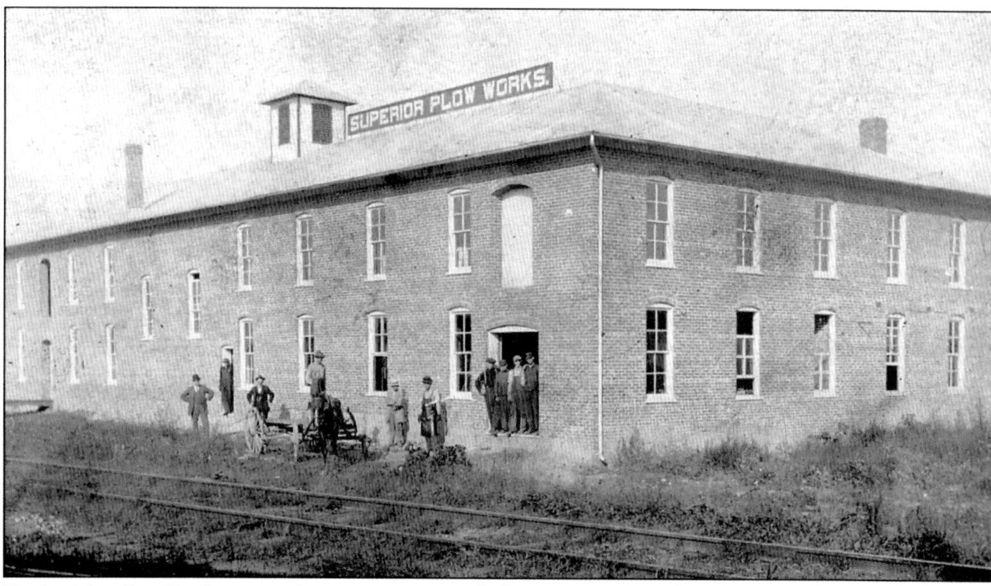

Backed by five Bridgewater businessmen, including carriage maker D.S. Thomas, Bridgewater Plow Works opened for business along the Chesapeake and Western tracks in 1908. According to a 1959 *Daily News Record* story, the company grossed $225,000 in that year as their diversification from hand plows to small gasoline-powered garden tractors paid off. Still standing, the building is a testament to a successful Bridgewater enterprise. (Jeffrey S. Evans Collection.)

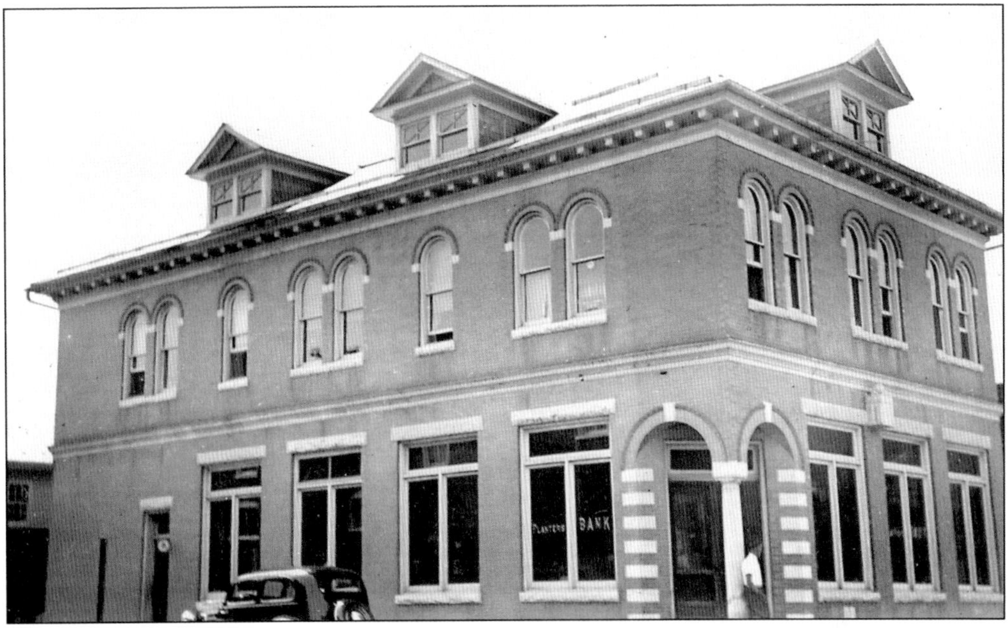

Inspired by the growth of business and industry and the arrival of the Chesapeake and Western Railroad, a group of businessmen formed the Planters Bank in 1898. By 1909, they opened this building, which was touted as "an up-to-date, thoroughly equipped bank building, with improved fire and burglar proof vault, time lock safe, and every modern safeguard for money and valuables." Shown here in 1935, the building still stands on the southeast corner of College and Main Streets. (Massanutten Regional Library Collection.)

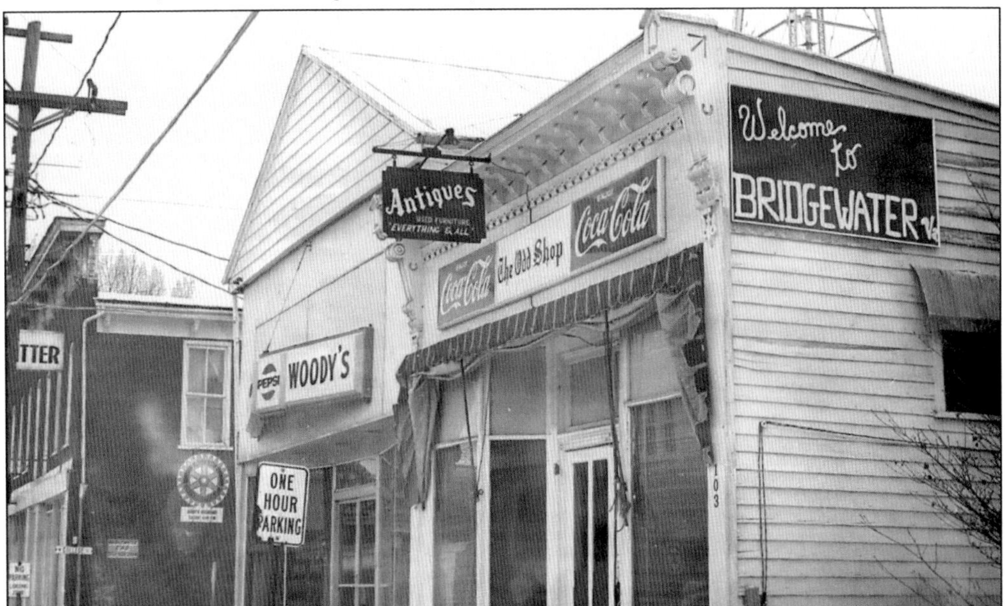

Many of the less substantial frame buildings that once lined Bridgewater's Main Street have given way to modern brick structures. Photographed in the 1960s, the sign on one building on the northwest corner of College and Main Streets seems to describe the structures: "Antiques." (Bridgewater College Collection.)

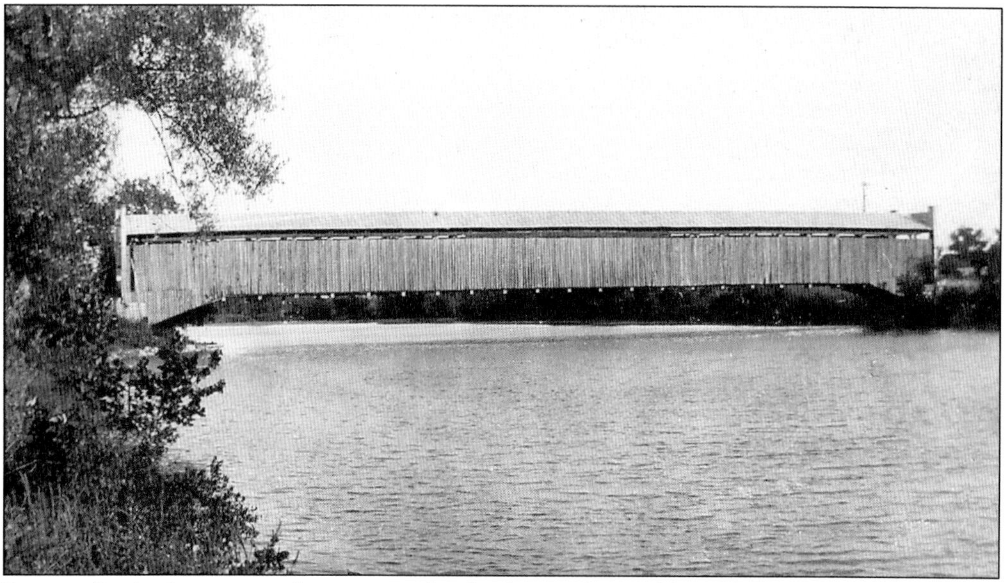

Reportedly the longest single-span wooden bridge in the world, Bridgewater's covered bridge stretched 250 feet and was completed in 1878 by William Grove. This fifth bridge over North River was declared unsafe in 1916, and by 1917, a new steel bridge replaced the more picturesque wooden structure. (Massanutten Regional Library Collection.)

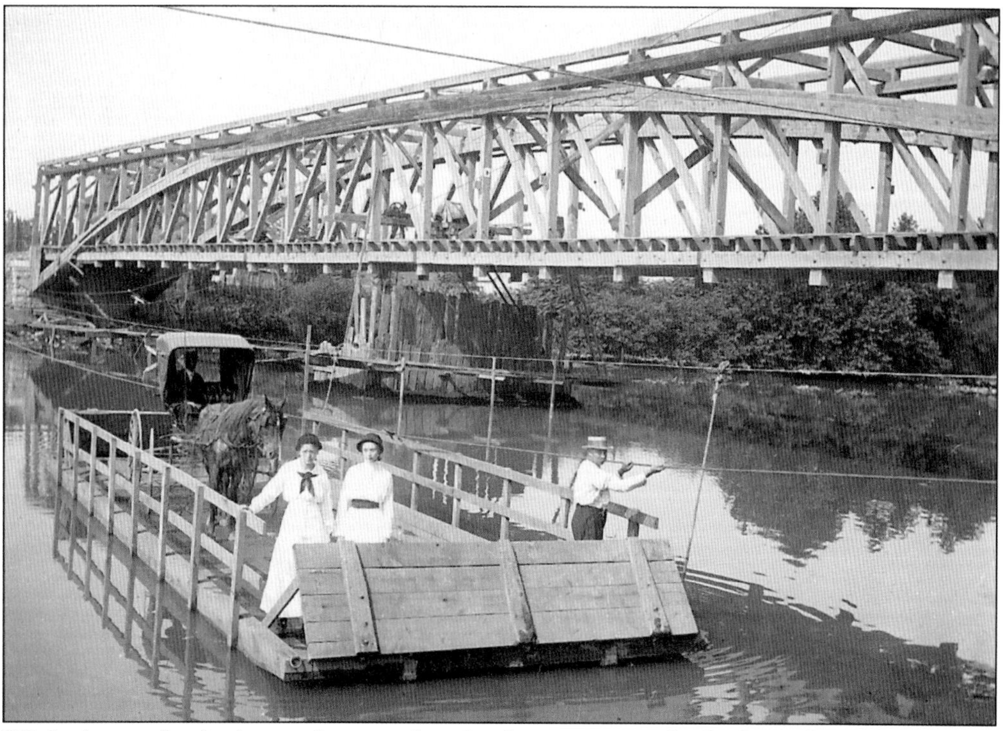

While the wooden bridge was being replaced, a ferry transported vehicles and passengers across North River. On April 6, 1917, the ferry's cable gave way and mail carrier J.S. Click, his automobile, and the mail all sank to the muddy bottom of the river. Fortunately, all were rescued. (Bridgewater College Collection.)

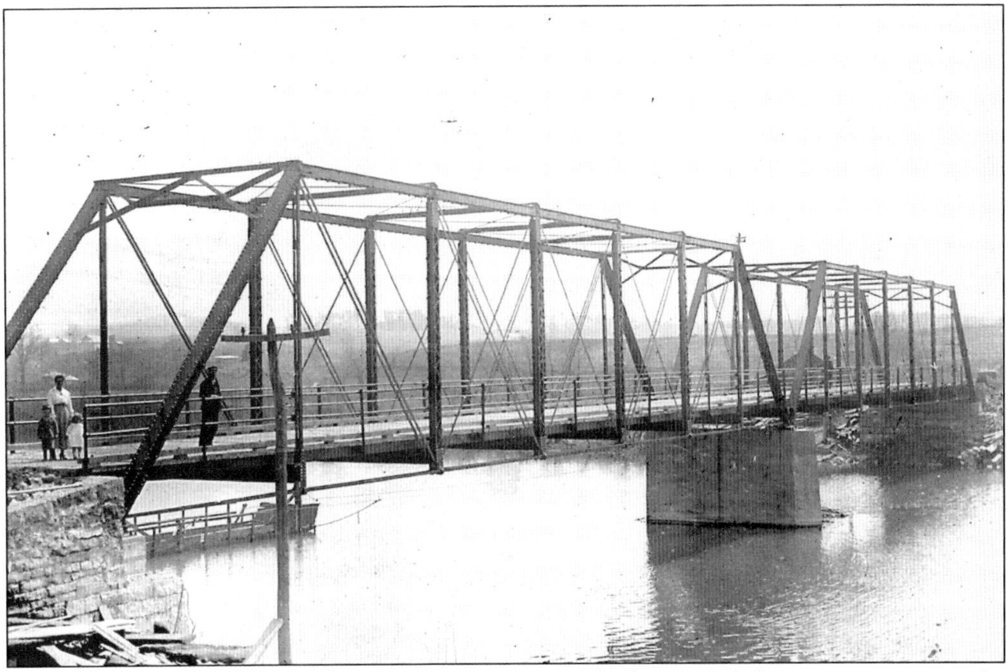

Nearing completion in 1917, Bridgewater's new steel bridge provided a stronger support for the growing automobile traffic along the Harrisonburg–Warm Springs Turnpike. Once found all over the county, these bridges are now becoming relics of the past. (Massanutten Regional Library Collection.)

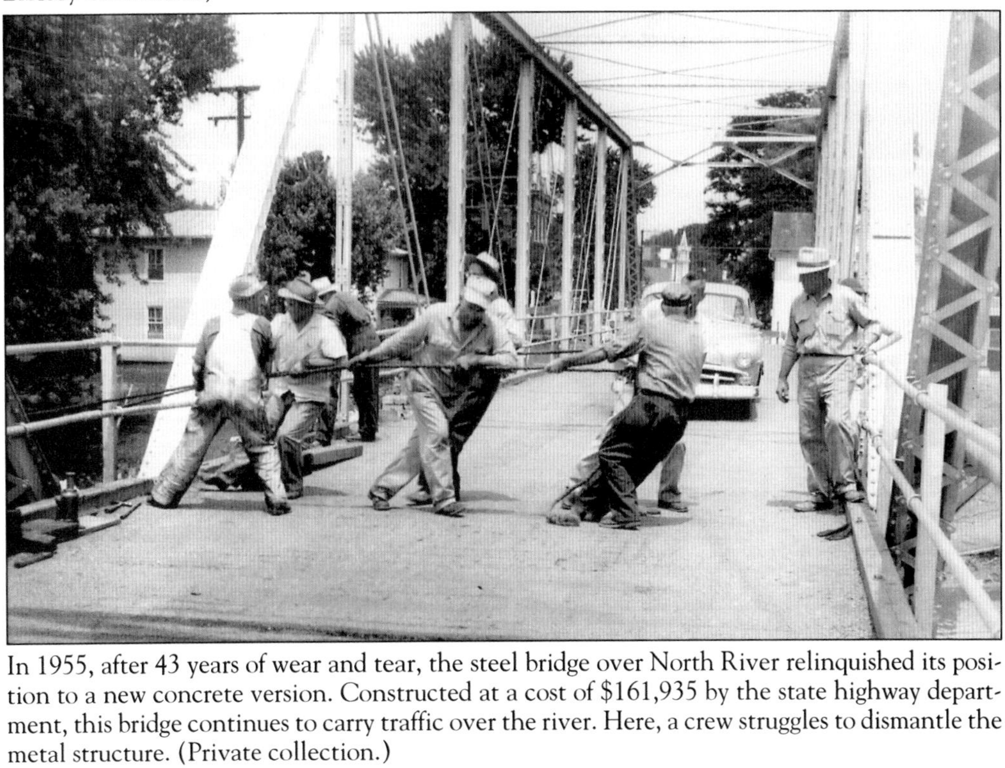

In 1955, after 43 years of wear and tear, the steel bridge over North River relinquished its position to a new concrete version. Constructed at a cost of $161,935 by the state highway department, this bridge continues to carry traffic over the river. Here, a crew struggles to dismantle the metal structure. (Private collection.)

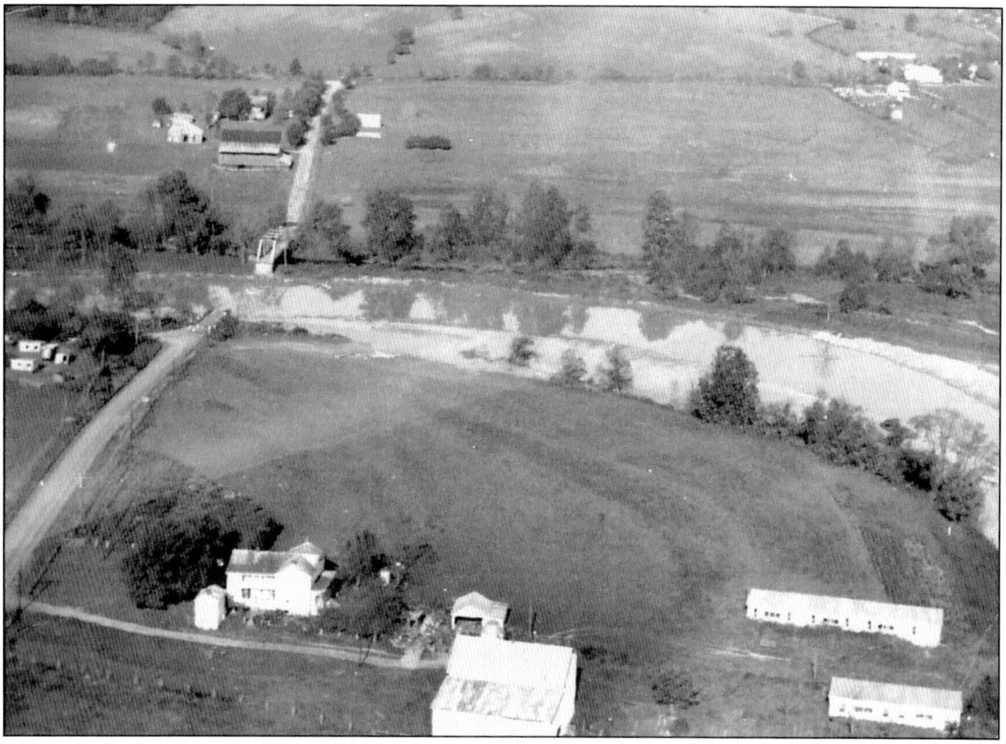

This aerial photograph of North River west of Bridgewater shows part of the damage caused by the flood of June 1949. This photo shows a portion of the steel bridge that was washed out and demonstrates how the river changed its course during its swell. The original river bend lies to the west of the flow seen here. (Private collection.)

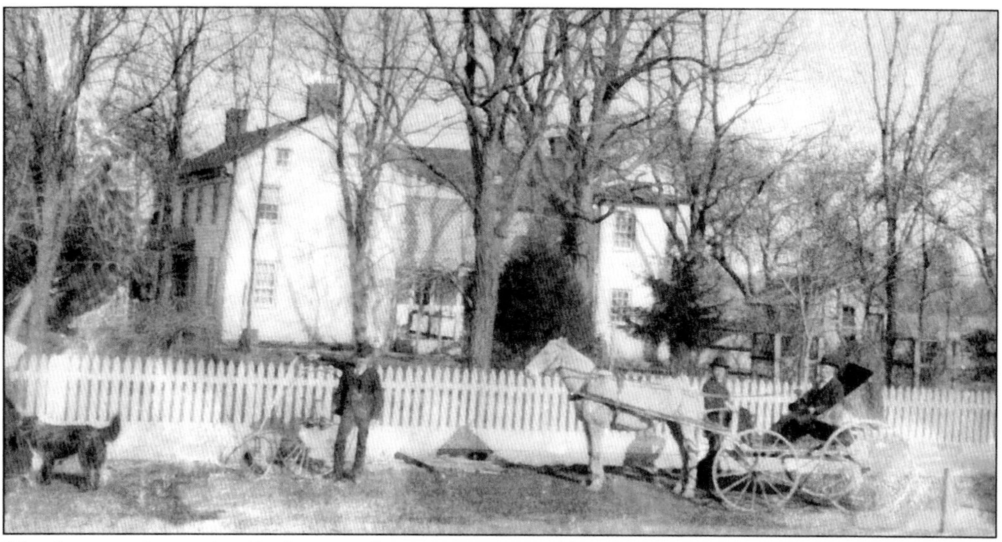

This house is located in Berlinton, the town promoted by George W. Berlin in the latter quarter of the 19th century. Berlin, an attorney who moved to Bridgewater in 1865, purchased the Byerly mill property on North River about a mile-and-a-half east of the turnpike. The house shown here, which still stands, appears as one of Berlin's properties in *Lake's 1885 Atlas* of Rockingham County. (Greg Evans Collection.)

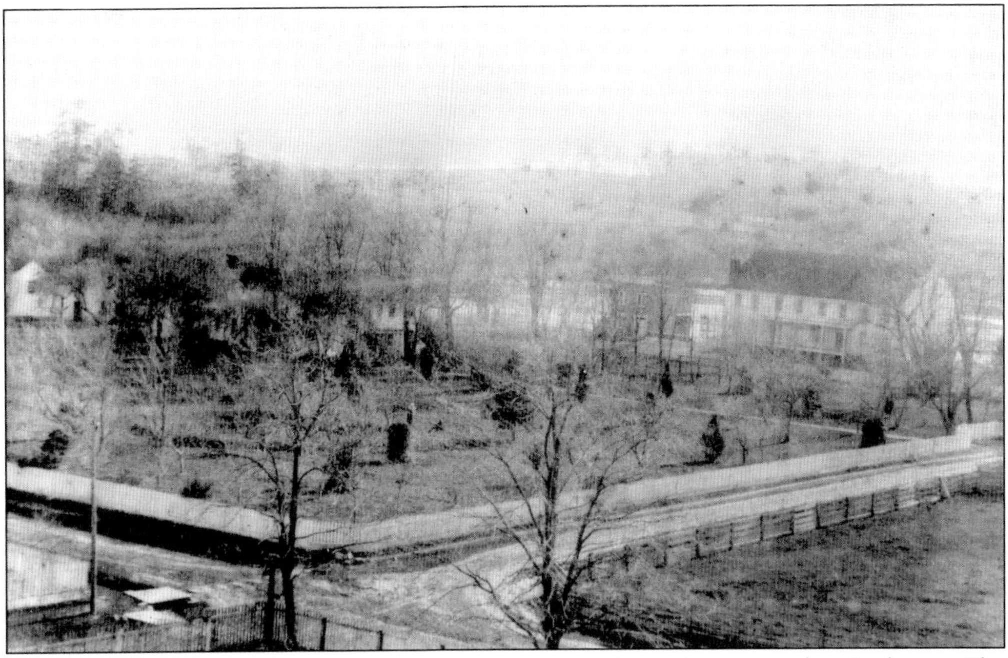

Looking southwest toward the river, this rare photograph shows the crossroads at Berlinton. The mill and its office appear along the river to the right, while the house pictured on the bottom of the opposite page can be seen to the left of the mill buildings. (Greg Evans Collection.)

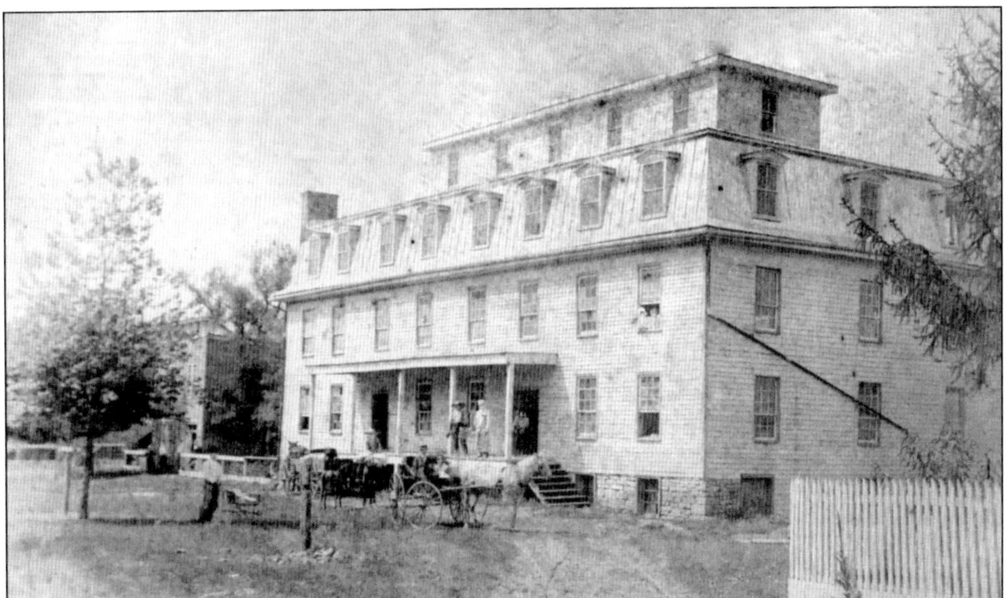

Nearly unrecognizable, this mill is the Berlin Mill pictured above after renovations in 1893. George W. Berlin advertised in May of that year the he had "now in operation a 'roller process' flouring mill." The structure shown here is the old mill with the roof raised to the popular mansard style of the 1890s. Sadly, this building was razed in the 1920s. (Greg Evans Collection.)

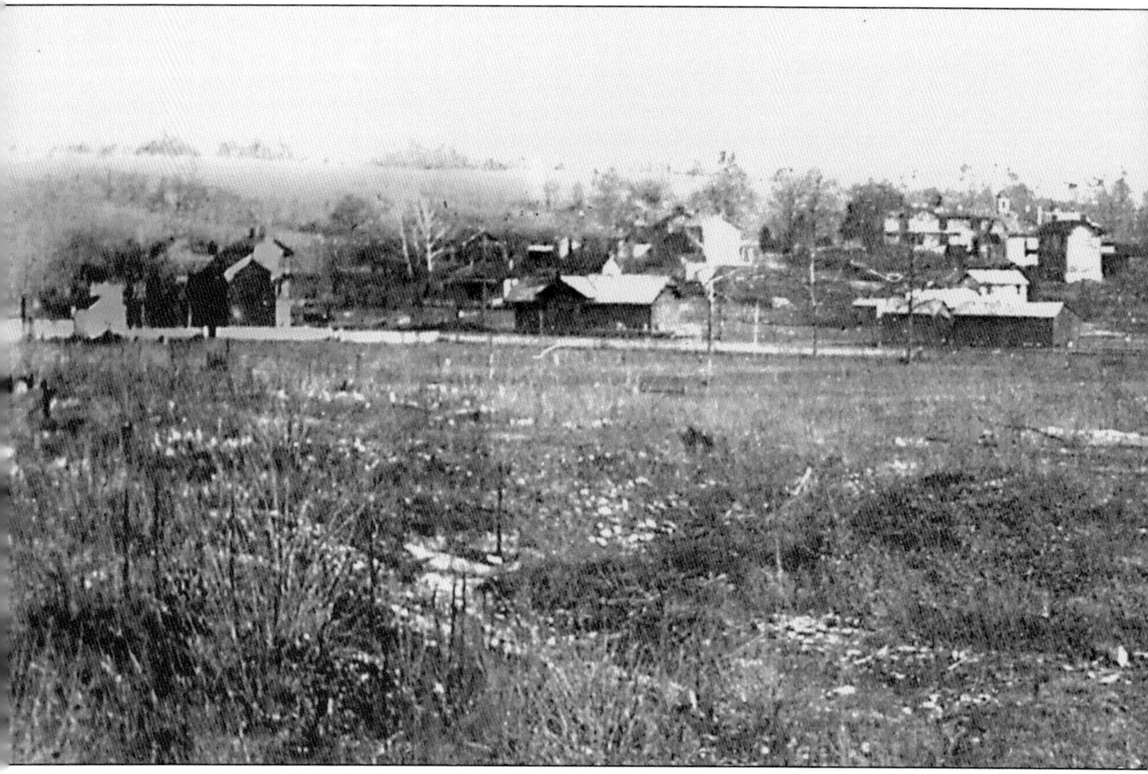

By the mid-1800s, the community of Pleasant Valley began to take form a few miles south of Harrisonburg. The family names of Byerly, Carpenter, Kaylor, Shaver, Saufley, Early, Wenger, and Rhodes were found here. By the early 1900s, when this photo was taken, Pleasant Valley had developed into a small commercial center amid the surrounding farms. The Pleasant Valley train depot, the second building from the left, was built in 1874 and was part of the line con-

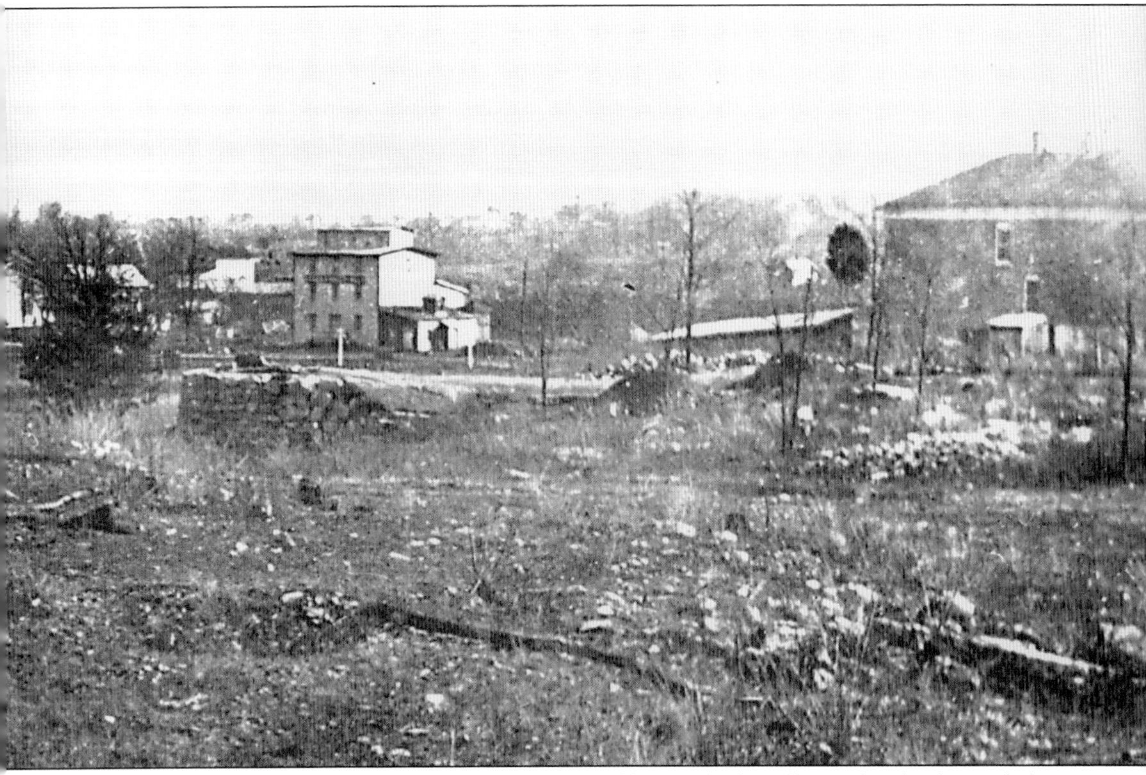

necting Harrisonburg and Staunton by rail. The building, which still stands, also housed the post office, farm supply storeroom, and a general store. The Osceola Mills, second building from the right, was one of several mills in the tiny community. The Pleasant Valley School is on the far right. (Kermit Early Collection.)

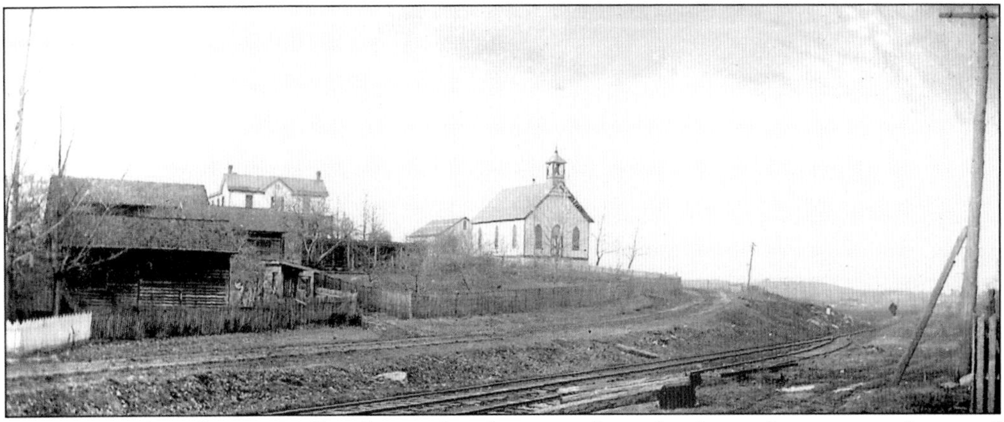

Taken from the Pleasant Valley depot, the photo on the right shows the view north toward Harrisonburg. Today, the fields beyond the railroad tracks are the site of the Pleasant Valley industrial park. During the late 1800s and early 1900s, trains in Rockingham County were an important mode of transportation for people making a cross-county trek. One Pleasant Valley resident recalled taking the train daily to Harrisonburg to attend school there; her father worked for the railroad. Extra trains were often scheduled for "Court Day" in Harrisonburg. (Kermit Early Collection.)

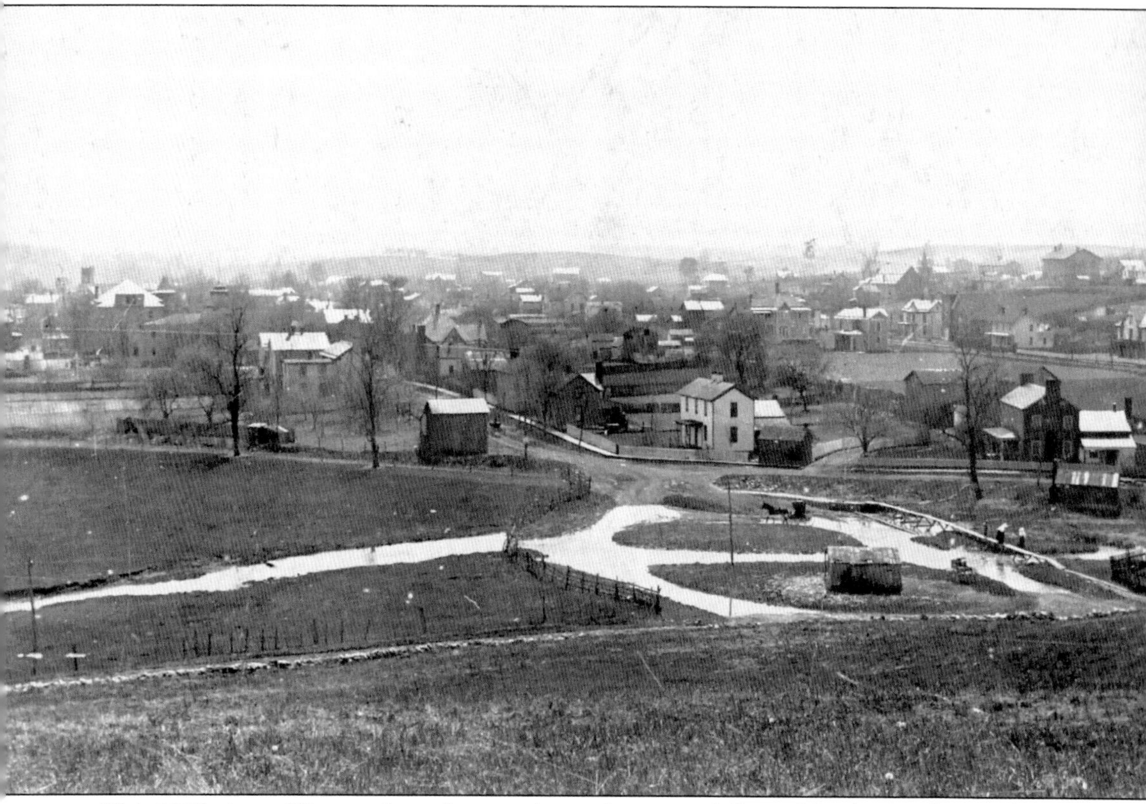

This 1907 view of Dayton from the east shows the unusual flow of Cooks Creek as it skirts the north end of town. While several individuals test the footbridge, a horse and buggy cross the ford onto Seminary Street (now College Street). First known as Rifetown, Dayton's earliest residents were the Daniel Harrison family, who first arrived in the area around 1748. Their stone house still stands on North Main Street. (Kent Botkin Collection.)

The west side of Dayton's Main Street in 1934 appears remarkably similar to the same scene today. Only the bank building at the far end of this photograph has been altered; the third floor has been removed. (Massanutten Regional Library Collection.)

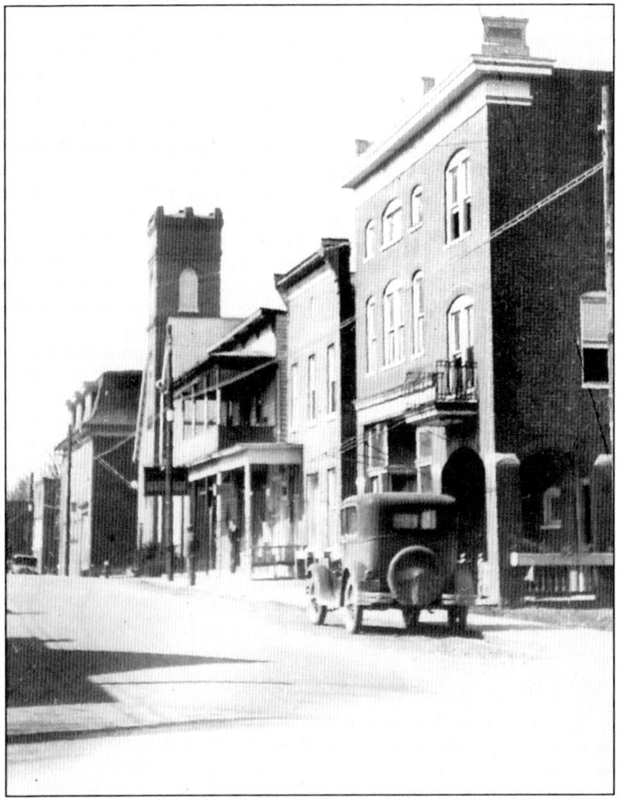

The Ruebush-Kieffer Company, the printing business Ephriam Ruebush and Aldine S. Kieffer started in Singers Glen in 1867, moved to Dayton in 1878. Following the fire of 1903 that destroyed the Waverly Hotel, the company purchased the property and contracted with Thuma & Dovel of Bridgewater and the Shrum Brothers of Dayton to build the edifice pictured here. Finished in 1906, the building still stands on College Street. (Eastern Mennonite University Collection.)

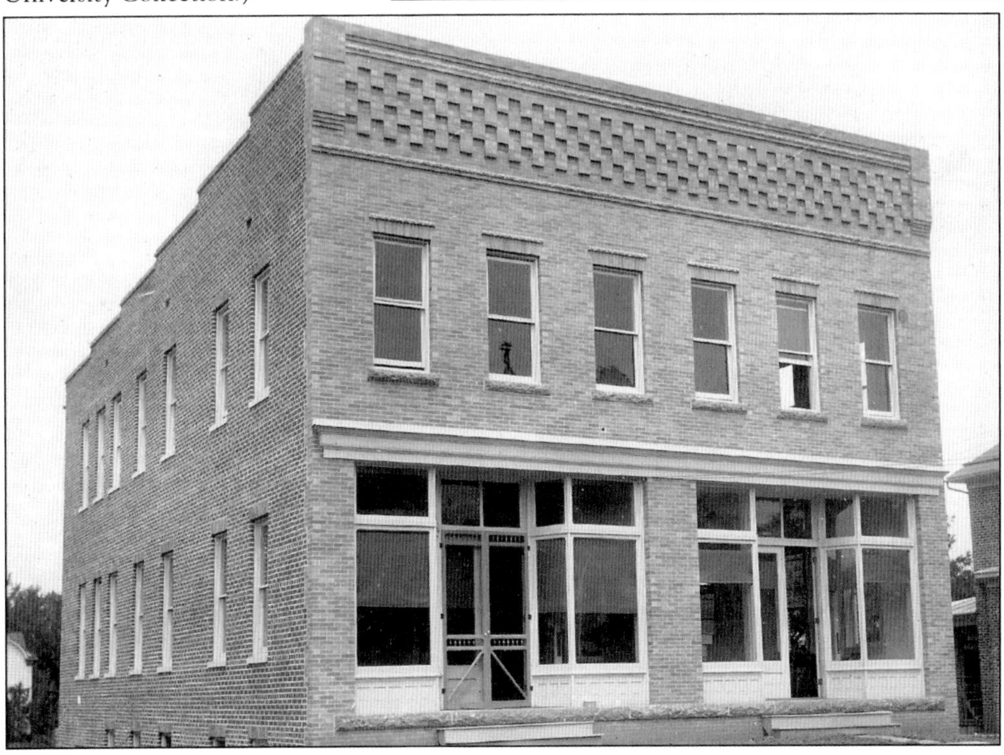

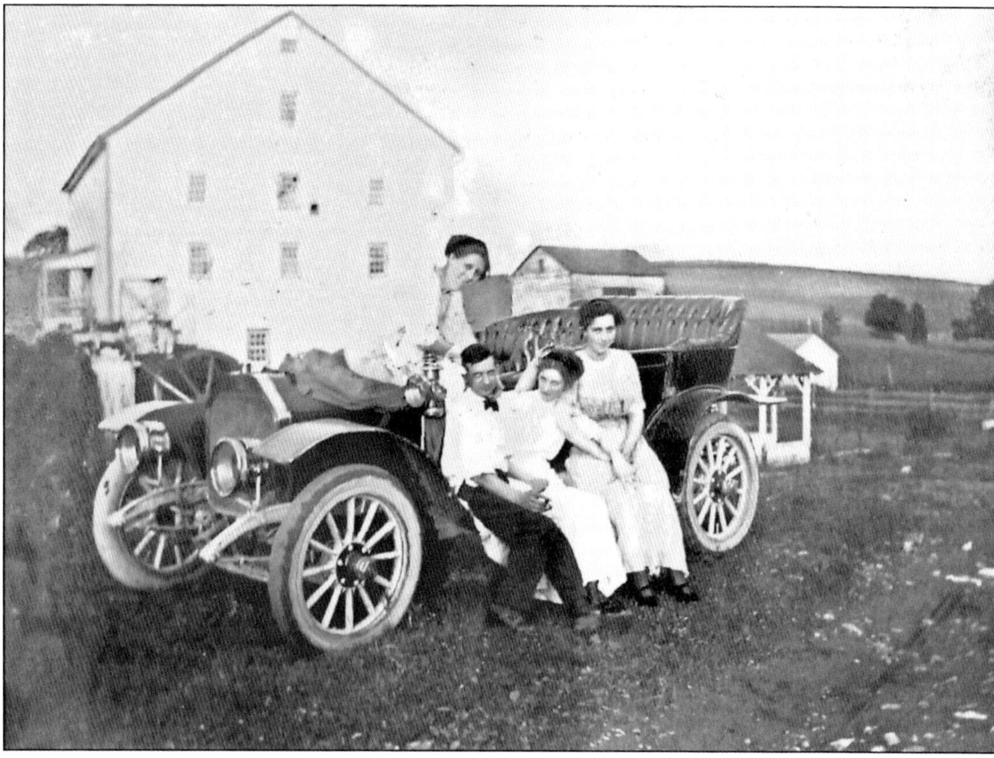

Soon after a new mill wheel was installed in 1909 at Silver Lake Mill in Dayton, this young man and three female companions enjoyed an afternoon around the mill and lake, motoring in their five-passenger touring car. The car's diamond-tufted leather upholstery and sleek overall styling undoubtedly helped the young man win friends. Over 200 firms in the United States were manufacturing automobiles in the early 1900s. (Private collection.)

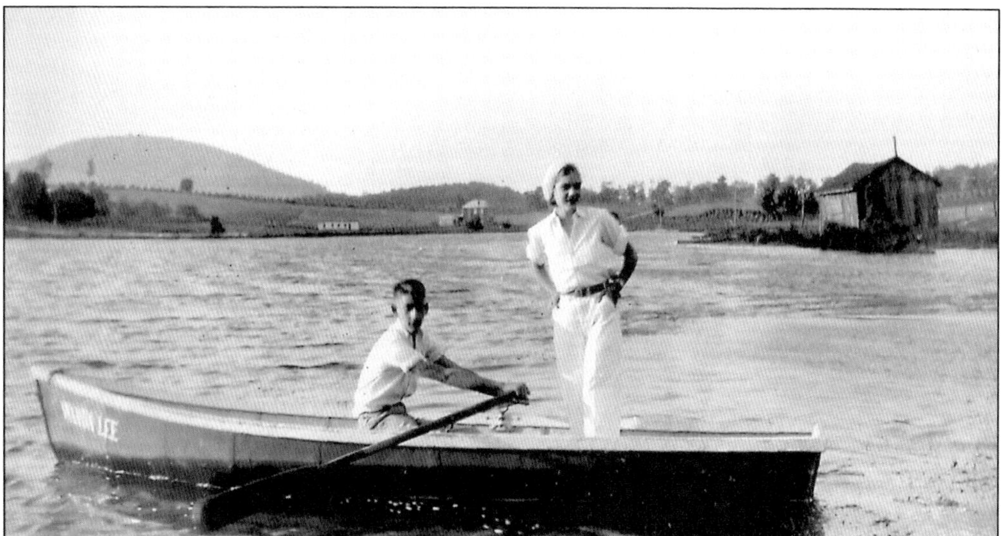

Jesse B. Grove Jr. and his sister, Elsie, spent many hours at Silver Lake around 1930. Their father, J.B. Grove, purchased the mill and lake in 1924. Along with grinding flour, Mr. Grove rented flat-bottomed boats by the hour to the public. (Private collection.)

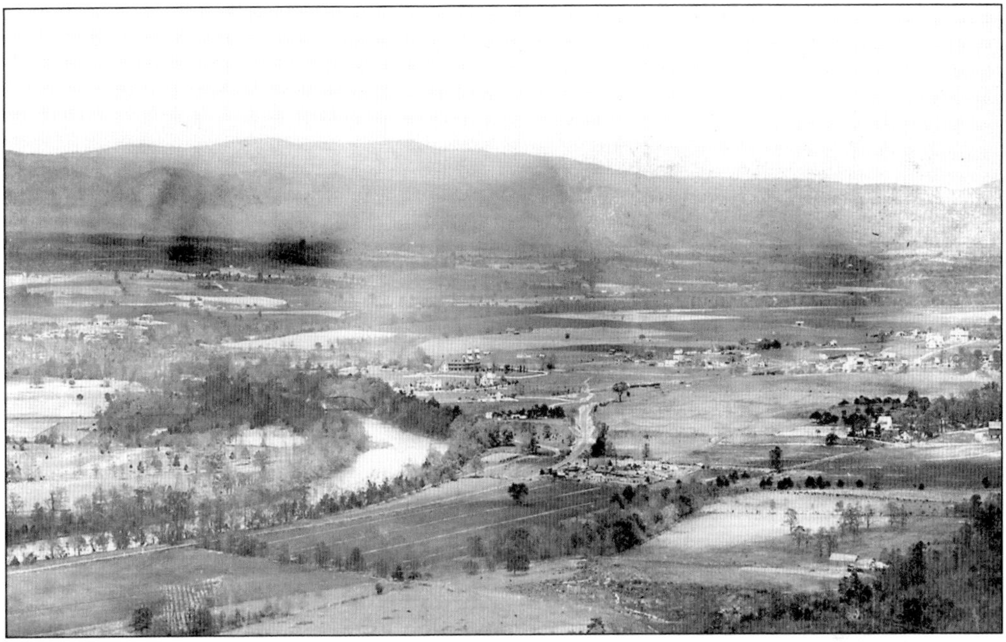

This panoramic photograph emphasizes Elkton's location along the south fork of the Shenandoah River in eastern Rockingham County. Known as Conrad's Store until 1881, the town is the center of economic activity in that section of the county. An enlargement of the photograph's center, below, shows the Gables Hotel. The elegant establishment began entertaining guests in 1891. The structure was sold at public auction in 1957 and razed soon after. (Massanutten Regional Library Collection.)

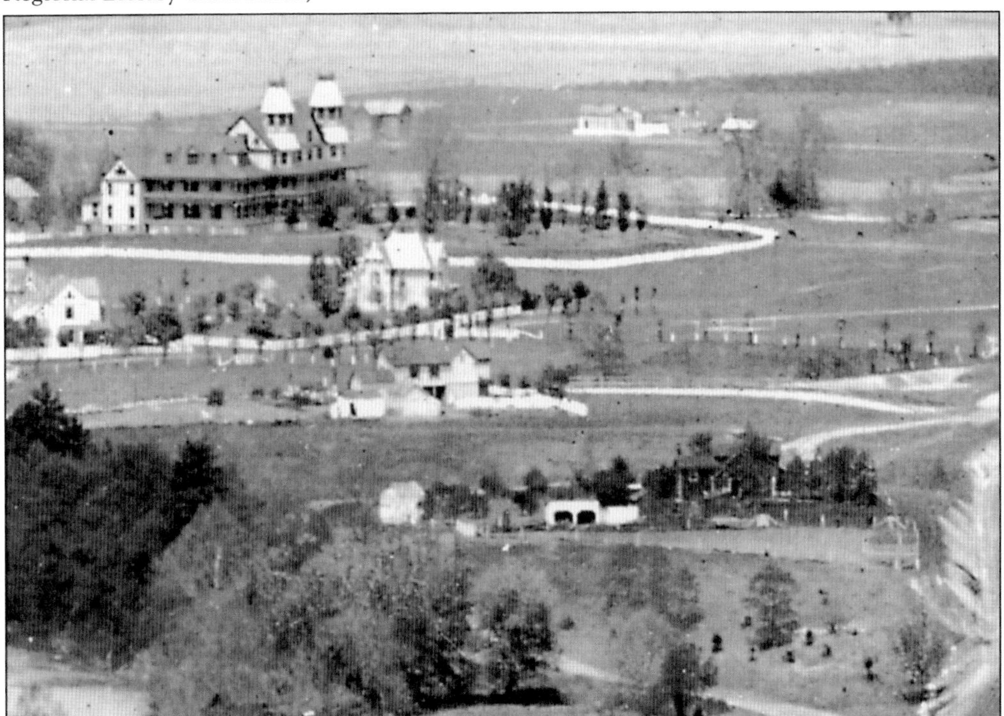

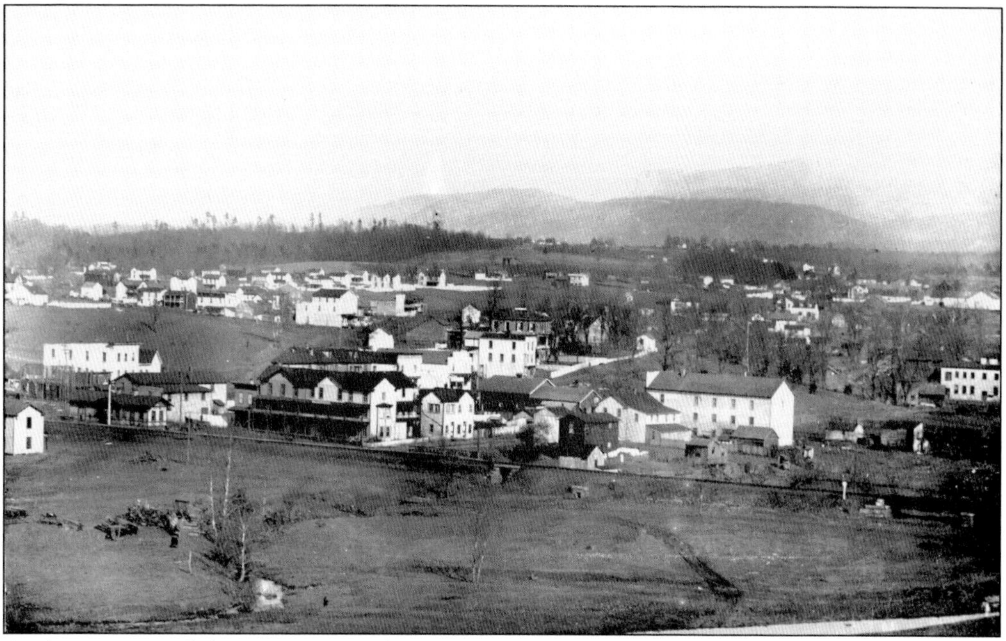

A closer view of the town around 1905 reveals more of the commercial and residential section of Elkton. The Virginia Hotel is just to the left of center in this photograph. The proprietor, W.E. Deal, boasted in 1909 that the hotel was newly renovated, and that patrons received famous Elk Lithia water from a nearby spring free of charge. (Massanutten Regional Library Collection.)

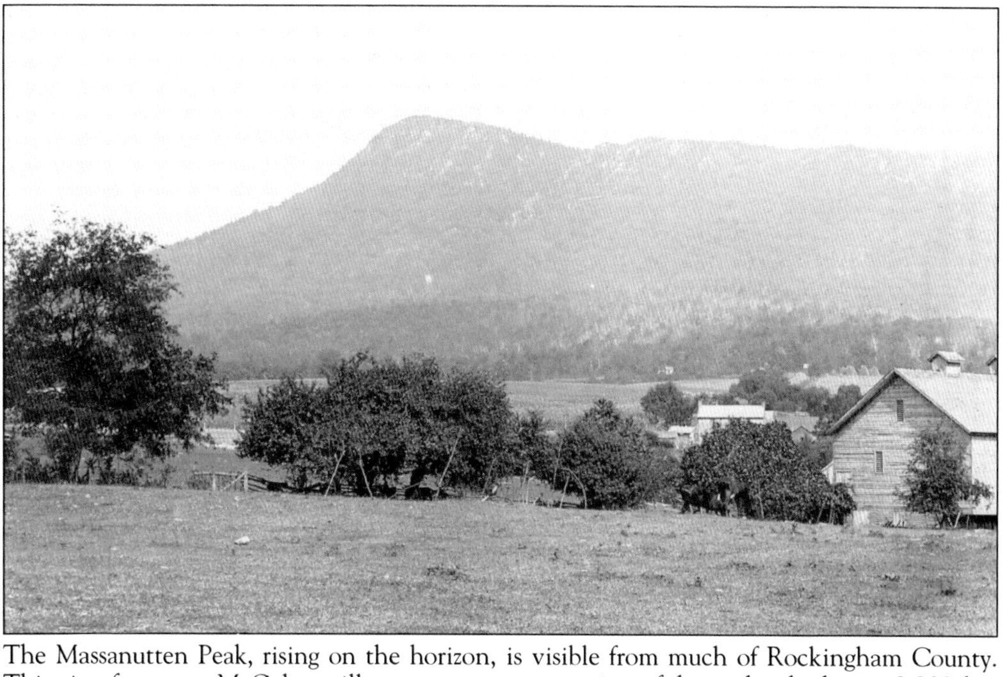

The Massanutten Peak, rising on the horizon, is visible from much of Rockingham County. This view from near McGaheysville presents an eastern view of the peak, which rises 2,900 feet above sea level. While not visible in this photograph, the peak's neighbor to the north, Laird's Knob, has an elevation of 3,400 feet. (Jeffrey S. Evans Collection.)

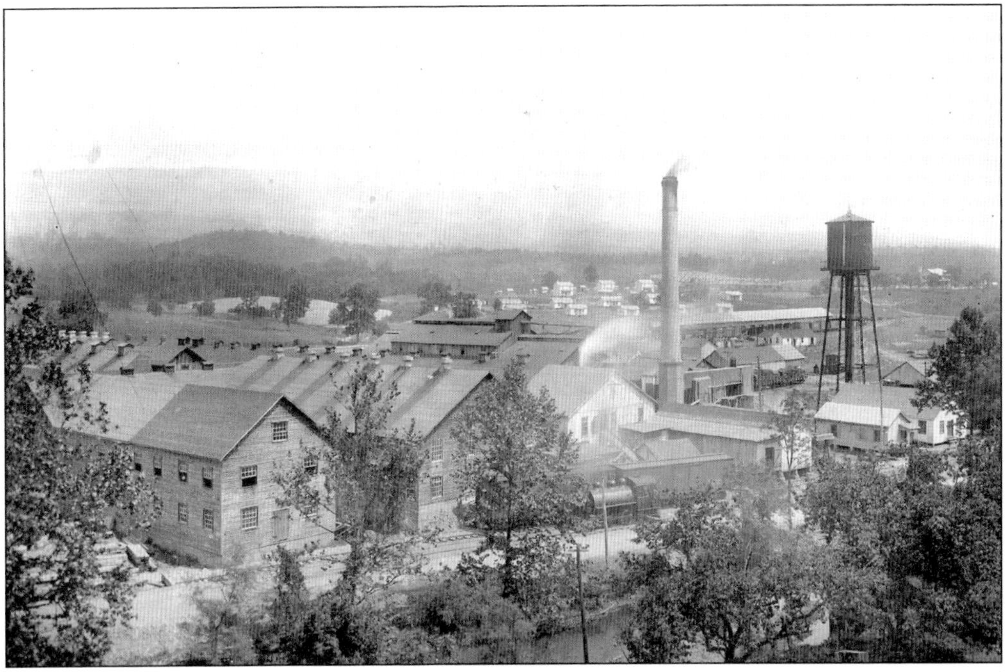

Touted as one of the most important businesses in Rockingham County in 1908, J.R. Cover and Sons tannery east of Elkton covered more than seven acres. The company, which was started in 1877 as a small sole leather tannery in Swift Run, used Texas steer hide and shipped their product to a Philadelphia warehouse, where it was distributed throughout the nation. (Harrisonburg-Rockingham Historical Society.)

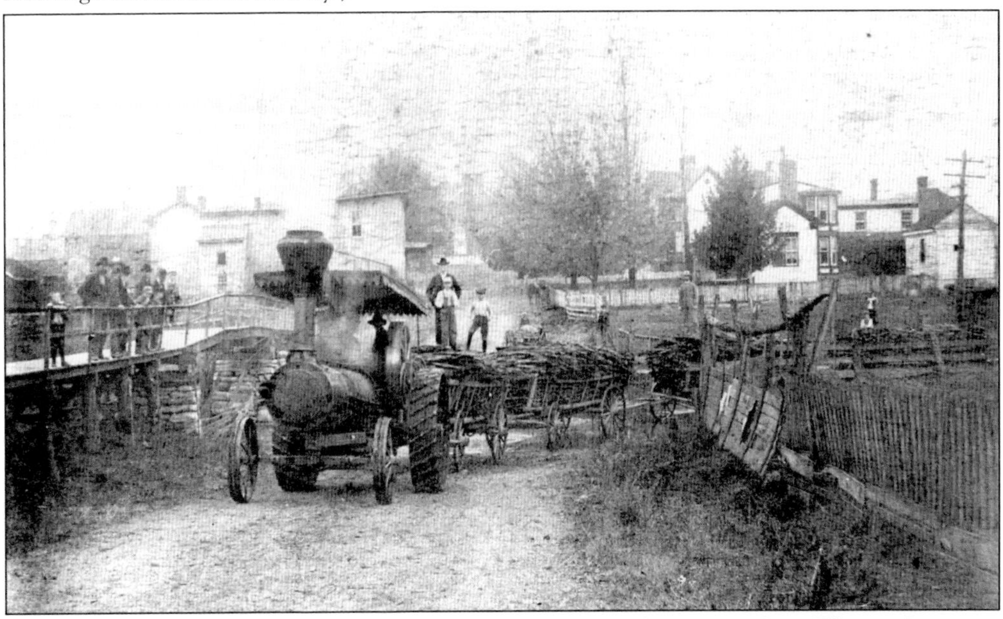

Although this photograph was shot in Mt. Clinton, across the county from Elkton, the steam engine pulling wagonloads of tanning bark is indicative of similar scenes at the Cover tannery. The Covers estimated in 1908 that more than 3,000 tons of chestnut oak and hemlock bark were ground each year to meet their demand. (Private collection.)

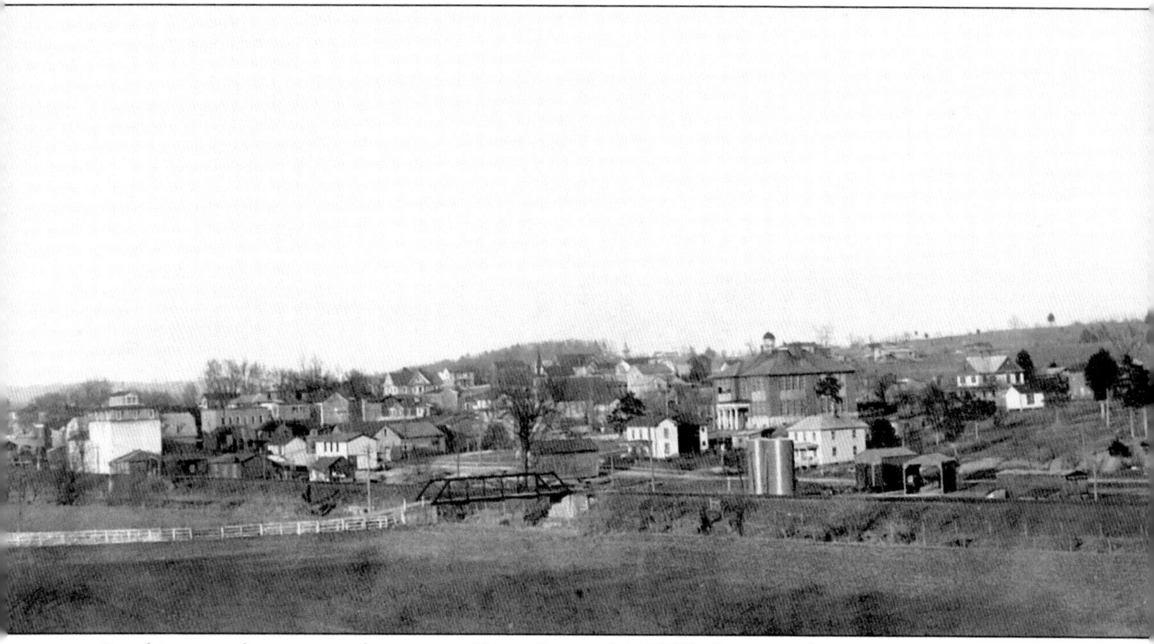

Looking northeast over the town of Broadway, this 1908 photograph presents an encompassing view of the main section of downtown. In its 1890 "Prospectus of [the] Virginia Valley Land and Improvement Company," the company's officials declared that Broadway "is clean, healthy and attractive, and absolutely free from all malaria." The company, it should be noted, was developing 400 acres adjacent to the town. (Eastern Mennonite University Collection.)

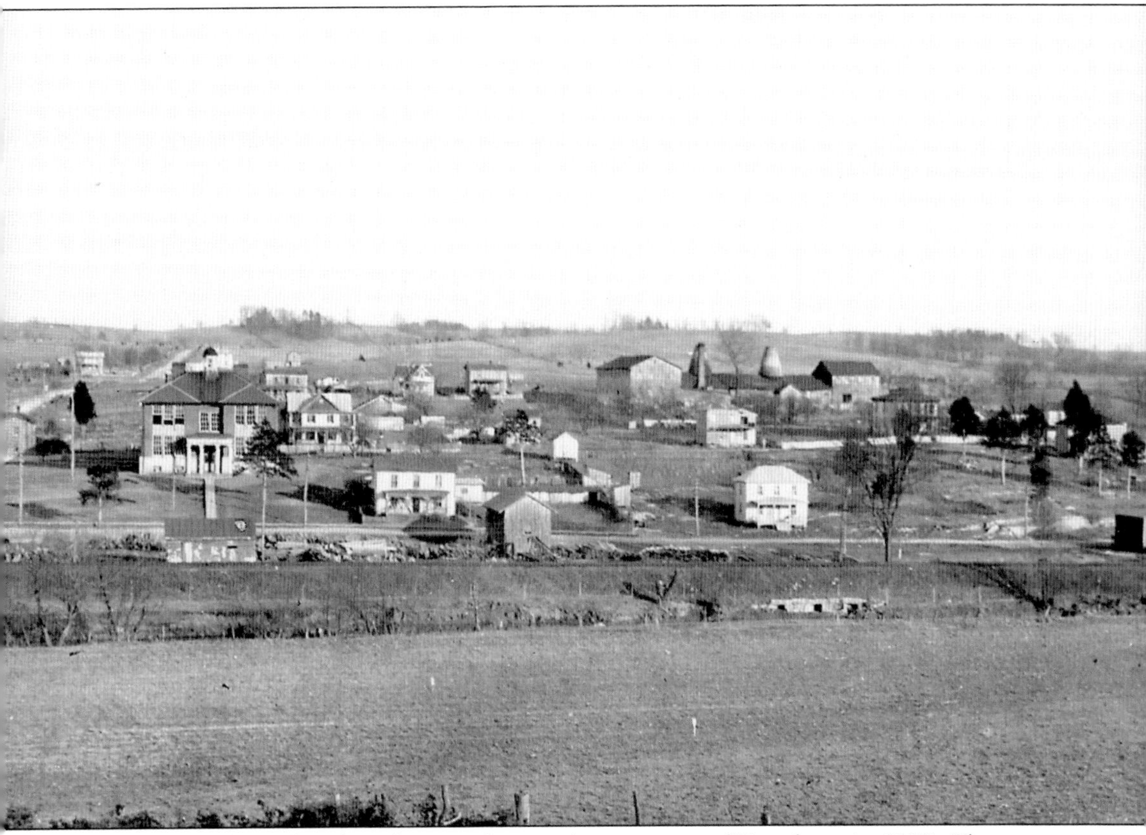

A half turn to the right, this photograph completes a view of Broadway in 1908. The most prominent sights here are the high school on the left and the manufactory located on the hill at right. The two kilns on this structure identify it as Radford's Mammoth Pottery touted in the Land and Improvement Company's promotional brochure. Linville Creek meanders in the foreground. (Eastern Mennonite University Collection.)

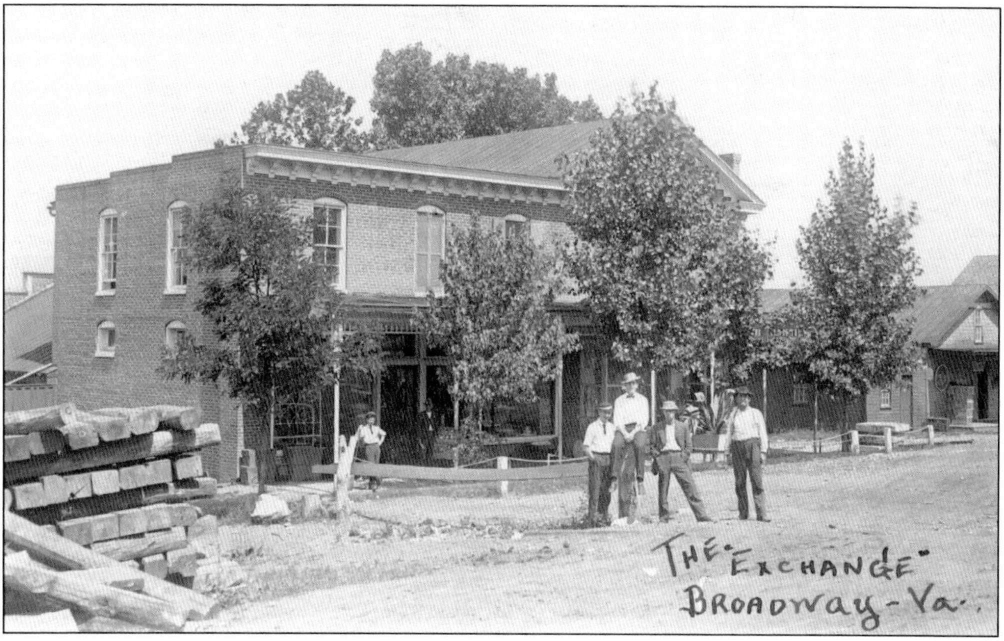

Previously known as the "Exchange," Beard and Company's general merchandise store was located in this building on Broadway's Main Street in 1908. J.E. Beard was also involved with the Broadway Milling Company and the Broadway Hardwood Manufacturing Company. His partners in the merchandise business were A.W. Whitmore and S.E. Long. (Jeffrey S. Evans Collection.)

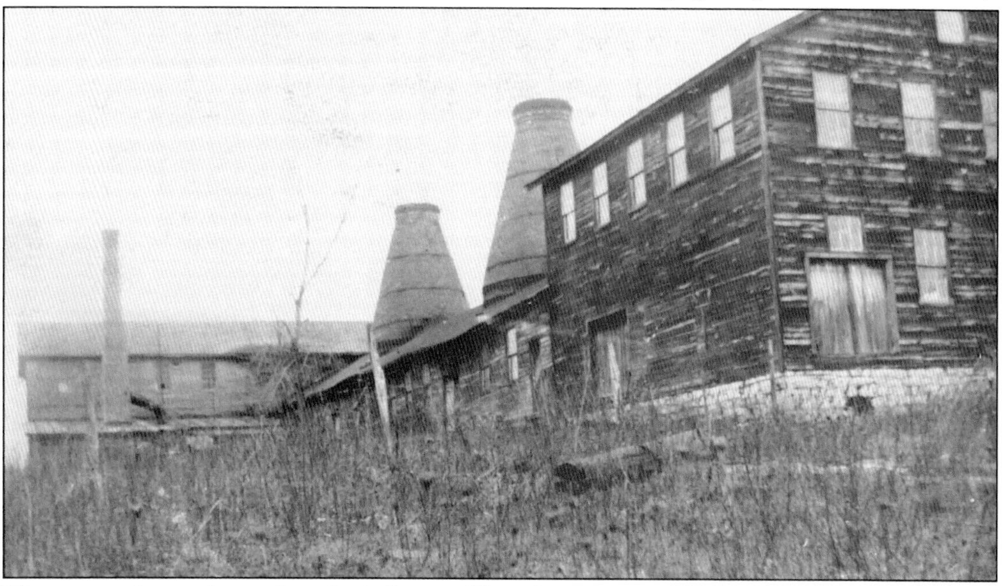

The pottery factory located on the hill east of Broadway operated for many years under different owners. A Certificate of Incorporation dated December 20, 1926, indicates that a new business, The Shenandoah Pottery Company, was to open in the old building later that year. Along with other activities, the company was to "carry on the business of manufacturers of sanitary ware, earthenware, porcelain, china . . . and ceramic ware of all kinds." The directors were C.C. Wood and Lena Wood, both of Broadway, and Fred C. Byford of Keyser, West Virginia. (Harold Wood Collection.)

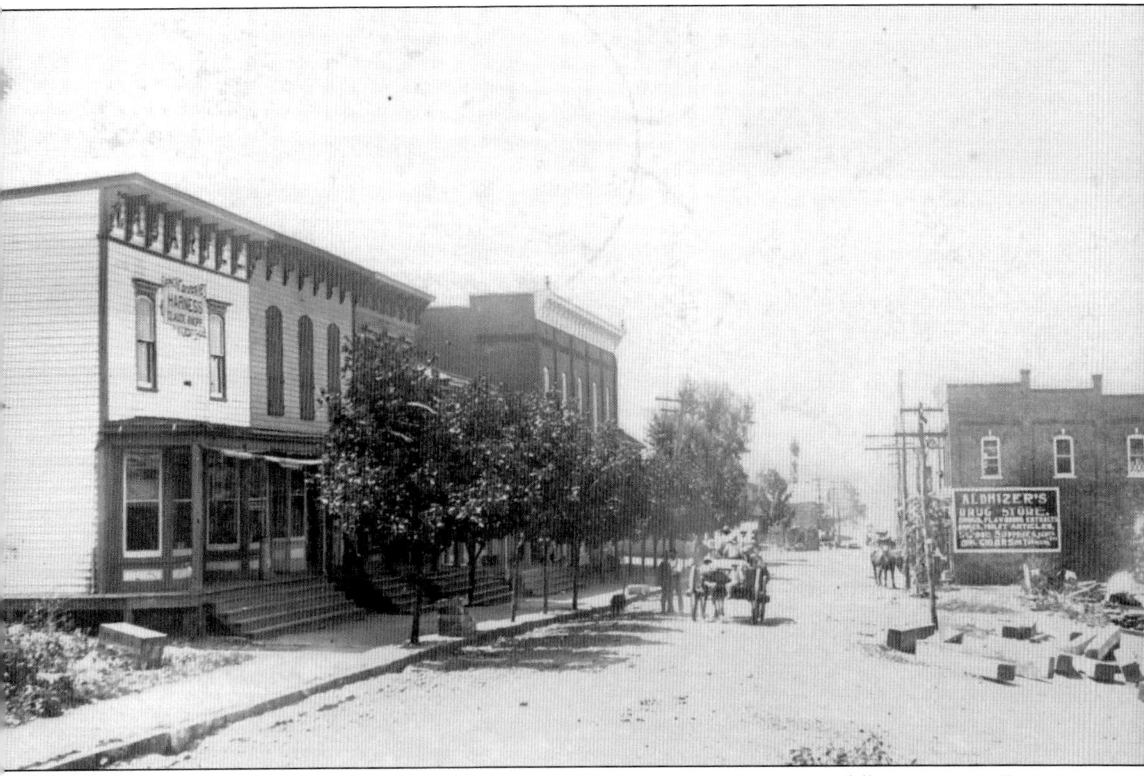

This *c.* 1910 photograph of Broadway's Main Street shows the George S. Aldhizer & Son Drug Store on the right and Claude Knopp's harness shop on the left. Aldhizer, a well-known citizen of the town, also served several terms as mayor and was director of the First National Bank. Knopp, a native of Rockingham County, opened his business in 1904 and offered a wide variety of saddles, bridles, and strap work as well as harness. (Jeffrey S. Evans Collection.)

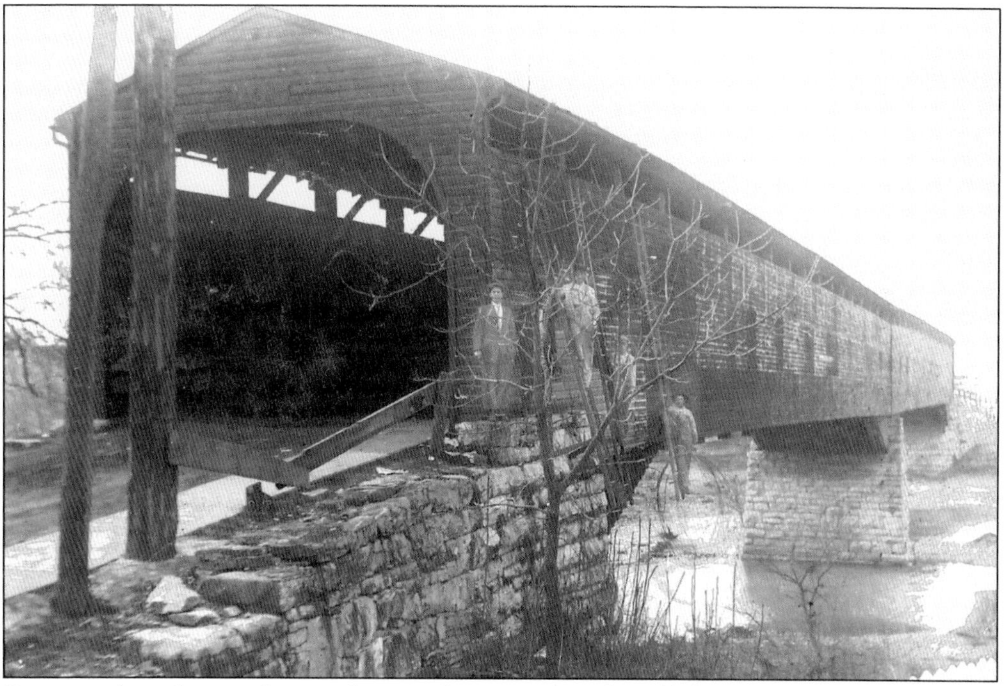

Surviving through several name changes, the town of Timberville became official in 1827 when a post office was established there. Previously the area was known as Williamsport, Thompson's Store, and Riddle's Tavern. Located on the south end of town, this covered bridge over the North Fork of the Shenandoah River was built in 1884 and stood until it was replaced by a concrete structure in 1935. (Jeffrey S. Evans Collection.)

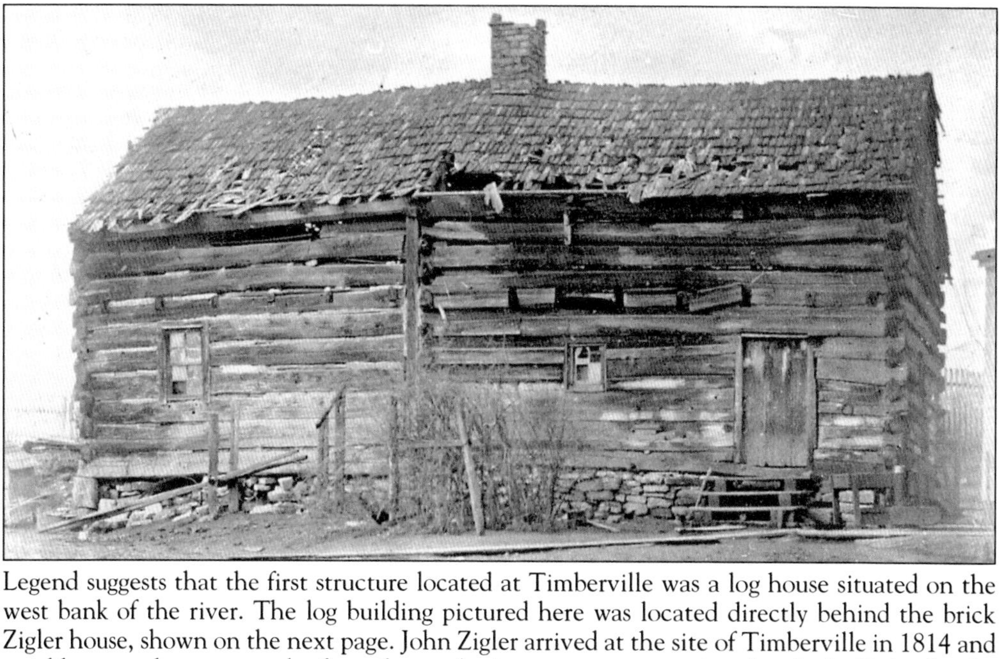

Legend suggests that the first structure located at Timberville was a log house situated on the west bank of the river. The log building pictured here was located directly behind the brick Zigler house, shown on the next page. John Zigler arrived at the site of Timberville in 1814 and quickly opened a tannery, the first of many business ventures associated with the Zigler family. (Jeffrey S. Evans Collection.)

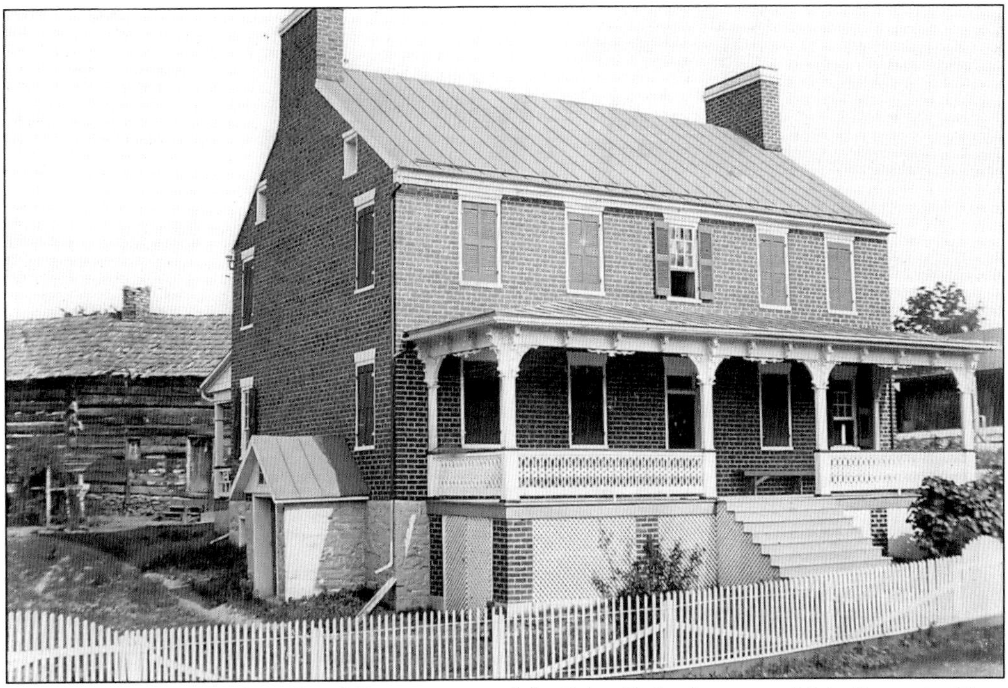

This pair of photographs offers different views of the John Zigler house on Main Street in Timberville. A comparison of these photos illustrates the changes that often take place in a property over a number of years. Above, the porch is noticeably higher and a picket fence separates the yard from the street. The original log house is visible in the background. The image below reveals that the ground around the house has been raised and the pickets replaced by a stone wall. The buildings in the background reflect the Ziglers' numerous business interests. (Eastern Mennonite University Collection.)

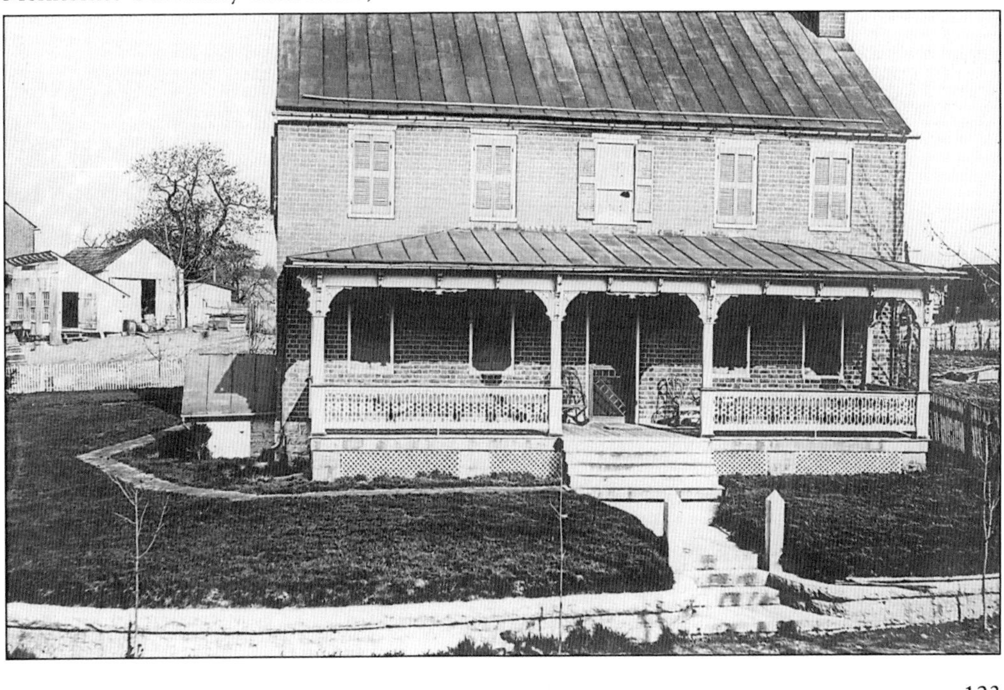

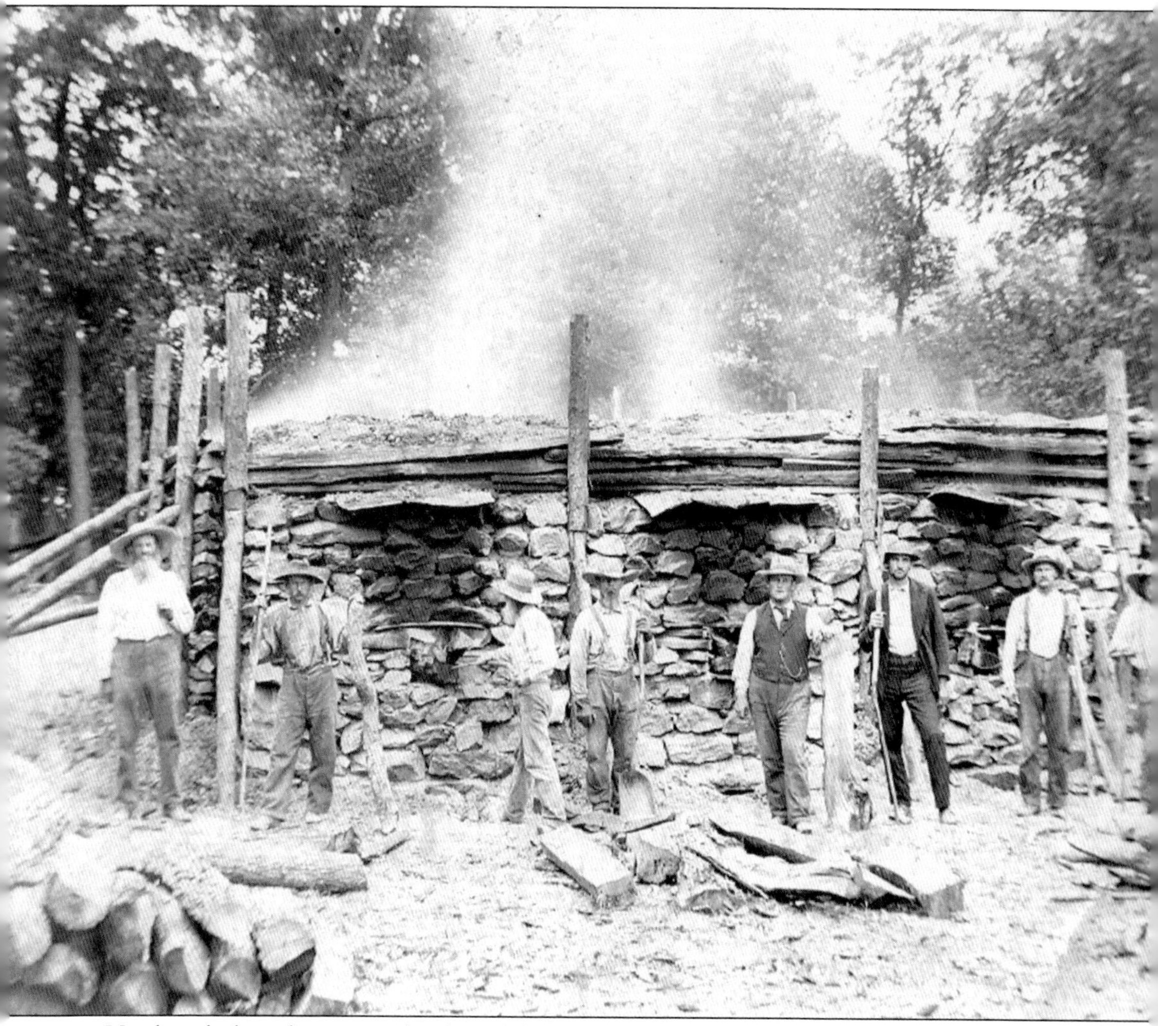

Unidentified workers man this lime kiln on the Zigler property around 1880. Farmers often "sweetened" their soil with lime before planting, and the abundance of limestone in Rockingham County made it profitable for them to burn their own lime. Of curious construction, this kiln was probably a temporary structure, suggested by the lack of masonry between the stones, and the earth piled on top helped insulate the burning stone. A kiln of this type would take four or five days of constant fire to burn successfully. (James Madison University, Carrier Library, Special Collections.)

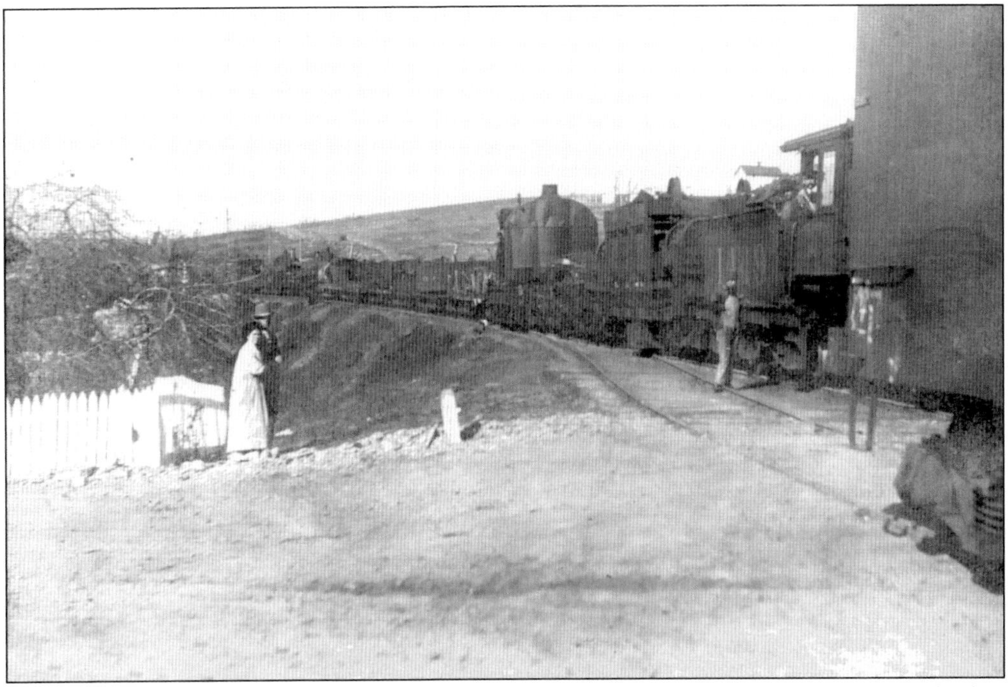

Pedestrians wait at the corner of the Zigler lot in Timberville while the Baltimore and Ohio train picks up freight at the depot. Writing on this photograph states: "Train in charge of engineer Dave Hupp and conductor Nipe." (Jeffrey S. Evans Collection.)

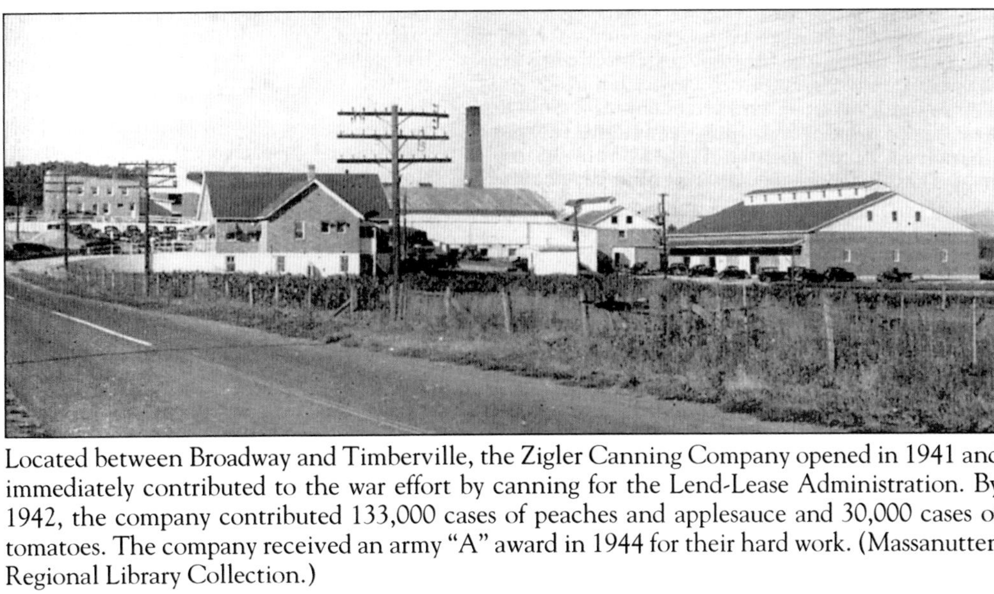

Located between Broadway and Timberville, the Zigler Canning Company opened in 1941 and immediately contributed to the war effort by canning for the Lend-Lease Administration. By 1942, the company contributed 133,000 cases of peaches and applesauce and 30,000 cases of tomatoes. The company received an army "A" award in 1944 for their hard work. (Massanutten Regional Library Collection.)

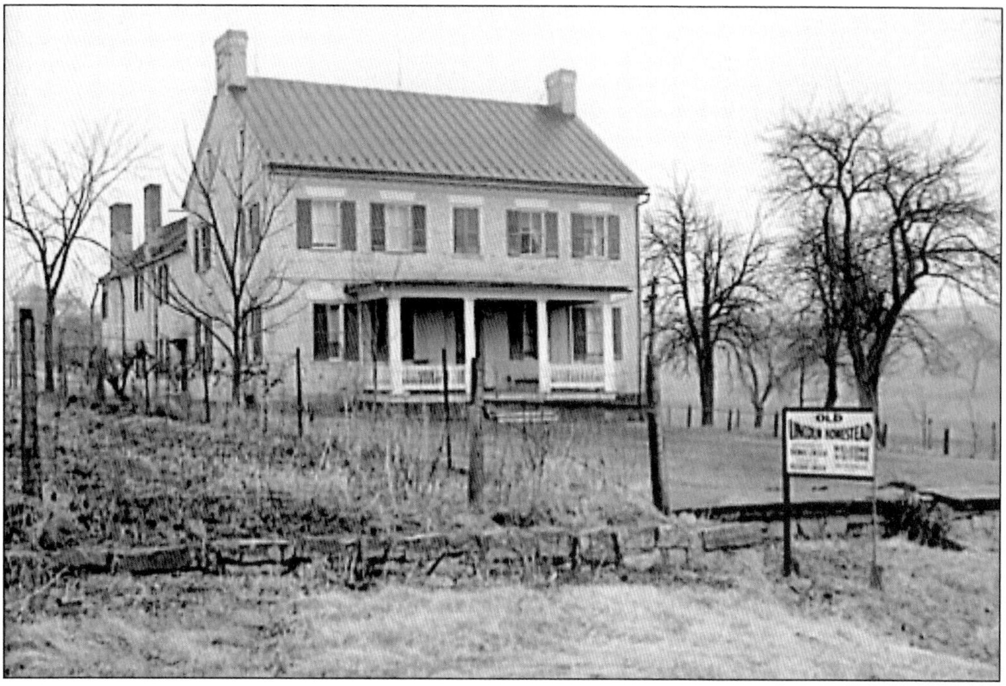

The Lincoln family homestead is a well-known feature on the landscape of northern Rockingham County. Capt. Jacob Lincoln built this house, home of President Abraham Lincoln's ancestors, in 1800. Jacob's brother, Abraham, moved his family to Kentucky in the early 1780s, where his Rockingham County–born son, Thomas, fathered the future President. (Library of Congress Collection.)

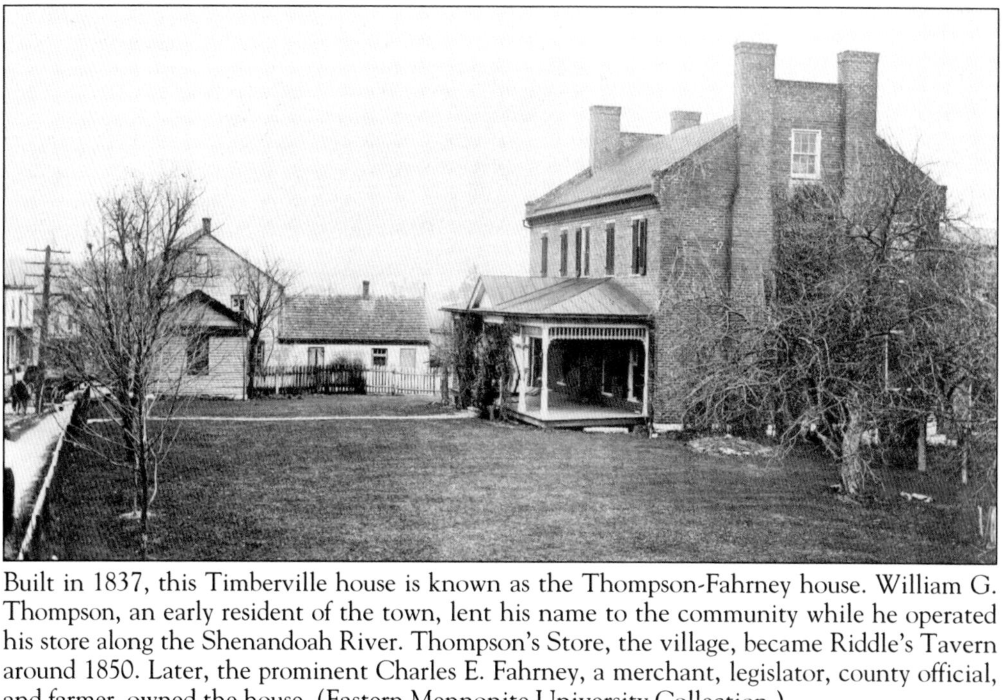

Built in 1837, this Timberville house is known as the Thompson-Fahrney house. William G. Thompson, an early resident of the town, lent his name to the community while he operated his store along the Shenandoah River. Thompson's Store, the village, became Riddle's Tavern around 1850. Later, the prominent Charles E. Fahrney, a merchant, legislator, county official, and farmer, owned the house. (Eastern Mennonite University Collection.)

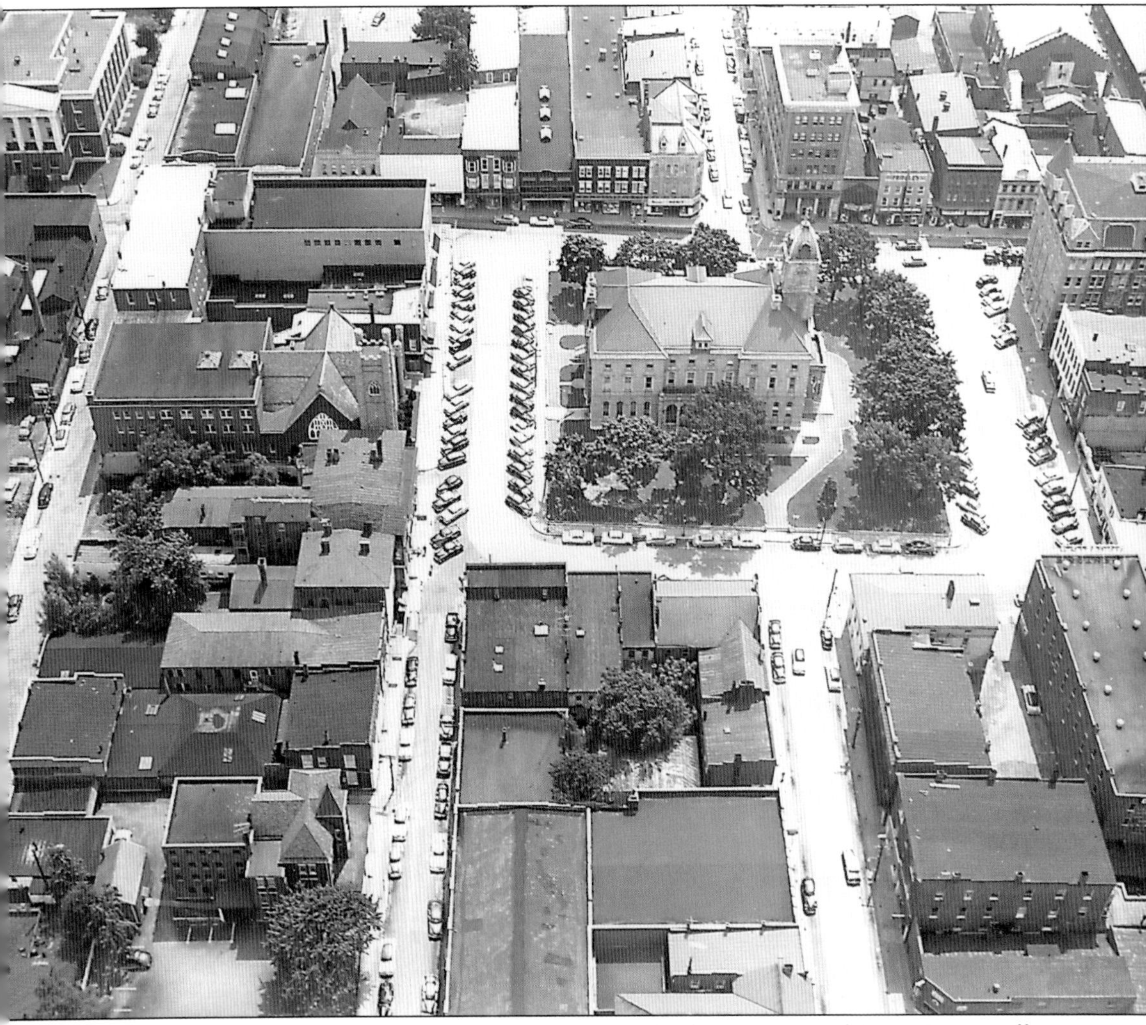

Presenting an interesting geometric pattern, this 1950s "bird's-eye view" of Court Square offers a unique final perspective on Rockingham County's courthouse. (Jim Suter Collection.)

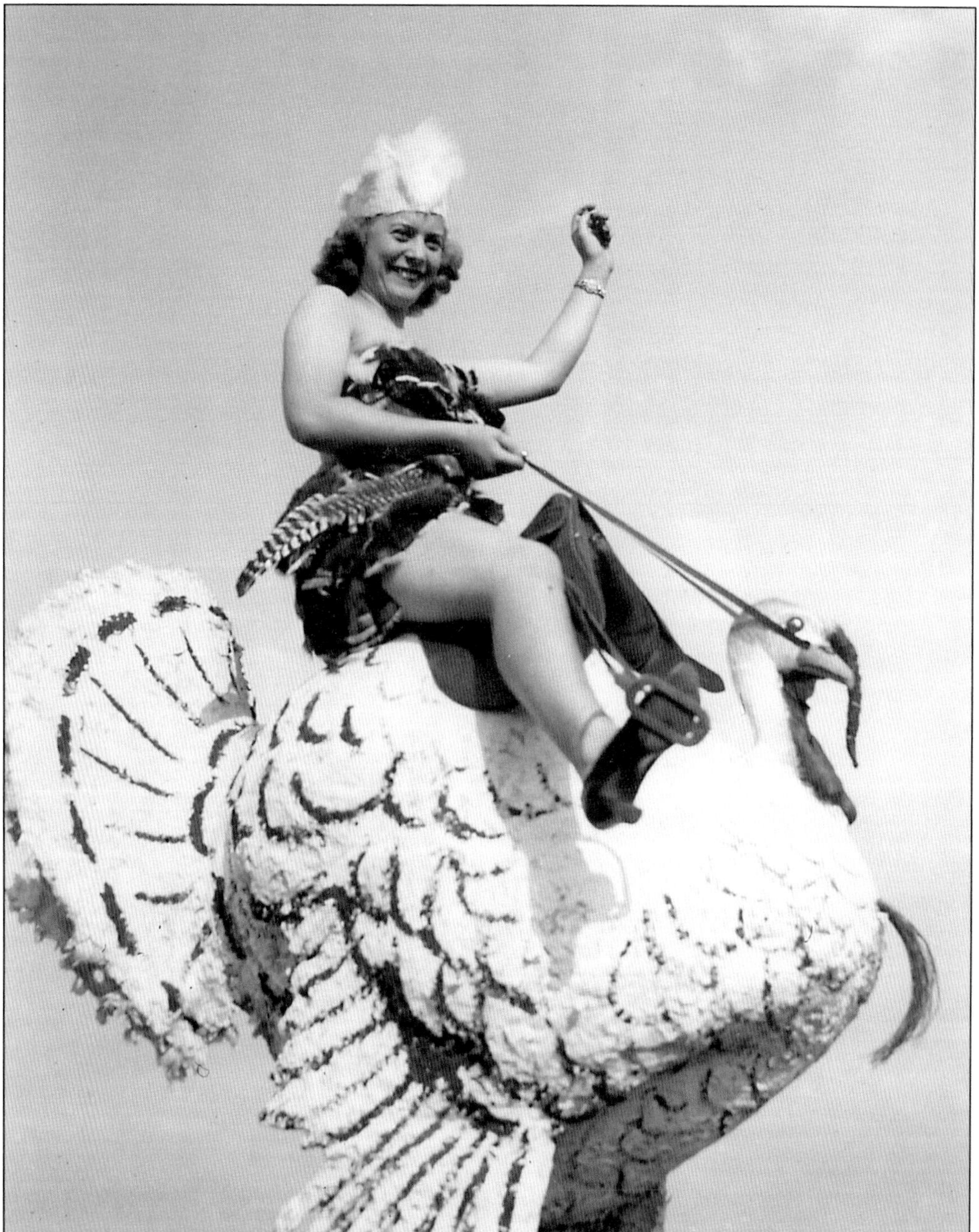

We grow 'em big in Rockingham County! (Harrisonburg-Rockingham Historical Society Collection.)